Blood Libel

Also by Ronald Florence

Nonfiction

Fritz: The Story of a Political Assassin
Marx's Daughters
The Optimum Sailboat
The Perfect Machine

Fiction

Zeppelin
The Gypsy Man
The Last Season

Blood Libel

The Damascus Affair of 1840

Ronald Florence

THE UNIVERSITY OF WISCONSIN PRESS

The University of Wisconsin Press
1930 Monroe Street
Madison, Wisconsin 53711

www.wisc.edu/wisconsinpress/

3 Henrietta Street
London WC2E 8LU, England

Printed in the United States of America

Library of Congress Cataloging-in-Publication Data

Florence, Ronald.
Blood libel : the Damascus affair of 1840 / Ronald Florence.
     p. cm.
Includes bibliographical references and index.
ISBN 0-299-20280-1 (hardcover : alk. paper)
1. Jews—Persecutions—Syria—Damascus. 2. Blood accusation—
Syria—Damascus.
3. Damascus (Syria)—Ethnic relations. I. Title.
DS135.S95F56   2004
956.91′4403—dc22   2004012628

Excerpt from "Torture" from *Miracle Fair* by Wislawa Szymborska, translated by
Joanna Trzeciak. Copyright © 2001 by Joanna Trzeciak. Used by permission of
W. W. Norton & Company, Inc.

For my teachers, Carl Astor and Wayne Franklin

The body is painful,
it must eat, breathe air, and sleep,
it has thin skin, with blood right beneath,
it has a goodly supply of teeth and nails,
its bones are brittle, its joints extensible.
In torture, all this is taken into account.
                    —*Wislawa Szymborska*

. . . whenever Allah wishes ill to his servants He appoints
their foolish ones as governors and their ignorant ones as judges . . .
                    —*Shaddad ibn ʿAmr ibn Aus*

Contents

Blood Libel

1

Damascus, February 1840

VERYONE IN Damascus knew Father Thomas.
The monk had lived at the Capuchin monastery for thirty-two years, long enough for his distinctive black habit with the white cordon, trim white beard, tonsure, and bag of medical instruments to be familiar in every quarter of the city. He had been trained as a pharmacist, and generations of Christians, Muslims, and Jews—some said as many as twelve to fifteen thousand children and adults—had felt the needle of his smallpox vaccinations. The father did not charge his patients, supporting himself on donations, and he had always been quick to post notices and run auctions to support those in need. Many thought him a saint.

The father was originally from Sardinia. Merchants in the *suqs* and friends in the Christian quarter called him Padre Tomasso, or sometimes *il cappuccino*. He was a small man, healthy but advancing in age; some found him quick-tempered and overly authoritative. But that was understandable in a man who lived alone in the monastery with only his servant, Ibrahim Amara, for company. When the two of them set off on one of the father's missions to the outlying villages, they looked like Don Quixote and Sancho Panza.[1]

At noon on Thursday, February 6, the father had been expected for dinner with a group of European prelates at the Christian quarter home of Dr. Massari, the personal physician to the pasha. Father Thomas was a punctual man, no doubt an inheritance of his offices, and when he did not appear at Dr. Massari's even after the dinner hour passed, the other guests were concerned enough to send out a search party.[2]

One could never be too cautious in Damascus. The city was fraught with dangers, especially for the non-Muslim minorities. Relentless epidemics of bubonic plague, cholera, smallpox, and impetigo took periodic tolls, and visitors found the streets and suqs a parade of the maimed, the blind, and the crippled—their missing limbs, ulcerated skin lesions, and suppurating sores the scars of what had not been or could not be treated. The fear of contagion was so great that visitors were quarantined for weeks in tiny lazarettes, and every letter was dipped in vinegar and water or punched and smoked.[3] Visitors intrepid enough to undergo the arduous quarantine faced the perils of bandits on the roads, the indignities of the infamous Ottoman bureaucracy, and the seemingly whimsical regulations of the courts and pashas. Even long-term residents lived in constant fear: the Christian and Jewish minorities were restricted to residence in their own quarters, where ancient walls, night watchmen, and locked gates were supposed to provide islands of security amidst the overwhelming sea of the Muslim majority.

The Christian quarter where Father Thomas and his host Dr. Massari lived—some called it the Armenian or European quarter—was a warren of narrow, crooked streets that butted up against the northern and eastern walls of the old city. It did not take long for word of the father's disappearance to spread through the densely settled streets. Before long a crowd gathered.

The Christian community of Damascus was small, perhaps twelve thousand individuals out of a population of one hundred thousand, and fiercely divided.[4] Ancient disputes over the nature, substance, and personality of God, the divine or human nature of Jesus, whether the Father was equal to or greater than the Son, the centrality of the resurrection or the crucifixion, and the language and structure of the liturgy still inspired passionate arguments in Damascus. The theological and liturgical disagreements were magnified by differences of social and economic status, language, geography, and commercial rivalries. The Syrian Greek (Orthodox) and Greek Catholic (Melchite) patriarchs resided in the city and led the largest denominations, but there were also congregations of Syrian, Armenian, and Latin-rite Catholics, Syrian and Armenian Orthodox, Maronites, missionary evangelical Protestants, and a small group of Roman Catholics for whom Father Thomas led services at the Franciscan church. That afternoon, for the first time that many in the city could remember, Christians of what seemed like every rite and denomination—men and women who rarely spoke to one another—stood side by side in the streets, shouting the same coarse rumors about the disappearance of the monk.

The delegation from Dr. Massari's house made a quick search of the Christian quarter. They found no trace of Father Thomas and went to the French consulate to report that the monk was missing. Although the father was a native of Sardinia, as a Roman Catholic clergyman in what had once been Ottoman territory, he was a French protégé and therefore entitled to the legal protection of the local representative of the French king.

The new French consul, Benoît Laurent François de Paul-Ulysse, Comte de Ratti-Menton, had only been in Damascus a few months. Before he did anything about the report that the monk was missing, he waited for his dragoman and chancellor, Jean-Baptiste Beaudin. Beaudin's official function was to translate languages and interpret the complex rituals at the pasha's divan, but he was also eyes and ears on the streets of the city for the new French consul. Beaudin had lived in Damascus longer than any other foreigner; was fluent in Arabic as well as French; could translate from Italian, English, German, Greek, Turkish, and Hebrew; and seemed to enjoy acquaintances or friendships with everyone who mattered in Damascus, including the pasha.

When Beaudin arrived at the consulate, he had already heard rumors in the streets. People were saying that the last time anyone had seen Father Thomas was on Wednesday afternoon, when the monk had been seen walking into the Jewish quarter. Some said he had been called there to vaccinate a child; others said that he had gone to post a notice on the door of the synagogue, an announcement of an auction to benefit a Dr. Terranova in the Egyptian military service.[5] Either story seemed plausible. The father regularly vaccinated children in every quarter of the city, and he often posted his notices on the door of the synagogue because the Jewish community had a reputation for generosity. Some in the Christian quarter claimed that the Jews only contributed to causes other than their own in the hope of reaping business advantages, but Father Thomas had always been willing to accept the charity.

Beaudin had also heard that on Wednesday night Monsieur Santi, a French pharmacist at the military hospital, had gone to the Capuchin monastery to return a book he had borrowed from Father Thomas. Santi had knocked on the monastery door for a long time, gotten no answer, and assumed the father was either ill or visiting patients at the Terra Sancta hospital next to the monastery. He went home without returning the book.[6]

On Thursday morning, according to the street rumors, the celebrants who showed up for morning mass at the monastery found the outside door latched. That was unusual—the father was usually up early for Matins—but not unusual enough to set off alarms. Those who arrived early probably assumed the father had overslept, and those who came later that morning could have concluded from the latched door that the mass was already over.

5

Sunset comes early in Damascus in February. It was already dark when Ratti-Menton and Beaudin left the consulate to investigate the monk's residence on Monastery Street. By then the crowd outside the French consulate was agitated, shouting: "Yesterday, Father Thomas was in the Jewish quarter; there's no doubt that he and his servant disappeared there!"[7] The two men had to sneak through the streets around the consulate to get past the crowds. At the monastery they found another boisterous crowd, again from a wide range of Christian denominations that were normally at loggerheads with one another. Ratti-Menton and Beaudin used a ladder from an adjacent building to get into the monastery. The outside door was latched but not locked or bolted.

They went first to the kitchen, where they found two places set for supper, presumably for Father Thomas and his servant, the only residents of the monastery. Crockery and flatware were laid out on the table, and dishes of food were set out, ready to be cooked, as if the monk and his servant had planned to return for dinner. The consul concluded that the table had been set for the night before, which meant that the monk and his servant must have disappeared some time in the afternoon or early evening on Wednesday—exactly what the rumors from the street said.

Ratti-Menton and Beaudin wandered from room to room in the monastery, through the father's bedroom and antechamber, the servant's bedroom, the refectory, a terrace with chairs and a table, and a salon with divans. The father's private dining room was well-stocked with dishes, flatware, glasses, cups, and candelabras. The bookshelves in his private rooms, the library, and the refectory were filled with fine volumes, many imported from Europe, including pharmacological and medical books and texts like Ovid. Cupboards in his apartment were filled with medical equipment and supplies. Closets in the father's rooms held many changes of clothing, good robes and chemises of fine wool, silk, cotton, and an umbrella. The servant's room also had an armoire stocked with robes and chemises in many colors. In the father's apartment they found medals, silver coins, and 119,000 piastres ($5,500–$6,000, a considerable sum in 1840).

It was quite an accumulation for a monk sworn to the simple life. Beaudin was familiar enough with Damascus gossip to know that if some thought him a saint, there were others in the city who thought Padre Tomasso a bit too obsessed with worldly goods for a monk.[8] But wealth, even a flamboyant display of silver coins, was not a crime. And nothing in the father's rooms or elsewhere in the monastery suggested that a crime had been committed. There was no evidence that the door had been forced; nothing seemed to be missing or disturbed. There was no blood, no footprints, no sign of violence or wrongdoing. An intruder would not have left the valuables behind, not in Damascus.

By the time Beaudin and the consul got back to the consulate, the news and rumors of Father Thomas's disappearance had spread through the Christian quarter like a fire, racing down the narrow alleyways, licking into hidden courtyards and up the stairways of the rickety second-floor galleries that overhung the streets. Few details were known yet; but as is so often the case, the fewer the facts, the more leeway for invention. As the evening wore on the rumor-mongering in the streets escalated until the crowds were shouting crude accusations.

Ratti-Menton was too new to Damascus to understand much Arabic. Beaudin must have translated for him. The crowd was still shouting that Father Thomas had disappeared in the Jewish quarter. Then they took up a harsher chant: "The Jews sacrificed the father!"[9]

A few voices suggested that the father might have gone off to one of the surrounding villages to vaccinate children, as he and his servant so often did. But the rising crescendo of accusations about the Jewish quarter drowned out all competing explanations. Late that night, when the streets should have belonged to the night watchmen, the crowd was still in the street shouting, "The Jews sacrificed the father!"

Beaudin and the consul could be sure that few would sleep well in Damascus that night.

2

The Usual Suspects

THE CHRISTIAN quarter of Damascus is bounded on the south by a broad, straight street, the remnants of the Roman Cardo Maximus. Bible-reading Christians know the Street Called Straight from the Acts of the Apostles.[1] On the same road, a few miles outside the city, is the very spot where the Jewish tentmaker Saul of Tarsus—who would later be known by the Latin version of his name, Paul—was walking on his way to Damascus to persecute Christians when "suddenly a light from heaven shone all around him." Saul fell to the ground and heard a voice call out to him: "Saul, Saul, why are you persecuting me?"

"Who are you, Lord?" Saul asked.

The answer came, "I am Jesus, whom you are persecuting. Get up and go into the city, and you will be told what you are to do."[2]

By 1840 only a few columns of the old Roman road still stood. The once-grand street was narrowed by the clutter of cramped shops, overhanging roofs blocked the light, and the once-fine paving was pockmarked where stones had been dislodged or stolen. But a guide could still point out the ruins of the house from which Paul had escaped during the night after the vision that led to his conversion, and a walk along the Street Called Straight could still be a moving experience for a Christian of devout faith.

Just across the famed street were the narrow alleyways and suqs of the Jewish quarter. Jews had lived in Damascus since the Roman era; a few families claimed they could trace their origins to biblical times. Through the centuries the small Jewish community had seen conquering peoples come and go, watched the rise and fall of empires. They had survived by finding a niche for themselves as merchants and craftsmen, trading in the suqs, and importing or exporting goods to the cities of Lebanon and the Holy Land and on the trade routes to Europe and Asia.

8

As a minority they had learned to live with the changes and with their second-class status as non-Muslims in the Ottoman Empire.

On market days the suqs of the Jewish quarter were filled with the goods for which Damascus was famous: stall after stall of sweetmeats, caramels, apricot paste, nuts, silk, brocade cloaks, sheepskins, felt rugs woven with arabesques of colored or golden threads, camel and horse saddles trimmed with buttons of precious metals and tufts of pearls, swords and daggers of steel pounded into the swirls that had once marked the famous Damascus steel. Sherbet sellers banged their brass bowls together to attract attention, and coffee sellers carried trays of tiny cups for sweet Turkish or bitter Arabic coffee or glasses of tea. Everywhere the eyes and nose of a visitor were greeted with a cornucopia of colors and scents—incense, ripe fruits, crushed spices, freshly killed meat, trodden dung, woodchips from the carvers and box makers, charcoal fires and quenched smoke of the smelters and blacksmiths, and the sandalwood, musk, violet, jasmine, and rose- and orange-blossom petals of the scent vendors.

For every product there was a separate suq. At the bazaar of the provision dealers, glass bowls were stacked with cones of rice and fantastically decorated eggs; engraved zinc pots and glass jars held curdled milk, clarified butter, and honey. Herbs and spices were displayed in open bags, sweets stacked on platters, fruits piled in baskets. Pottery crocks held *mahnik*, marinated lamb sausages. Separate shops under an overhead arch blackened with smoke sold the fried mutton that Damascenes ate for breakfast. In the coffee suq the beans were pulverized in giant mortars, with two men alternately swinging huge sledges as pestles. One suq sold wooden cases and keys. There was a suq of silversmiths, another of dealers in *tumbak* flakes for the *nargilehs*, or water pipes, of men of leisure. There were suqs for carpets and for the delicate yellow slippers and red gondola-shaped overshoes that Damascenes preferred. Under wooden roofs that kept out the winter rains and blocked the intense summer sun, merchants would buy and sell and exchange gossip and news from early morning until sunset. Some merchants had places in the fabled covered khans, built to receive the great caravans from the east, where warehouses and apartments shared space with the camel and donkey stalls. Others sold from a favored spot on the side of a road, spreading out goods on a blanket or a tiny cart, adding to the spectacle of color and variety while they hoped they were not in violation of ancient rights or bureaucratic regulations.

It was said that there was nothing that could not be purchased in the suqs of Damascus, but increasingly the merchandise was not produced locally or brought on the famed camel trains from the east but imported by ships calling at Beirut or Alexandria. The hammers of the forgemen and the silent stitching of the slipper makers and saddle makers were a shadow of what they had once been. A few looms still wove *alaja*, a local blend of cotton and silk, but the local weavers could no longer compete with the cotton fields of Egypt, the mills of Manchester, and the Jacquard looms of France. Urban men had begun wearing fezzes imported from France. Bedouin headdresses were made in Birmingham. The cashmere shawl went out of style. Coffee no longer came from Yemen but from Dutch Java or Spanish America; sugar for the coffee came from the British or French West Indies.[3] Only tourists bought swords in the suqs; everyone else knew that the secret of true Damascus steel had been lost for centuries. The marketplaces that had once been outlets of local industry were now mostly a forum where merchants could meet and haggle. Foreigners complained that everything for sale was priced at least six times what it ought to be, not understanding that for the merchants of Damascus the haggling in the suqs was not only an opportunity to fine-tune the prices that in another culture might be set by more structured market mechanisms but an opportunity to assess character, to determine with what manner of man one was dealing.

On Friday morning Jean-Baptiste Beaudin went to the governor's palace just south of the great Umayyad Mosque to report the disappearance of the monk to Sherif Pasha, the governor of Syria and the adopted son of Muhammad Ali, the viceroy of Egypt, whose recently expanded territories included Syria. Despite the forbidding reputation potentates in the former Ottoman Empire enjoyed, Beaudin could be fairly confident that he would receive a warm welcome at the pasha's palace, the grandest Ottoman-style home in the city. Beaudin and Sherif Pasha were longtime acquaintances, and they had been known to spend evenings socializing together. The pasha also seemed to respect the new French consul. The politics of Damascus had come a long way from the xenophobic days when Europeans were not allowed in the city unless they wore native Arab dress.

Sherif Pasha did not question the French consul's right to investigate and prosecute the disappearance of the monk. The capitulation treaties were ancient and undisputed: the French had won the right to protect Capuchin missionaries in the Ottoman Empire during the reign of Louis XIV, and subsequent treaties between the French kings and the sultans had extended French protection to all Roman Catholic clergy. The pasha had heard about events in the Christian quarter and had already made his own inquiries, sending an official into the Jewish quarter to ask questions. He offered to provide assistance to the French consul in the search for suspects or witnesses.[4] But Beaudin and the pasha both knew the investigation would have to wait. Friday was the Muslim sabbath, not a day for business in Damascus, even police business. With its great Umayyad Mosque, Damascus was a semi-holy city. For the Muslim majority, Friday was the day of rest and prayer, the day when even those who were less than diligent in their daily prayers would make amends by going to the mosques to hear the imams give their weekly sermons or read suras from the Qur'an. The Muslim sabbath was also a day for gossip and talk, when men could gather in coffeehouses and at private divans, sharing news and rumors over tiny cups of sweet coffee and tea and nargilehs packed with flaky leaves of tumbak. By the end of the day, few in Damascus would not have heard the news of the disappearance of the monk and the accusations from the Christian quarter.

Damascus had always been a city of fear. People in the streets and in the markets wore façades of friendliness, and ubiquitous greetings of "As-Salām 'alaikum!" and "'Alaikum as-Salām!" in return were as automatic as breathing, but the formal mask of politeness only held ancient frictions, jealousies, and hatreds in check, like a steady drizzle that keeps a smoldering fire from erupting into flame. If a fragile social truce smoothed over tensions among groups in the city, Christians still warned their children about Jewish bogeymen, Jews did not venture into the Christian quarter alone at night, and members of the religious minorities were cautious and circumspect in the Muslim quarters.

Even the architecture of the city was informed as much by fear as by the relentless summer heat, the bitterly cold winter winds, and the traditional Islamic goal of putting no barrier between the earthly realm of man and the celestial realm of God.[5] In Father Thomas's native Italy, cities were forums of open squares and public places, inviting people to meet. Damascus was a city of fortress-homes, their heavy mud or stone walls encircling the courtyard, a private family refuge secure against the world of assassins, rapists, thieves, blasphemers, apostates, and tax collectors outside. From the street, visitors' eyes were drawn to the rickety upper floors, tottering over the narrow streets like the sails of over-rigged tall ships. But even those seemingly fragile galleries, usually the bedrooms and private parlors of the women of the family, were protected and insulated by the heavy walls of the first floor. The only windows onto the street were occasional high clerestory slits for light. Entranceways were deliberately inconspicuous, tucked away in twisty alleys, the doors modest, sometimes with a dissembling pile of debris in front. The exterior walls were exposed mud and stone, sometimes covered with a thin layer of straw and plaster; soil and sand blown off the desert would collect in chinks in the walls, sprouting flowers and vines that grew untended.

The exterior walls of the finest homes were decorated with florid Arabic script. A few homes in the Jewish quarter matched the fashion with inscriptions from the Psalms transliterated into Arabic, but most homes in the Jewish quarter below the Street Called Straight eschewed decor in favor of plain yellow stucco, either out of poverty or in the hope that anonymity would protect them from the curious. From the outside it was hard to tell whether a mean door concealed a courtyard crowded with the cramped hovels of the poor or one of the famed homes of the wealthy. Raphael Farhi, a merchant banker who was rumored to be the wealthiest Jew in Damascus, had his home built with an entrance so concealed that all but the most trusted visitors were received at a decoy house to the left of the main entrance with its own courtyard and receiving room. Only Farhi's family and friends ever saw the real house, built to the traditional Damascus plan of a cross, the rooms in each corner constructed of Italian marble imported on mules from the seacoast, with interior walls carved in florid arabesque patterns. The doors were gilded, clusters of golden fruits and flowers dangled from the cornices and ceilings, rooms were furnished with silk and gold divans and decorated with bowls, pitchers, nargilehs, perfume-bottles, and water-goblets of silver. The house was rumored to have cost 1.5 million piastres, enough to inspire endless rumors and jealousy, and to blind outsiders to the poverty of most of the Jewish quarter.[6]

Saturday morning was a quiet time in the Jewish quarter. Many stalls in the suqs were closed for the Jewish sabbath, leaving whole neighborhoods without the noise, color, and bustle of the displays of goods, or the complex ballets of haggling.

For rich and poor alike in the Jewish quarter, the sabbath eve would have been marked by the best meal of the week: a fat lamb or kid, a breast of veal, perhaps a plump fowl. It was not by coincidence that the chicken suq was also called the Friday suq.[7] In the Syrian tradition, the meat or fowl would be cooked with lemons and sweet fruits, flavored with cinnamon and allspice, braised by servants in the private kitchens of the well-to-do or roasted in a communal oven, and served with *bazargan*, a salad of bulgur and walnuts flavored with tamarind or pomegranate. Men, women, and children would bathe before the sabbath dinner, observant men would visit the *mikveh* or ritual bath, all would dress in their best clothes. Houses would be swept and scrubbed and tables set with the finest linen to greet the sabbath queen. After the woman of the family lit and blessed the sabbath lights—in Damascus they used wicks in oil rather than candles—the head of the family would recite the paean to a "woman of valor" from Proverbs and bless the children. After dinner they would sing and tell stories to celebrate this greatest of all of God's gifts: a day of each week devoted to rest, study, prayer, spirit, and song.

Saturday was the day when rich and poor alike stayed home from the suqs, when whole families would be together, men and women walking side by side to one of the synagogues. The women would take seats in the high balcony while the men sat around the *bimah* below, but the railing in front of the balcony was low enough and open enough that the women could still see and be seen. The Jewish women of Damascus were not closeted like the women of the Muslim quarters, who by tradition were never seen outside their homes.

On Saturday, February 8, 1840, the peace of the sabbath in the Jewish quarter was suddenly shattered by the appearance of the *taffekji-bashi*, the chief of police, leading a detachment of soldiers and police and accompanied by Francis Salina, a physician from Aleppo who served as assistant dragoman to the French consul. Some thought the police and soldiers had consulted local *shaykhs*, Muslim holy men, who told them that the monk and his servant had been killed by the Jews in their own quarter.[8]

With the authority of the pasha behind them, the soldiers searched houses of the Jewish quarter with impunity, sating their curiosity about the rumored wealth that had long been cloaked in the anonymity of yellow stucco. They forced their way into courtyards and private living quarters that had never been seen by anyone except family members and close friends. Inside the houses they opened cupboards and armoires, tore down wall hangings, ripped up carpets and floorboards, penetrating into private chambers and pawing over clothing, books, furnishings, and intimate possessions as they searched for secret passages and concealed rooms. They dug up fresh graves in the Jewish cemetery, looking for the missing monk and for signs of violence on the corpses they disinterred. In the wealthier homes soldiers lounged on the divans, drinking brandy and smoking. They never said what they were searching for, leaving those who watched in horror to speculate on the purpose of this wholesale violation of the community and the sabbath.

In the course of the search, the police and soldiers questioned two Greek Orthodox men, Mikha'il Kessab and Namah Kallam, who said that they had arrived in the Jewish quarter fifteen minutes before sunset on Wednesday, the day the monk supposedly disappeared, and had seen seven or eight men with their faces covered with handkerchiefs walking quickly down the main street. They said they had overheard one of the men, only a few steps away, ask Father Thomas's servant where he was going, and the servant's answer: "I'm going to bring my master home."[9]

The information was not especially useful, except to remind the search party that *two* people had disappeared: Father Thomas *and* his servant. As horrifying as the search was for the Jewish community, the search party came away empty handed. The only evidence they took back with them was a copy of the notice about the charity auction that Father Thomas had supposedly posted on the synagogue door. The searchers found it not on the door of the synagogue but high up on the wall outside a barber shop near the synagogue.

Yet in one respect the raid was surely a success: if anyone in the Jewish quarter was not already terrified from the rumors that had coursed through the streets of the city for two days, the search made sure that every Jew in Damascus was aware of the vulnerability of their community. Who wouldn't wonder what it meant and what would come next? Were the stories about the monk's disappearance only a false rumor that had been started to give the police and troops a pretext to search? Were they only curious, or were they looking for gold and other valuables? Or were the rumors and the search a pretext for demanding another bribe from the community? And what if the searches were not as benign as curiosity or a pretext for booty or extortion? What if there was a truly nefarious purpose?

That evening, while the Jewish community marked the end of the sabbath, holding onto the last sweet smells of the *havdalah* rosewater to blot out memories of the armed search, Sherif Pasha ordered a Muslim prisoner named Sa'id-Muhammad-al-Talli released from the palace dungeons.[10] Al-Talli had been in prison for two months for nonpayment of a debt of 1,200 piastres (approximately $55). In exchange for his freedom al-Talli agreed to assist in the investigation of the disappearance of Father Thomas, claiming that he knew "all the bad characters amongst the Jews" and that if he were released he would use "his best endeavors to discover the perpetrators of the crime." Jean-Baptiste Beaudin personally urged the pasha to release him. The French consul may have paid al-Talli's outstanding debt.[11]

It was not al-Talli's first time in jail, nor was it the first time he had offered the police his knowledge and connections in the underworld of Damascus for a price. A spendthrift and "addicted to intemperance," Al-Talli had a shadowy reputation. He had once been the collector of the *kharāj*, the poll tax paid by Christians and Jews. The offices of tax collector were traditionally auctioned in the Ottoman lands—tax collectors kept everything they levied in excess of the amount they agreed to pay the treasury—which gave the tax collectors enormous leeway to offer special privileges or exact punishing demands from those subject to the tax. Al-Talli had taken advantage of the position to cultivate relationships in the Christian and Jewish quarters. Long after he had lost his official position, he still claimed to be on terms of "great intimacy" with prominent Jewish merchants, although by then most of his dealings seemed closer to extortion than legitimate business. Many in the Jewish and Muslim quarters considered him thoroughly unsavory. The pasha and the French consul were willing to overlook al-Talli's notoriety if his information was useful.[12]

On Sunday the detachment of soldiers and police returned to the Jewish quarter, accompanied by the French consul, Beaudin, and al-Talli. The consul had been disappointed by the lack of arrests on Saturday and blamed the chief of police for being soft on the Jews. This time Beaudin and al-Talli pointed out places that should be searched, and acting on al-Talli's information, the search party seized a Jew named Solomon al-Hallaq (the barber), whose shop was near the synagogue. It was over al-Hallaq's shop that the soldiers had found the auction notice Father Thomas allegedly posted. Al-Hallaq was a poor man partially supported by charity from the Jewish community. He had been married only six months, and his wife begged for mercy, but he was arrested with three other men of what the French consul called "the common class" and taken to the French consulate for questioning.[13]

Again, the consul and the soldiers did not explain their actions. When the search party left, the residents of the Jewish quarter could only wonder what would come next.

3

The Jewish Quarter

O N MONDAY, the day after the first suspects were arrested in the Jewish quarter, the pasha summoned the chief rabbi of Damascus to the *serail*.

Unlike the other rabbis of the city, who spent much of their time as merchants in the suqs or held the title of rabbi as an honorific, Rabbi Jacob Antabi was a full-time rabbi supported by contributions from members of the community. It was not a lucrative calling, and the rabbi was not a wealthy man, although one of his daughters was married to Aslan Farhi, the son of Raphael Farhi. To those looking in from outside the community, Antabi's daughter's marriage and his lofty title of chief rabbi (*grand ḥakham*) made him a member of the elite of the Damascus Jews. When Beaudin and the French consul made a list of the powerful families in the Jewish community and their wealth, they included Antabi.[1]

The position of chief rabbi was in fact far less exalted than the title seemed to imply. It was an elected office, and even within the Jewish community the chief rabbi enjoyed little of the hierarchical rank and authority of an archbishop or cardinal. The formal role existed only because the Ottoman Empire granted substantial local autonomy to *millets* like the Jewish community. In return the Ottoman bureaucracy required that each community be represented by an individual who could be called to account. It was in that capacity that the rabbi was summoned to the governor's palace to appear before Sherif Pasha at his divan.

For the Jewish community, it was hard to know what to expect of Sherif Pasha. He was not a Damascene, or even a Syrian, but was born in Albania, the son of an Ottoman army officer who had been killed in battle when Sherif was four months old. Muhammad Ali, the viceroy of Egypt, adopted the child and raised him with his own children.[2]

In 1831 Muhammad Ali, then governor of the Ottoman province of Egypt, claimed he had not been adequately compensated for his military efforts on behalf of the sultan during the Greek rebellion (his son Ibrahim Pasha had sent back a bag of rebels' ears from Crete to show the prowess of his army)[3] and revolted by extending his own authority to include Gaza, the Holy Land, and Syria. When the sultan sent an Ottoman army to crush the rebellion, Ibrahim Pasha led the Egyptian armies in a grand, sweeping attack through the lands of greater Syria. To the shock and astonishment of the Sublime Porte and a watching and wary Europe, Ibrahim Pasha soundly defeated the Ottoman armies, driving deep into Anatolia, the belly of Turkey, and stopping only when his supply lines were stretched perilously thin and his advances had outstripped even the ambitions of his father. Ibrahim Pasha immediately set out to modernize the administration of the areas now ruled by Egypt, selecting Damascus as the administrative capital of greater Syria. Muhammad Ali appointed his adopted son Sherif Pasha as the new governor of Syria.

The new pasha, his brother, and his father considered themselves reformers and were especially proud of their tolerance of minorities. Under the Ottomans, the Christian and Jewish minorities had been *dhimmis*, a legal classification that effectively made them second-class citizens, subject to special taxes, without the right to testify against a Muslim in court, and restricted by a host of minutely precise regulations that circumscribed what clothing they could wear; the size, design, and decorations of their churches and synagogues; whether they could carry weapons or ride horses or donkeys in the city; and how and where they could observe their own religious rites. Before Muhammad Ali the minorities were at best tolerated and were encumbered by special taxes, including a capitation tax, a tax on those who killed animals for food, and a special tax on Christians because they were assumed to eat pork. They were constantly humiliated by dozens of petty restrictions and customs. A Christian or Jew meeting a Muslim in the suq was required to give up the favored position near the wall and move into what was called "the kennel," the middle of the street where sewage, garbage, and foraging feral dogs shared the roadway. Members of the minorities could not raise their voice when talking with a Muslim, had to wear black clothing and turban, and could not have a seal engraved in Arabic, a language considered too noble for minorities who were allowed only Greek or Hebrew. If a minority-owned house was higher than a Muslim neighbor's, it was liable to be pulled down. The corpses of Jews or Christians could not be carried past the door of a mosque.[4]

Most of these regulations had been lifted under the new Egyptian administration, which even allowed bells and crosses on Christian churches, the blowing of the *shofar* and Purim celebrations in the streets for the Jews, and wine shops in the suqs. The restrictions that remained were symbolic, residual sumptuary customs that frowned on Jews and Christians wearing the green caftan or white turban of a Muslim, and an expectation that the minorities would refrain from public displays that might be objectionable to the Muslims, such as the ringing of church bells or parades with the cross on the Muslim sabbath. Special taxes were still imposed on the minorities, but even these were not strictly enforced.[5]

The liberalization was accompanied by wholesale reorganization of the administrative offices. The traditional policy of the Porte toward rebellious pashas followed an old Turkish proverb: "The hand you cannot cut off—kiss." The sultans flattered and awarded honors to those they could not ruin, waiting for an opportunity to regain authority and leaving the provincial pashas to exercise wide-ranging authority. Corruption had been so widespread that the sultans issued decrees banning the acceptance of *baksheesh* and asked officials to take oaths on their holy books that they would not accept bribes or gifts or show partiality in the performance of their official duties. For the administrative and fiscal posts that were auctioned or contracted, Ottoman administrations had favored Jews. As late as 1830 Raphael Farhi, who held the post of *sarraf* or chief accountant in Damascus, had collected official receipts and made payments for the pasha directly from a strongbox in the center of a vast room, surrounded by clerks on stools or sitting cross-legged on the floor, keeping accounts in Arabic and Turkish.[6]

Just two years later the Jews had lost most of the key administrative positions they had held under the Ottomans. In Egypt, following Napoleon Bonaparte's policy of drawing on local Christians for administrative positions, Muhammad Ali had favored the Copts for administrative positions; in Syria he and his sons turned to the Greek Catholics. The Egyptian reforms included an abolition of the old system of selling tax-collection rights and the appointment of civil servants in their place; Greek Catholics got these new positions and the influence and commercial advantages that accompanied the administrative positions. The Greek Catholics and Orthodox had long been rivals of the Jews in the Ottoman lands, and it was now the Christian merchants who profited from the increase in imports from Europe. Hanna Bahri, a wealthy Greek Catholic from Homs, was granted the prize position of sarraf and became a chief adviser to the pasha. He soon enjoyed such status at Sherif Pasha's divan that he was awarded the title *Bey* and all were required to rise when he entered the room, privileges that had never before been accorded to a non-Muslim. Bahri appointed local Greek Catholics, the principle commercial rivals of the Jews, to the positions of tax collectors and customs agents.[7] Damascus had never before seen so much change so quickly. In the words of a poet of a later generation, "The oppression we suffered before was chaotic / Now it is refined and well-organized."[8]

Only Rabbi Antabi's version of his interview with the pasha has survived, and what was perhaps a lengthy exchange of small talk in the tradition of the divan may be telescoped in his recollections. From the rabbi's account, the pasha told the rabbi that since Father Thomas had disappeared in the Jewish quarter, he expected the rabbi to see to it that the missing monk was produced.

Although he was on his knees before the pasha, Antabi answered defiantly: "Is the Jewish quarter closed off?" He answered his own question. "It is open on every side. Thousands of people go in and go out, day and night, so how can the law hold us responsible?" He pointed out that he was powerless to check every visitor to the quarter and had no troops to help with an investigation. He bitterly quoted Genesis: "Am I my brother's keeper?"

The pasha's answer was to strike the rabbi on the head.

"It is obvious to me," the pasha said, "that you killed him [Father Thomas] to take his blood and that that's your custom. Don't you know about the expulsion from Spain and other expulsions, and about the thousands of Jews killed because of this issue? And yet you stick to this custom of killing people secretly! I have sworn that now I too shall kill you without number until not even two Jews are left here."

With that he dismissed the rabbi.[9]

That evening Rabbi Antabi called for a meeting of the entire Jewish community of Damascus. The meeting was as unprecedented as the reason for it. The Jewish quarter did not even have a place where the whole community could gather, no grand synagogue that focused the Jewish community with the imposing grandeur of the great European synagogues or the Ben Ezra synagogue in Cairo. The synagogues in the quarter were small, built or adapted in accord with the constraints imposed by the Ottoman administration, which required that non-Muslim religious buildings be inconspicuous. Within the Jewish community different social groups were loyal to each rabbi. In each group the richest men bought the right to the best seats in their synagogues; poorer men made do with whatever seat they could find.

That evening much of the Jewish community of Damascus crowded into Rabbi Antabi's synagogue, tucked in at the end of a narrow lane off the Street of Stones (*Tal al Hijara*), a long, narrow street that twisted and turned through much of the Jewish quarter. Everyone was on edge from the talk in the streets and the rumors from the serail as the rabbi stepped up to the ark where the prayer scrolls were kept and suddenly opened the curtain and the metal-decorated wooden doors, revealing the torahs in their *tiqs*, the ornately decorated wooden container encasing a Sephardic torah scroll. His act was so striking—the torahs were normally only brought out to be read at regular services or on the most solemn of occasions, like the *Kol Nidre* prayer—that the attention of the nervous crowd quickly focused on the rabbi. Someone blew a *shofar*, the horn made from the antler of a ram or antelope that is blown on the most important of Jewish holidays.

With the ark open behind him and the plaintive call of the shofar echoing in the ears of his audience, Rabbi Antabi told the community that the rumors and terrible accusations that had been directed at the Jewish community were a "true catastrophe," that the peril hanging over the Jews of Damascus was the gravest danger the community and the Hebrew nation had ever faced, and that it was imperative that anyone with knowledge of the disappearance of the monk come forward. Anyone who had information and did not come forward, he said, would be excommunicated.[10]

No one could mistake the gravity of the rabbi's message. "Excommunication" doesn't fully capture the social and religious breadth of the Hebrew decrees of *niddui* or *ḥerem*, Spinoza's punishment and traditionally the punishment reserved for a Jewish man who vindictively refuses to give his wife a *get*, or Jewish divorce. A man under *ḥerem* is a total outcast from the community: he may not enter the synagogue or participate in collective prayers; no other Jew may do business with him, enter his house, speak to him, or stand within four paces of him. It was the strongest threat the rabbi could make.

Sometime after the dramatic meeting, Antabi heard that a Jewish seller of tumbak had seen Father Thomas and his servant leaving the city before sunset on the evening they supposedly were killed. The monk and servant had been on their way to Salihiye, a village (actually almost a suburb) outside the city walls to the north, below the slopes of Mount Qassioun that looms over Damascus. The tumbak seller, a young man named Isaac Yavo, had a stand in the Hamidieh Suq, the traditional market for nargilehs near the rug market and the western gate of the city, far from the Jewish quarter in the southeast corner of the city.

When he was questioned, Yavo remembered speaking with the monk's servant that afternoon. Yavo had said, "You have not bought any tumbak of me for some time; buy some now."

The servant had answered, "I need none now, for I bought some today."[11]

Isaac Yavo's mother was wary. Even in the face of the rabbi's threat of excommunication, she was reluctant to have her son testify. Because the monk was a French protégé, any testimony would take place at the French consulate, and no one knew quite what to expect from the new consul.

In the few months he had been in Damascus, Count Ratti-Menton had been helpful in his dealings with the Jewish community. Two Algerian Jews had applied for permission to marry, and the consul had given his support on both petitions. As one would expect from the representative of the nation that had given the world the Rights of Man and had been the first to grant its own Jews full citizenship, Ratti-Menton had written that his own principles agreed with "the emancipation of this portion of humanity."[12]

The only other information anyone had about the new French consul was that he had held previous assignments as vice consul or assistant consul in Genoa, Palermo, Naples, Tiflis, and Gibraltar and that some Palermo businessmen had praised his "zeal and energetic activity."[13] From outward appearances his had been a traditional climb up the diplomatic ladder, but there was another side of Ratti-Menton's career that the French foreign ministry, traditionally protective of its diplomats, had cautiously shielded. Even the other consuls in Damascus seem not to have known that Ratti-Menton had left some of his previous posts under questionable circumstances, including rumors of unpaid debts, two declarations of bankruptcy, a request by the host government that he depart Tiflis, and a scandal involving his overly persistent efforts to marry a wealthy heiress in Sicily. The blemishes on his service record—and an awareness that in the eyes of many his Italian ancestry and birth in Puerto Rico diminished his credentials as an authentic French nobleman—might have explained Ratti-Menton's eagerness to assert his position and authority in Damascus. With a somewhat shaky career behind him, he had plenty of room for a triumph on his record.

If Count Ratti-Menton was something of an unknown to the Jewish community, his chancellor and dragoman, Jean-Baptiste Beaudin, was known perhaps too well. Beaudin was a Frenchman by birth, but he had lived in Damascus long enough to straddle two cultures. His Arabic drew compliments in a society where poetry is cherished, and he was married to an Arab woman, yet he eagerly pointed out that his wife was of "European descent," and for many years he had been in the employ of the legendary Lady Hester Stanhope, the niece of William Pitt who had created a sensation with her lovers in London before she arrived unveiled and on horseback to begin a flamboyant life in Damascus.[14]

Beaudin's house on a narrow alley in the Christian quarter was the social locus of the Christian community and a magnet to visitors from abroad. With its walls of mud and tiny, red-shuttered, grate-covered windows, the house was properly inconspicuous: the low door looked like a stable entrance, and as often as not a visitor would find a puddle in front of the door, a typical Damascus ruse to ensure privacy. Once inside the visitor would discover a grand courtyard of marble, with sycamores and Persian willows for shade, cooling fountains, doors leading to six large rooms with vaulted roofs, and balustrades of polished cedar and marble to separate the lower portions for servants from the upper chambers with their fine Persian carpets and mattresses of silk. Tame swallows and doves sipped at the fountains.

In the evenings Beaudin held court there for the local consuls, prelates, and dignitaries, including the pasha. With the skills of a chameleon, Beaudin could one moment be the perfect Paris dandy, flaunting the newest turn of phrase in French or Italian and discussing the latest fashions in Paris, and a moment later reappear in flowing robes, a turban, and yellow Damascus slippers, draping himself on a divan, fingering the amber beads of a chapelet and languidly smoking a nargileh while he commented in poetic Arabic on the price of tobacco in remote desert villages. To admirers from as far away as France and Britain, Beaudin's exotic life in the desert city evoked the Romantic ideals of loneliness, despair, isolation, and rebellion. Visitors trekked across the mountains of Lebanon to call on him, as they had once trekked after Byron and Shelley. Beaudin did not discourage the comparisons. The poet Lamartine was enchanted: "Beaudin is one of those rare men whom nature has fitted for everything. He possesses a shrewd and clear mind, a firm and upright heart, and indefatigable activity."[15] He was not the only visitor to be seduced by Beaudin's charm.

If he was lionized in the European quarter and outside Damascus, many in the Jewish quarter found Beaudin mystifying and unpredictable, which in Damascus meant terrifying. The dragomans in Damascus were notorious for accepting bribes from foreigners to reveal secrets or counteract influence at the court. Beaudin was considered a master of the art and was so respected at Sherif Pasha's divan that he did not wear the distinctive high caps trimmed with sable fur (*kalpak*) by which the dragomen were traditionally identified. His salary as dragoman and chancellor to the French consulate was not sufficient to support his lavish house and entertaining, and the shop he maintained in one of the suqs and heavy borrowing from the pasha only left him further in debt. He remedied his constant financial woes by collecting debts, usually from Jewish merchants, on behalf of foreign brokers. His methods were persistent, and if some of the debts were legitimate, there were many in the Jewish community who claimed that Beaudin abused his position and his friendship with the pasha to cross the line from debt collection to extortion.[16]

The Jewish community had also seen Beaudin with the French consul on their second search of the Jewish quarter, adding his own commentary to the guidance of Muhammad al-Talli, and they knew about Beaudin's friendship with the pasha. If the pasha sent troops to aide the French consul's search of the Jewish quarter, it was hard not to wonder how far their cooperation extended. It was one thing to volunteer to testify at the French consulate, but what if Yavo's testimony were taken instead at the serail? No one who had lived long in Damascus would volunteer for that.

Still, Yavo's testimony was crucial to exonerate the community from the accusations that were floating freely in the Damascus cafes and streets. To negotiate the terms of Isaac Yavo's testimony and obtain guarantees that he would be safe, Rabbi Antabi prevailed upon a respected member of the Jewish community, Isaac Picciotto, a young but wealthy merchant with excellent connections in Europe. Picciotto spoke Italian and French, and his family had a long record of service as consuls representing Austria, Denmark, Prussia, and other European powers in the commercial center of Aleppo. From the reputation of his family in consular circles, and his own status as an Austrian protégé, Picciotto had every reason to anticipate that he and Count Ratti-Menton could come to a satisfactory agreement about Isaac Yavo's testimony. Ratti-Menton readily assured Picciotto that there was nothing to fear if the young man testified, but Isaac Yavo's mother was sufficiently concerned about the potential perils of the situation that it was only after Picciotto and Rabbi Antabi repeatedly secured the personal assurances of the French consul that she finally agreed to let her son testify.[17]

The agreement was cause for celebration in the Jewish community: if young Isaac Yavo, a witness with no special interest, testified that he had seen Father Thomas at the Hamidieh market on the other side of the city at the very time when the monk was alleged to have disappeared in the Jewish quarter, it would totally undermine the unsubstantiated accusations that the father had been murdered in the Jewish quarter. Relief from the horrid accusations and the pasha's threats seemed at hand.

The preparations for Yavo's testimony were not the only defense the community mustered.

Even before Rabbi Antabi called the meeting of the Jewish community in his synagogue, a small group of prominent men in the quarter met privately to formulate a response to the threatening rumors. Meir

Farhi, a wealthy and respected merchant, called the meeting, bringing together a group of local merchants with considerable personal fortunes and experience with the bureaucracy: his brothers Murad and Joseph, David Harari and his brothers Isaac and Joseph, Aaron Stambouli, and Shahade Lisbona. The Hararis were rumored to be second in wealth in the Jewish community to the Farhis, and Stambouli and Lisbona were on the next rung of wealth and influence.[18] Each man at the meeting had done enough business to be familiar with the baroque administrative procedures of the Ottoman Empire, and all were friends, or at least acquaintances, of highly placed local officials like the chief of police, the new sarraf, or the pasha. Many of the men had held quasi-administrative positions. Shahade Lisbona, an exception to the Egyptian appointment of Greek-rite Catholics, still held a contract with the government for financial services.

The men at the meeting knew that a response to the rumors and arrests would have to come from within their own community. The Jews of Damascus had heard and read about the wealthy, influential Jews of the West, like the Rothschilds with their dominant banking positions and social recognition in England, France, Germany, Austria, and Italy, and Moses Montefiore, who had been honored by the monarchy in England. They also knew the familiarity was not reciprocated.

It was not that the world didn't know about the Jews of the ancient Holy Lands. Throughout the diaspora Jews had been encouraged to give *tzedakah* each week to support the Jews of Palestine. In the tiniest remote *shtetls* and villages, families would deposit a few coins each week in a blue tin box to support those who spent their days in study and prayer at the Western Wall or in the yeshivas of Jerusalem or Safed. The "Next year in Jerusalem!" of the Passover Haggadah and the poignant plaint of the Psalms, "If I forget thee, O Jerusalem, may my right hand wither," were in the prayers of every Jew.

But there were no special prayers for the ancient Jewish community of Damascus less than two hundred kilometers north of Jerusalem. Indeed, Syria was so remote in the imaginations of the Ashkenazi and even the Sephardic Jewish communities of Europe and the Americas that those who were aware of the Jews of Damascus thought of them as a people apart, an offshoot of the mainstream of Judaism. The few European Jews who had traveled in the Middle East rarely ventured to Damascus. Even the intrepid Moses Montefiore, famed for his trips to the Holy Land, declined to visit Damascus, in part from fear of epidemics and the dreaded lazarettes but also because the local regulations in Damascus required foreigners to wear native dress in the city, which meant Montefiore would not be able to appear at court in his favored uniform of a Lieutenant of the Guard.

The little the world may have heard or read about the Jews of Damascus made them seem a lost tribe. The melodies of their chanted prayers and hymns, borrowed from the Arabic traditions of melodic improvisation, sounded more like the lilts of the suq or an Arab neighborhood than the canonical melodies of the traditional Jewish services. The daily language of the community was neither the Yiddish of the Askenazi Jews nor the Judeo-Spanish of the Sephardic Jews but Arabic. A few families in Damascus traced their family histories to the expulsion from Spain and retained traces of Judeo-Spanish in their private speech, and there were a few others in the community, like Isaac Picciotto, who had spent time in Europe or who did extensive business with European merchants and, as a result, knew Italian or French. The majority of the Jews in Damascus spoke only Arabic in their homes, in the suqs, and in their prayer houses. The only language they had in common with European or American Jews was Hebrew, a language most Jews considered too sacred for secular matters.

Knowing they had to rely on their own resources, the group of merchants agreed to offer an award of 50,000 piastres (roughly $2,500, a generous sum in 1840) for information on the disappearance of Father Thomas. Although they did not seem to have a plan for what to do after they posted the reward, at the very least the offer would buy them time. Even before they announced the reward, they tried lobbying officials of the pasha's government in an effort to halt the spread of the calumnies and accusations that had been directed against their community. They knew where to expend their efforts: the wealthy merchants had all held administrative positions before the arrival of the Egyptian administration, and Raphael Farhi was still doing considerable banking business with Ibrahim Pasha and Sherif Pasha.[19]

One delegation called on Hanna Bahri Bey, the wealthy Greek Catholic merchant from Homs who had replaced Raphael Farhi as sarraf and had become a policy adviser to Sherif Pasha. Bahri listened to the appeal from Shahade Lisbona and Raphael Farhi but distanced himself from the matter, saying that the accusations against the Jews were "not a matter that concerned him" and that the Jews would have to handle the situation themselves.[20]

The group had greater expectations of Ali Agha, the chief of police, who had a reputation as a bon vivant, was friends with many in the Jewish community and was rumored to have been favored in his financial and mercantile transactions by the Farhi family. It is not clear what Ali Agha promised the delegation that called on him, but the French consul later accused him of being lax in his searches of the Jewish quarter and of "allowing himself to be bought by the Jews."[21]

Finally, the group went to the French consulate to present the offer of the reward for information on the disappearance of the monk. They had already printed thirty notices announcing the reward and put them up in the Christian, Muslim, and Jewish quarters of the city, and they were prepared to post bond for the reward.

While they were waiting to be received by the consul, Shahade Lisbona passed a message, wrapped around a 500 piastre note, to one of the consul's close advisers, a Christian named Ayyub Shubli.[22] Like everyone who had done business with officials in the Ottoman Empire, Lisbona had offered comparable baksheesh to Ottoman and Egyptian officials dozens, if not hundreds, of times. It was the way business was done. From the pettiest official to the pasha himself, the appropriate baksheesh was an essential token of respect, a discreet incentive to ensure that a petition or plea received prompt notice. Five hundred piastres was a generous, though not excessive, sum. Shubli had himself no doubt passed similar notes with the appropriate baksheesh countless times and perhaps received them almost as often.

But instead of quietly pocketing the 500 piastre note, Shubli held it up. Acting surprised, he said that it appeared that Lisbona and the delegation were trying to bribe him. At that point an altercation broke out: shouting, accusations, and counter-accusations. The French consul and his advisers acted as though they had never before seen or heard of baksheesh passed to an official. The consul accused Lisbona and the Jewish community of attempting bribery to deflect attention from the disappearance of the monk in the Jewish quarter. They later called Lisbona back to the consulate for interrogation. Asked why he had offered the money to Ayyub Shubli, he said that he wanted to distance himself from the affair because he had been "afraid."[23]

The others in the delegation were not arrested, and Raphael Farhi and Isaac Picciotto were permitted to call at the serail and at the French consulate to urge solidarity and responsibility on those who had been arrested in the earlier search of the Jewish quarter. Farhi and Picciotto may have also attempted to gather intelligence. But the joint mission on behalf of the community was in tatters. Instead of demonstrating the concern and good intentions of the Jewish community, and buying time until the actual whereabouts of the monk could be learned, the delegation had called attention to their wealth and their willingness to pay whatever was necessary to smooth over the situation.

Word of the episode spread quickly. To many in Damascus the delegation of Jewish elders and their bribe seemed proof of the guilt of the Jews.

4

Interrogation

R ATTI-MENTON had studied law in Paris before he joined the diplomatic corps, and while he had never practiced law, he knew that the barber Solomon al-Hallaq, who had been identified as a suspect by Muhammad al-Talli, was a good candidate for interrogation. The barber was young, not well educated, too poor to be able to bribe the jailers, and socially isolated from the wealthy Jews who might seek to influence his testimony. In the imposing environment of the consulate, and in the face of the authority represented by the pasha's police and troops, the French consul could expect that the barber would confess or at least point his finger at others who were behind the disappearance of the monk.

But when Ratti-Menton asked the barber about the disappearance of Father Thomas, the barber answered that he knew nothing about it. The consul asked again and got the same answer.[1]

The consul changed tack. He asked the barber about Father Thomas' flyer: Why was the notice on the wall over the barber's shop? The barber said that he assumed Father Thomas had put it there.

If that was the case, Ratti-Menton asked, why was the notice high up on the wall?[2] Everyone knew that Father Thomas was a small man. And he posted his appeals for funds on the doors of churches and synagogues, not outside barber shops. The barber said that maybe the notice had fallen off the door of the synagogue and someone had put it back up on the wall over the shop.

How was it fastened to the wall? The barber answered that it was put up with two sealing wafers, one red and one lilac.

And how did the barber know the color of the sealing wafers, which were behind the notice and hidden by the paper? The barber said he did not remember. Maybe he had put the notice back after it fell off the wall.

Ratti-Menton asked how that could be. He pointed out that the sealing wafers appeared to be used for the first time. He had retrieved copies of the same notice from the Greek Catholic and Greek Orthodox churches, and neither of them had been put up with sealing wafers like those used for this notice.[3] The implication was that the barber had put the notice up himself, which meant that Father Thomas had not come to the Jewish quarter to post his notice but had been lured there, presumably to meet a nefarious end.

The barber answered that he did not know anything else, that he had told them everything he knew about the father. Beaudin tried questioning the barber directly instead of translating the questions of the consul. It made no difference who asked the questions. Solomon al-Hallaq repeated that he knew nothing about the monk. They asked questions for three days without getting answers.

It was not an auspicious start for the investigation.

Westerners like Ratti-Menton found the Ottoman legal system incomprehensible in theory and barbaric in practice. The guarantees to the accused which are the bedrocks of Western criminal law—the presumption of innocence, and the rights of the accused to be represented by a lawyer, to know the precise charges that have been brought, to be confronted by an accuser, to be protected from self-incrimination, and of habeas corpus—held little significance in the Ottoman legal system. Instead, the underpinning of the system was faith in the omniscience and omnipresence of a compassionate and merciful Allah, who would protect the innocent and allow or perhaps even hasten the condemnation of the guilty. Faith in the benevolent protection of Allah precluded the need for the accused to be represented by a lawyer. It also meant there was no reason to limit the range of questions that could be asked of the accused, or the means used to persuade testimony from witnesses. Procedures that a Westerner would have labeled torture were in the Ottoman system only an incentive to induce a suspect to give truthful testimony. Under the ubiquitous protection of a merciful and compassionate Allah, the innocent were assumed to have nothing to fear.

Although we instinctively react with horror to the use of torture in judicial investigations, medieval French and English criminal proceedings, the ancestors of our own legal system, used much the same methods. In the courts of twelfth-century France, the accused swore an oath promising to tell the truth. Then with the understanding that the oath had summoned God to bear witness, and that God would surely protect the innocent, the accused would be forced to walk over a bed of hot coals or through a gauntlet of swords. A witness who told the truth was presumed to have nothing to fear from the coals or swords. Today our courts retain only the sworn oath that a witness takes before giving testimony. At Sherif Pasha's court in 1840, a merciful and compassionate Allah was still expected to protect the innocent.

The workings of the Ottoman legal system could lead to abuses, and they frequently did when official attitudes favored efficiency over the civil and judicial rights of witnesses and suspects. The typical investigative procedure was to round up the usual suspects then utilize whatever means of interrogation would elicit a confession or accusations. Those named by the witnesses or suspects would in turn be arrested and interrogated until they too confessed, at which point the crime was declared solved. The investigation and the trial were essentially the same procedure. Since the pasha was the chief administrative and judicial officer of Syria, interrogations that took place before him effectively constituted the trial. After the interrogation, a formal statement would be prepared in the form of questions and answers, which when signed by the accused constituted the trial record.

Although Ratti-Menton was eager to show off enlightened French investigative and judicial procedures to the Egyptians, after three days of fruitless interrogation at the consulate he concluded that he had no choice but to turn the barber over to "ordinary jurisdiction," by which he meant the pasha and his interrogators.[4] Ratti-Menton probably considered the partial surrender of his legal authority as the protector of the Roman Catholic clergy a small price to pay for the potential payoff in information if the pasha's interrogation methods were more successful than his own. He and the pasha may have already come to an understanding that they would cooperate in prosecuting the case.

Solomon al-Hallaq was taken to the serail, where the pasha offered him 50,000 piastres and a full pardon if he confessed to the murder of the monk. If he refused, the barber was warned, the pasha "knew what to do."

The barber answered, "Go to the important people in the quarter; they will settle everything." The barber, who presumably knew about the reward the wealthy Jewish merchants had posted, may have thought the same wealthy leaders of the Jewish community would pay whatever extortion was demanded. Later the barber told Muhammad al-Talli, "Tell the pasha to arrest the important people in our nation; those people know [the answers]." Asked whom he meant, the barber answered, "You know them better than I do."[5]

The pasha was not satisfied with al-Hallaq's enigmatic answers. As he had promised, he knew what to do when the barber refused to confess.

Europeans called it the *bastinado*; the local term, in Arabic, was *falaga*. The procedure had been refined over centuries of use to an exquisitely effective means of persuading cooperation from a person under interrogation. The subject would be bound face down on a wood bench, and the interrogator would stand at his feet with a *kurbash*, a whip constructed of tapered strips of hide. The very best kurbashes were made of hippopotamus hide, expensive and difficult to come by in the Middle East but highly valued because the tough hide could be shaped into exceptionally fine yet rugged lashes.[6] The finer the lash, the more effective the bastinado.

The first stroke of the kurbash was usually against the wooden bench. The impact of hide against wood softened the individual strands of the kurbash, making the lashes more effective, and the loud snap focused the attention of the subject, amplifying his anxiety. The next blow fell on the soles of the feet with their sensitive nerve endings. Wealthy subjects, whose feet were accustomed to the soft yellow leather of Damascus slippers, sometimes confessed before the first blow fell. Or they would bribe the interrogators to lighten up on the number or severity of strokes. Damascenes joked about a man receiving the bastinado and crying out, "My back, oh my back!" When bystanders said, "You fool, it is not on your back but on your feet that you are suffering," the man answered, "Ah! But if I had some powerful patron at my back, I should not be under the stick. It is this lack that makes me wail about my back."[7]

The barber Solomon al-Hallaq, without a patron and too poor to post a bribe, could expect no mercy. After he was flogged with 150 to 200 lashes of the kurbash, al-Hallaq changed his testimony.[8] His new story was that on the afternoon the monk disappeared, a servant of David Harari's named Murad al-Fatal had visited the barber in his shop near the synagogue and asked him to come back to Harari's house to bleed his master. Al-Hallaq claimed that he did not really know David Harari. They recognized one another well enough to say "As-Salam 'alaikum!" when they passed on the street but were not of the same circle. He was only a poor barber, and Harari was a wealthy merchant, a man whose investments and holdings, along with those of his brothers, were worth hundreds of thousands of piastres.[9]

The barber told the pasha that he and Murad al-Fatal walked together back to David Harari's house on the Street of Stones. Once there the barber walked into one of the many rooms of the house and saw Father Thomas stretched out on a raised section of the floor. The father's arms were tied behind his back, his mouth was gagged, and he was being held by several men, including David Harari, Harari's brothers Isaac and Aaron, their uncles Rabbi Joseph Leniado and Joseph Harari, and two other rabbis, Moses Abulafia and Moses Salonicli.[10] Many of the men al-Hallaq named were members of the delegation of wealthy merchants who had gone to the French consulate to offer a reward for information on the disappearance of the monk.

The barber said that David Harari asked him to slit the throat of the monk but that he had refused, pleading that he lacked the courage.

"After you were asked to slit the throat of the priest," the pasha asked, "Did you stay there or leave?"

"I didn't stay there. I went to close my shop and go home."

"If the father had cried out, would someone have heard him outside?"

The barber answered, "The house is surrounded by Jewish houses. No one could hear anything. And finding himself alone among them, he would be afraid to cry out."

Later, under questioning by Beaudin, the barber admitted that Aaron Harari had given him one of Father Thomas's notices and the sealing wafers and that he had put the notice up on Thursday and told no one, not even his wife or his father. He said that David Harari had promised to give him 1,000 piastres and told him that if he went to prison they would take care of his family.

"How did they promise?" Beaudin asked.

The barber explained that on Sunday afternoon, when the soldiers arrested him in the Jewish quarter, David Harari managed to pass near him and said, "Don't be afraid, we'll give you money."[11]

The pasha ordered the men named in the barber's testimony arrested. After hearing about the new interrogation, the French consul went to see Sherif Pasha to congratulate him on the "laudable zeal" with which he was pursuing the case.[12]

For the Jewish community the new testimony was a terrible blow.

Over the centuries the Jews of Damascus had been no strangers to accusations from the Muslim majority and especially from their commercial rivals in the Christian quarter—usually of usury, avarice, greed, or xenophobia. While none of the accusations was welcome, they could at least be explained from the outsider merchant roles the Jews had long played in the community. For centuries the Jews of Damascus had sold and imported merchandise and had lent money to Christians and Muslims, even redefining transactions to use discounted notes or to sell fictitious goods to circumvent the Muslim ban against interest. If most of their transactions were welcomed, and for the most part filled necessary functions in the commercial and financial life of the city, in a predominantly Muslim culture in which merchant and financial activities were frowned upon by the notables, it was not surprising that the Jews were sometimes the targets of bitter accusations, charged with usury and price gouging and with adulterating scammony, a resin drawn from the local convolvulus plant that was much in demand as a laxative in Europe.[13]

Of all the accusations ever leveled against Jews, the "blood libel"—the myth that Jews kill Christians and use their blood for obscure ritual purposes—was the most terrifying and inexplicable. It was a Christian myth, believed and propagated by Christians. Its most probable origin may be in a corruption of the Christian Mass, perhaps a twisted confusion of the ancient and long-discontinued Jewish practice of animal sacrifice, the Agnus Dei of the Christian Eucharist, and the exhortation of John 6:53 ("if you do not eat the flesh of the Son of Man and drink his blood, you have no life in you"). Just as gossip undergoes strange mutations from one telling to another, so that a story of minor consequences becomes embellished into murder and mayhem, so too a myth that began in some bizarre misinterpretation of the Christian Mass with its mysterious transubstantiation of wine and bread into the blood and flesh of Jesus became the horrifying accusation of ritual murder. For centuries in Europe the myth waxed and waned, popping up without apparent roots in a village or city, ultimately to be proved spurious, only to resurface in a neighboring village or perhaps halfway across Europe. No matter how many times the charges were proved baseless, the myth would reappear, a weed that could not be killed with the truth.

In the Christian quarter of Damascus the myth of Jewish ritual murder had been one of those stories passed from generation to generation in quiet whispers, like the warnings parents gave their children about Jewish bogeymen. The inspiration for the whispers came each year during Holy Week, when giant statues of the crucified Christ were paraded through the streets to the accompaniment of drums, and the Catholic and Orthodox priests preached fiery sermons that contrasted the Christians who belonged in the city where Paul had his miraculous vision and conversion with the eternally homeless Jews, condemned to wander the world. The priests would read from the gospel of John how Jesus "came to his own and his own people did not accept him" and how at the time of the Jewish Passover Jesus had gone to Jerusalem and found "the moneychangers sitting there."[14]

On Good Friday the Catholic priests would focus on the prayer Pro Perfidiis Judaeis, the only prayer in that day's liturgy that was not dignified by kneeling. Their sermons would reach a crescendo with the passage

> Pilate said [to the chief priests and the guards], "Take him yourselves and crucify him: I find no case against him."

The Jews replied, "We have a law, and according to that law he ought
to be put to death, because he has claimed to be the Son of God. . . ."
He said to the Jews, "Here is your king!"
They cried out, "Away with him, away with him, crucify him!"[15]

Some Damascus priests went further. When they invoked the image
of the Jewish moneylenders outside the Temple, they accused the Jews,
all Jews, of usury, reminding their audience that in their own community the Jews were often the bankers and moneylenders. When they
read the narration of deicide in the gospel of John, they would expand
the alleged role of the Jews to include the actions of the Roman soldiers
who were supposed to have pierced Jesus' body while he was on the
cross. In the fervor of Holy Week it was only a few more steps to accuse
the Jews of replaying the crucifixion by murdering Christians or of
mocking the most sacred of Christian rituals, the Eucharist, by using the
blood of Christians in perverse rituals of their own.

As horrible as they were, the Holy Week sermons were predictable.
Every year, at the time of the sermons, there would be ugly incidents on
the streets of Damascus. Bands of Christian thugs would demand black-
mail and threaten to raise mobs against the Jews. The hierarchy of
insults, a pride among some speakers of Arabic, would escalate. One
long-term resident remembered that if it was "tolerably reasonable" to
call a man a donkey, "somewhat severe" to call him a dog, and "contemptuous" to call him a swine, it was "withering in the last degree" to
call him a Jew.[16] In bad years Jews who ventured out onto the streets
would be beaten or publicly humiliated. The Jews of Damascus learned
to avoid the streets and the suqs from Maundy Thursday through
Easter Sunday.

These annual Holy Week accusations were repulsive and hateful.
Yet the sermons of the priests remained abstract attacks, generalized
and deliberately vague accusations of what, even in the passions of
Easter week, were metaphorical crimes. The priests no doubt intended
to incite hatred and fear of the Jews, and they succeeded. But they did
not accuse specific members of the Jewish community of an actual
crime. The passions they aroused were of the moment, a fervor that
accompanied the strong emotions of Holy Week. When Easter and
Passover passed, the violence on the streets and the coarse imprecations
would end, and emotions would gradually subside. The relations
between the Jewish and Christian communities in Damascus would
perhaps never be more than civil, but the Jewish community had lived
long enough as a minority in Damascus to celebrate what did *not* hap-
pen: the Jews were not subjected to the humiliating anti-Jewish sermons
that some Italian Jews were forced to attend, the rabbis of Damascus

were not forced to dress in grotesque costumes to be humiliated by the public at carnival, and the Jews were not forced to participate in outlandish carnival races for the entertainment of the Christians. More important, there were no mass murders of Jews, no forced conversions, no mass expulsion. In comparison to those unspoken threats, the Easter nastiness probably seemed mild. The Jewish merchants knew that after Holy Week they could return to the cafes and their stalls in the suqs and khans, and that in time the markets and streets would again be alive with shouts, negotiations, and polite greetings.

For the Jewish community of Damascus the blood libel had been a whispered caution, an awareness of evil, slanderous tales that were all the more bizarre and incomprehensible because they were so at odds with fundamental Jewish values, thought, and law. The abhorrence of cannibalism and the absolute prohibition against the consumption of blood are fundamental concepts of Hebrew scripture and Jewish laws. The laws of *kashrut* absolutely forbid an observant Jew from consuming blood: an egg contaminated by a single drop of blood is not kosher and cannot be eaten, and meats like liver must be specially treated to remove any trace of blood. The absolute rejection of the human sacrifice that had marked earlier religions was as central to the history of Judaism and the Jewish people as monotheism. The Akedah, the binding of Isaac by Abraham on Mount Moriah, is a seminal event in Judaism precisely because God ultimately does not demand human sacrifice of Abraham. The absolute impossibility of the Easter accusations made them all the more incomprehensible; it was as if the accusations in the streets and the sermons were a wicked game some Christians enjoyed playing during Holy Week.

Despite decades or centuries of the repulsive and appalling Easter accusations, the Jewish community of Damascus had no experience of an actual prosecution of an alleged blood libel.[17] And the manhunts and arrests in February 1840 came not amidst the predictable passions of Holy Week but months before. Suddenly, without warning, the charges whispered in the streets were not abstract imprecations against Jews in general but were targeted directly at the rabbis and the heads of the richest merchant families of Damascus, men respected as leaders of the Jewish community, men whose families had lived in Damascus for hundreds of years, men who had distinguished themselves with their commitments to charity and civic responsibility and who now suddenly found themselves charged with the ritual murder of a man who, if not exactly a saint, was widely admired in Damascus.

The immediate damage of the barber's testimony was limited by the lack of corroboration, but the barber's identification of leading members of the Jewish community escalated the rumors and accusations that had been daily fare in the suqs and coffee houses. With rumors in the streets everywhere, it was clear that the pasha and the French consul would not drop the matter and that a wave of arrests would follow. The Jews—even the wealthier and more powerful members of the community who had once held high offices—also knew that they were powerless before any legal procedures in the pasha's court. It was hard not to fear that the Jewish community would never again live in peace in Damascus.

In the Jewish quarter there was suddenly talk of leaving or going into hiding. There were secret passageways and concealed apartments in the back alleyways of the city and Muslim families that could be paid to hide a person until the crisis cooled off. There were also villages outside Damascus where a person could disappear. A few families like the Farhis or the Hararis were wealthy enough to be able to hire a camel train to cross the desert to Jerusalem, Alexandria, or Beirut. There was even talk of travel by ship from Beirut or Alexandria to Constantinople, Italy, or France.

But even flight was not an escape. Travelers had already reported from Beirut that the rumors from Damascus had inspired attacks on the Jews and the plundering of synagogues in the Djabar neighborhood. Germanos Bahri, the brother of Hanna Bahri Bey, held a similar office in Aleppo, where he spread word of the accusations and investigation in Damascus, prompting demonstrations against the Jews there. News from Damascus had prompted the Greek Catholics and Muslims in Jerusalem to threaten the Jewish community there.[18] A few of the Damascus merchants had family or commercial connections in Italy, but the papal territories still had ghettos. France had never had ghettos, but Ratti-Menton was not an inviting example of the welcome that might await a Jewish family in France. And flight, even travel to another city of the Middle East like Aleppo or Jerusalem, meant leaving everything behind. Damascus was the only world the Jews of the city knew, Arabic the only language they spoke; the customs and food and pace of life in Damascus were familiar and treasured. Despite the talk, the only ones who fled were a few families who did not have capital or property in the city.[19]

The barber's new confession invigorated the investigation for Ratti-Menton, Beaudin, and the pasha. If they had begun their pursuit of the Damascus Jews from motives of ambition, greed, and political opportunism, they seem to have convinced themselves of the truth of the street rumors and their own accusations against the Jews. Once they had decided to prosecute the Jews, procedures like the bastinado, which may have had a rationale as tools of investigation, became instead techniques to persuade witnesses like Solomon al-Hallaq to agree to the details of a broad indictment. The kurbash and the tourniquet can leave a subject all too eager to please his interrogators. Witnesses knew they had only to agree to the narrative and names the pasha, Beaudin, and Ratti-Menton suggested and the pain would stop.

By the end of the week, the pasha and Ratti-Menton had stepped up the searches of the Jewish quarter, with the pasha's troops and police making daily forays into the homes south of the Street Called Straight. This time the searches focused primarily on the homes of the "better class of Jews" who had been named in the barber's "confession": the Harari brothers, their elderly uncle Rabbi Joseph Leniado, and Rabbis Moses Salonicli and Moses Abulafia.[20] The French consul and his aides accompanied the troops on their searches, and mobs of Christians, twenty or thirty at a time, followed along, adding their jeers to the hubbub.

While the soldiers searched more of the private homes, the French consul focused his attention on the women of the Jewish community. Although the Sephardic Jewish communities of the Middle East shared much of the honor/shame code of gender relations with the Muslim majorities, the Jewish women were not veiled and sheltered like the Muslim women.[21] The Jewish women of Damascus were known for their beauty and elegant grooming. They braided their thick, dark hair with gold coins and wore elaborately brocaded robes over embroidered bodices and white trousers. Many of the Jews were desperately poor, but among the wealthier families the women often wore fine gold and diamond jewelry. In a culture where banks were virtually unknown, much of the wealth of a family might be in a wife's jewels. One visitor wrote that Raphael Farhi's wife wore a diamond "worth the price of a German principality" on her forehead and another on her finger "worth the price of a New York uptown establishment—ladies, dresses, and all."[22]

To a European, the elegantly dressed Jewish women who ventured out in public, especially in the relative safety of the Jewish quarter, must have seemed a sharp contrast to the unseen Muslim women hidden away in their homes or behind veils. Ratti-Menton was not married. During the searches of the Jewish quarter he stared at the younger Jewish women, pretending to look them over as candidates for marriage. He boldly approached some of the women in their homes, making suggestive comments. He tried to persuade David Harari's daughter, a beautiful young girl, to leave with him by promising her that he would "interest himself on behalf of the deliverance of [her] father." At the home of Rabbi Joseph Leniado he insisted that Leniado's wife Esther uncover her face, sang an Arabic love song to her, and demanded to be kissed. When she refused he said, "Your husband is old; I would be willing to take you, or else my dragoman would." Francis Salina, the assistant dragoman of the French consulate who accompanied Ratti-Menton as his interpreter, also tried to extort jewelry from some of the women, including Mouna Farhi. At one point during the search, Ratti-Menton turned to his entourage and said, "If it weren't for this Father Thomas case, we could never have been able to see these Jewish women."[23]

The consul's remarks and gestures might have been acceptable flirting in Paris. As a European aristocrat among those whom he probably saw as quaint or backward, the count probably thought himself charming, perhaps irresistible. To Damascus sensibilities his behavior was shockingly offensive, adding to the terror and horror of men and women who were forced to watch the violation of the sanctity of their homes and to witness respected members of their community arrested for an incomprehensible and horrifying accusation.

Harari's servant, Murad al-Fatal, was the next to be interrogated. Al-Talli was still at the serail, where he could counsel the witnesses before and after they were questioned by the pasha. After a session on the bastinado, al-Fatal admitted that he had been sent to fetch the barber that night. But he said he had not come back to the house with the barber and that he knew nothing else about the matter.

Who was at your master's house that afternoon? the pasha asked. Al-Fatal said that he had seen no one. His master had an abscess on his gum and didn't go out.[24]

Perhaps in respect of their standing in their community, the other men arrested in the sweep were not flogged; instead they were held in individual cells, where they were forced to stand without sleep, guarded by a soldier with a bayonet who made sure they did not slump or support themselves against a wall. They had all been without sleep for thirty-six hours when they were individually questioned.[25] All of the men denied any knowledge of the alleged incident.

David Harari, at whose house the barber claimed the monk had been murdered, told the interrogators he had not seen Father Thomas for two or three months, that he had not seen the others that afternoon, and that while his house was on the Street of Stones as the barber had testified, there had been no gathering there. He said that on Wednesday evening he had been late in the suq. After finishing his business he had gone to the customs house to clear some fabric, and from there he had gone to the house of Giorgios Ankhouri and stayed until late.

Joseph Leniado, Harari's uncle and a rabbi by training, explained that his daughter had died on February 1 and that it was the custom in his family to sit *shiva* for seven days. His shiva had not ended until Thursday afternoon; he had not gone out at all on Wednesday and hence knew nothing about the missing monk. To support his alibi he gave the names of two Christian merchants who had called at his house on the evening the monk was allegedly murdered. One, who was from Damascus, confirmed the alibi. The pasha refused to accept a written deposition from the other merchant, who was from a town three days away from Damascus.

Isaac Harari said that he did not travel in the same circles as the barber and that as a busy merchant he did not have time for anything like what the barber had described.

Joseph Harari said his house was also on the Street of Stones but that as an old man he rarely went out. It had been three months since he had seen Father Thomas, and, in any event, he certainly had no complaints against Christians. He had been raised among them; they slept at his house and he had slept at theirs.

Rabbi Moses Abulafia, who was also a merchant, said he had come back from the suq to his house on the corner of the Street of Stones and School Street (*al-Katateeb*) toward sunset that night and had seen no one. He pointed out that the Hararis were not his "society" and that he had not been with any of them for six months. He allowed that it was possible that the barber had seen him on the street, but he did not remember seeing the barber for a month and a half or maybe two months.

Rabbi Moses Salonicli told the pasha he had no idea what the barber was talking about, that he had gone home around ten-thirty or eleven that day and that he had not seen Father Thomas at all.

Aaron Harari said that his house was close to the English consulate, that he rarely went to his brother's house in the Street of Stones, and that it had been more than a week since he had seen the barber. He said that everyone walks in the area of their houses, especially in the late afternoon when they leave work in the suqs. Hence the assertions of the barber were completely without foundation and undoubtedly made up.

When the men had made their individual denials, the barber was brought in and asked if he had seen them in front of David Harari's house. The barber repeated his earlier testimony that he had seen them all together with Father Thomas on the Street of Stones near the houses of two of the Hararis brothers on Wednesday between noon and midafternoon.

The arrested men said to the barber, "My friend, how can you say that you saw us? You should beg God to forgive you."[26]

The pasha later questioned Giorgios Ankhouri, who had been named in David Harari's alibi. Ankhouri said David Harari had come to his house not on Wednesday as he had testified but on Thursday afternoon. The pasha also questioned the official at the customs house, who said that it was on Thursday that David Harari had come to clear three bales of cloth, not Wednesday as Harari had testified.[27] But even the pasha was not willing to hold the men on the basis of a few contradictions in their alibis. Everyone except Solomon al-Hallaq and David Harari's servant was released. Al-Hallaq and the servant were held in the barracks next to the serail.

Raphael Farhi, whom many regarded as the leader of the Jewish community, visited the barber and the servant Murad al-Fatal at the serail. No food, clothes, or bedding was given to those in detention, and Farhi may have brought food and warm clothing. After Farhi left, Murad al-Fatal retracted his earlier testimony, leaving the barber's story uncorroborated. Al-Fatal later said that he had changed his testimony from fear: while the pasha could have him beaten, Raphael Farhi was powerful enough to make him lose "everything" in the Jewish quarter.[28]

The French consul, furious at the interference in the investigation, had Raphael Farhi placed in preventive detention in the French consulate. Farhi, a British protégé and well connected abroad, was spared any questioning, and Ratti-Menton noted that in his case Article 365 of the French penal code, which forbade the use of force to compel testimony, would be strictly observed. Farhi was also allowed to have a servant go back and forth to his house daily to bring food and changes of clothing and bedding.[29]

With Raphael Farhi in detention, five respected elders of the community and two rabbis accused as the murderers of the monk, and two poor men of the community still in custody and potentially subject to more torture to coerce further testimony, the Jewish community of Damascus was desperate. Their sole hope was to come up with an alternate explanation of the disappearance of the monk.

5

The Tumbak Seller
& the Watchman

ANY IN DAMASCUS remembered that not long before he
disappeared, Father Thomas and his servant had gotten into
an argument with a leader of the Muslim muleteers named
Ibn I'wah at the Khan Assad Pasha, the largest of the *caravanserai* of
Damascus. The khan, with its imposing wooden doors large enough to
admit camel trains, sculptured doorway, and the encircling black and
white stone walls of the ground-floor warehouses, formed an uninten-
tional theater-in-the-round. The balconied second floor that served as
an inn for traders visiting Damascus was an ideal gallery for an audience to watch a dispute on the trading floor below. Although Father
Thomas was widely respected as a pharmacist and healer, he had a reputation for haughtiness and belligerence, and an excited crowd in the
khan had watched the monk's servant seize the muleteer around the
throat and hold him until "blood came." They had also heard Father
Thomas curse the muleteer "in his faith." The muleteer answered by
knocking Father Thomas down and swearing that he should "not die
but by his [the muleteer's] hands." The mostly Muslim crowd in the
khan jeered at the monk, and one bystander, a Muslim merchant named
Abu-Yahya-al-Kaphar, joined in cursing and threatening Father
Thomas. Al-Kaphar, a former druggist who sold general merchandise
from a small shop in the khan, was heavily in debt and had a reputation
for being morose. Street rumors blamed his ill humor on troubles with
his two wives, one white and one of color.

A day or two after Father Thomas and his servant disappeared, al-
Kaphar's shop did not open for business and remained closed for many

40

days. Rumors blamed the Jews for his disappearance until someone broke into the shop, which was locked from inside, and found al-Kaphar hanged inside. Spokesmen from the Jewish community urged that the apparent suicide be investigated, suggesting that al-Kaphar, either alone or with the muleteer, might have taken revenge for the incident in the khan by murdering Father Thomas and then have committed suicide because he feared he would be apprehended, convicted, and executed by the pasha.

It seemed a promising area of investigation until the pasha announced that he would not investigate the suicide or question the muleteer.[1]

The testimony of the tumbak seller Isaac Yavo was the last hope left for the Jewish community. Yavo was young, had no connection to the leaders of the Jewish community, and no reason to lie. Once he testified that he had seen the monk leaving Damascus through the gate near the Hamidieh suq at the same time that Father Thomas was alleged to have disappeared in the Jewish quarter on the opposite side of the city, it would put an end to the entire matter.

The story Isaac Yavo told the French consul and Beaudin was simple. On Wednesday, February 5, the day Father Thomas was supposed to have disappeared in the Jewish quarter, Yavo had seen the monk and his servant Ibrahim Amara leave the city through the western gate. Yavo explained that his tumbak stall was near the gate, in one of the many stalls that had been built between the columns of the old Roman road there, just south of the citadel on the northwest corner of the city.[2] Yavo went to his stall every day. Tumbak was a good business: nargilehs were popular in Damascus.

He said he did not know the monk, although he recognized him because the father and his servant often came through the gate on their way to the outlying villages where Father Thomas administered vaccinations. He had seen them that Wednesday a half-hour before sunset on their way out of the city.[3] The place where he had seen them was at least a thirty-minute walk from the Jewish quarter.

Yavo's story was so at odds with the testimony of the barber and the rumors and clamors in the streets of the Christian quarter that Ratti-Menton and Beaudin interrogated the young tumbak seller again the next day and the following day, trying to break his story. Yavo stuck to his account.

After three days of interrogation, Count Ratti-Menton was at another dead end in his investigation. His questioning of the barber had gone nowhere until the pasha had taken over with his more persuasive techniques. Now the consul's interrogation of this new witness, far

from shedding light on the disappearance of the monk, had only confused the investigation, exonerating instead of condemning the accused
Jews. Instead of releasing Yavo after his testimony, as he had promised
to do in his negotiations with Isaac Picciotto and Rabbi Antabi, Ratti-
Menton had the young witness taken to the serail.

The pasha did not welcome Yavo's testimony. In his own interrogation of the young tobaccanist the pasha pointed out that the gate where
Yavo claimed to have seen Father Thomas was in the western part of
the city, while the Jewish quarter, as everyone knew, was in the east.
Since everyone knew the father had disappeared in the Jewish quarter,
the pasha announced, it was obvious that Yavo was lying and part of a
Jewish conspiracy. He demanded of Yavo, "Who dares to give evidence
in favor of the Jews? Who bribed you to give this false evidence?"

Yavo answered that no one had paid him. The story he told was
what he had seen. He was a poor shopkeeper. He worked every day at
his stall by the western gate. He saw people come and go from the city.
That afternoon he had seen the monk and his servant leaving the city.
He had talked to the monk's servant. He often saw them on their way
out to villages where they gave vaccinations. He had no reason to lie.

Furious at the contradictory testimony, the pasha ordered Yavo
flogged until he revealed the names of those who had suborned his
false testimony.[4]

The usual session of the bastinado was 200 lashes. If the witness was
uncooperative, a second session of 150 lashes was usually enough to
persuade cooperation. The interrogators sometimes added an additional inducement, typically, in Damascus, the tourniquet, a thin cord of
hide that was tightened around the head by twisting with a stick until
the subject's eyes bulged out of their sockets. The tourniquet was so
painful that even the most recalcitrant subject would usually decide to
cooperate.

The soldiers in the military barracks next to the serail were experienced with the bastinado. They knew that when the feet of a subject
were so lacerated from the kurbash that further flogging was futile, they
could shift to the buttocks or the backs of the thighs. They were also
masters of the technique of suddenly pausing, without warning, during
the flogging. To the subject the unanticipated surcease after what had
seemed interminable and unbearable pain could seem a temporary victory. That pause in the flogging was often the moment when a subject
would let down his guard, relaxing the tricks that had gotten him
through the pain of the lashes. The subject might even feel a sudden
bond with the interrogators who only a moment before had been tormentors. The brief moment of bonding could produce a confession.

If the subject did not confess, the pause would end as suddenly as it began. Without warning the kurbash would snap against the wooden frame of the bastinado, waking the subject from the temporary reverie of the surcease and reminding him that the next blow would fall on a sensitive part of his body, that the excruciating pain he had thought unbearable only moments before would begin anew. It was another moment when a subject was at his most vulnerable.

Isaac Yavo was strong young man. With determination, a strong man can withstand flogging for a long time. There are tricks to steel resolve against the pain. Focusing on a memory, an image of a loved one, a pleasant moment or place, or a dream can help. A man can pray for unconsciousness. He can recite a prayer over and over and find solace in the words and the thought that his repeated mantra is a flag of defiance.

At some point during his flogging, Isaac Yavo began to recite the Sh'ma, the central declaration of the Jewish faith: "Sh'ma Israel, adonai eloheinu, Adonai ehad" (Hear O Israel, the Lord our God, the Lord is one).[5] Yavo was not a learned man, but he probably knew that it is a *mitzvah*, a good deed, for a Jew to die with the words of the Sh'ma on his lips. It doesn't take long on the bastinado for a man to start thinking of death.

While Yavo was being flogged, in another cell in the barracks interrogators questioned another potential witness to the disappearance of the monk, the night porter who was paid by the Jewish community to monitor the streets of the Jewish quarter. The night porter had his post at a gate near the end of the Street of Stones, only twenty meters from the Street Called Straight. Anyone who wanted to come or go from David Harari's house had to pass by his station. Like Yavo, the watchman was a poor man without the means to bribe the guards and interrogators. He was not young but sixty years old. No formal record seems to have been kept of his interrogation, and, reflecting his lowly social status in the community, the few references to him that have survived do not even mention his name.

The watchman testified that he had not seen any of the people who were supposed to have come and gone from David Harari's house that night, including the monk.[6]

Two days after his interrogation by the pasha, the serail announced that Isaac Yavo had died in his cell in the dungeon. There was no official investigation of his death. The explanation on the street was that Yavo had received five thousand lashes. When the Jewish burial society came to the serail to claim his body, they had difficulty completing the ritual washing in preparation for burial because the flesh "fell entirely off from his bones." Ratti-Menton later claimed that the pasha regretted what the soldiers had done to the young man, and would certainly have opposed it if he had known, because he hoped to persuade Yavo to admit who had told him to lie.[7] The night watchman also died in the dungeons, five days after he was flogged.

The last hopes of the Jewish community died with these men.

6

The Long Wait

A FTER YAVO'S DEATH, a delegation from the Jewish community went
to the Hamidieh suq where Yavo had reported seeing the monk
and his servant leaving the city. There they searched out
Christians and Muslims who lived or worked in the area and found several witnesses who confirmed Yavo's deposition. When the delegation
returned to the Jewish quarter and suggested that these new witnesses
could be called before the pasha to testify, someone suggested that it
would be prudent to confirm that the witnesses were actually willing to
testify. Especially after the earlier incident when an effort to post a
reward had been turned into accusations of bribery, it would be an
extreme embarrassment for the Jewish community if the witnesses
failed to support Yavo's story.

The delegation returned to the Hamidieh suq and asked the witnesses if they would testify. The answer they got was, "No, no; we have
seen them; but if we be called before the Pasha, we shall say, we have
not." By way of explanation, the witnesses told the delegation from the
Jewish quarter that Yavo was dead because he said he saw the monk,
and they were not willing to "endanger our lives for your sakes."[1]

While the Jewish quarter saw their last hope for a defense collapse,
the French consul interrogated a black slave named Kittèh who lived in
the house of a Jew named Sérazettoum. Unable to get satisfactory
responses to his questions—interrogation was not Ratti-Menton's
strong suit—he had the slave taken to the serail, where the pasha promised her "the richest presents, and even marriage" (probably concubi-
nage) if she would only confess.

Kittèh insisted that she knew nothing and that she was sure no murder had been committed in her master's house. The pasha switched
from "good cop" to "bad cop," drawing his sword and threatening to

cut her head off if she didn't tell the truth. "I am a Muslim," she said, "and only the slave of these Jews. If I knew anything against them I should not deny it."

In frustration the pasha sent her to the bastinado until he and Ratti-Menton finally concluded, as the French consul put it, that she was an idiot and would never say more than "I know nothing."[2]

The pasha and the consul had been eager for more testimony because the barber Solomon al-Hallaq's uncorroborated accusations were not enough to convict the prominent Jews he had named in his confession. Now the pasha decided on a new tactic.

Without warning, Sherif Pasha dispatched a squadron of soldiers to the Hebrew Boys' School in the Jewish quarter, where they arrested sixty-five boys, students in the equivalent of a *ḥeder*, a Jewish elementary school. Some of the boys were as young as five years old. The boys were taken to the serail and locked up in two crowded cells, with no blankets or extra clothes against the February cold, no hygiene facilities, and a meager ration of ten drachms of bread and water twice a day. Their anxious parents were not allowed to visit them.

Interrogators repeatedly questioned the children until one little boy said his father killed the monk and threw him in a pit in the courtyard of their school. A search party was dispatched to the school, where they found a subterranean vault with little peepholes where the children sometimes played. The vault was excavated with the little boy watching. Nothing suspicious was found.[3]

The Jewish community knew the incarceration and interrogation of the boys was a sham. The boys were hostages, held to put pressure on the community. Sherif Pasha may have drawn inspiration from the biblical story of the ransoming of the first-born in Egypt and the Jewish ceremony of the redemption of the first-born, reasoning that if sons were that important to the Jews, surely the Jews of Damascus would surrender the guilty parties to gain the release of their own sons.[4]

To increase the pressure on the community the pasha also ordered approximately seventy Jewish men arrested—estimates at the time varied from fifteen to three hundred—including the Jewish gravediggers and butchers. Some of the arrested men were subjected to the bastinado and interrogation; others were held in the barracks as hostages. The pasha seems to have believed that with the butchers and gravediggers incarcerated, the life of the Jewish community would grind to a halt and they would have no choice but to confess to the murder of Father Thomas. If he knew that only a trained ritual butcher could slaughter animals in accord with kosher laws, the pasha seems not to have realized that the community could go without meat. In reality, the pressure point was at the serail: with so many arrested, there was a shortage of cells in the dungeons of the serail and the adjoining barracks. Some of the incarcerated men had to be held in common cells with chains and collars around their necks.[5]

Delegations from the Jewish community called on the pasha, begging him to release the innocent children. In the tiny, crowded cells, in the bitter cold of a Damascus winter, epidemic disease was a danger. Older boys were mixed in with younger boys; tyrannical behavior or sexual exploitation was not out of the question. And, of course, neither the children nor their mothers could answer the pasha's questions. None of them knew anything about the monk.

The pasha was adamant. He refused to release any of the hostages.

There had been crises in the Jewish community before, disputes with other minorities, friction with the Muslim majority, run-ins with local officials, and threats against the Jews. The possibility of violence was always close to the surface in Syria and the Holy Land. There had been pogroms against the Jews in Safed in 1834 and 1838. In 1834 Daniel Picciotto, the Netherlands representative in Syrian Tripoli, had joined with his English and French counterparts to protest the plundering of Jews by resident Egyptians there. And visitors to Damascus had observed that the city was a "seat of fanaticism."[6] Still, there had never been a situation like this. No one in the Jewish community knew what to expect next. Nothing is more frightening than the unknown.

The Jews of Damascus were accustomed to life as a minority. Despite the occasionally demeaning regulations, including a rule that forbade a Jew from holding any office with authority over a Muslim, the Jewish community generally got along well with the Muslim majority. Unlike the Christians, who sometimes challenged the regulations by ringing church bells or holding church processions on the Muslim sabbath, the Jews cautiously avoided what Muslims or the Ottoman or Egyptian officials would see as rebellious or offensive acts. There had always been some resentment of their status as merchants, bankers, moneylenders, and officials in the provincial government administration, but the Jews did not object to being marked by wearing specially colored garments, did not erect magnificent synagogues or worship publicly, were the first to discharge Muslim slaves when requested, and were the last to dress like Muslims, even when it was permitted. Jews also paid local Muslim notables sums of money as an "insurance fee" to protect themselves against riot and assaults, were careful not to demand the expanded political rights that some of the reforming edicts seemed to promise, and were willing to demonstrate loyalty to the Muslim state. In Damascus, unlike most cities of the Middle East, the Jews even took Arabic names.[7]

The fundamental cultural and theological similarities between Judaism and Islam also created bridges between the communities. Both religions were fiercely monotheistic, worshiping a single God without what they perceived as the dilution and idolatry of the Christian trinity and saints or the interlocution of the Christian priests. Jews instinctively agreed with the inscriptions from the Qur'an on the Dome of the Rock: "Praise be to God, who begets no son, and has no partner" and "He is God, one, eternal. He does not beget, nor is he begotten, and has no peer." The Jewish kashrut laws were familiar to a Muslim who observed halal dietary restrictions, especially in the bans against the consumption of pork or blood. Jews and Muslims, unlike the Christians, circumcised male children, the Jews on the eighth day after birth and the Muslims after the eighth birthday.[8] There were intersections and subtle but recognizable borrowings in the theologies and liturgies of the two faiths: the emphasis on the written word and the recognition of Moses as a major Islamic prophet, and Abraham (Ibrahim) was a patriarch in both traditions. The Akedah, the story of the binding of Isaac by Abraham in the Hebrew Bible, had its parallel in Allah's refusal of Ibrahim's offer to sacrifice his son, which is celebrated in the Islamic festival of Id al-Adha. In Damascus Muslim men fervently observed the holiday by slaughtering a ram, slitting its throat while saying, "In the name of Allah, Allah is great." In 1840 the holiday fell one week after Father Thomas disappeared.

The Jews and Muslims of Damascus rarely enjoyed close social relationships. They did not intermarry, they lived in separate areas of the city, and they were generally formal in their business relationships. For most Muslims connection with the state, as in accepting an administrative position, was considered demeaning, and the Muslim notables disdained merchant trade in favor of landowning or socially prestigious membership in the societies of Muslim religious experts, descendants of the prophet, or the chiefs of the local military garrison. But even those who kept their distance from merchant activities purchased goods from Jewish merchants and borrowed money from Jewish bankers. Within that nexus of formality and mutual respect, the Jews and Muslims usually lived peacefully side by side, separate descendants of the children of Abraham.

The same could not be said of the Jewish and Christian communities in Damascus. Each was a minority within the Muslim culture, restricted to residence in its own quarter and subject to sumptuary laws and other restrictions as dhimmis. But if the two minorities might have had much to gain from cooperating with one another, they were locked in a commercial and political competition and separated by ancient fears and myths. Christian and Jewish merchants competed openly in the suqs and in the import and export trade that was increasingly important as the expanding port at Beirut opened Damascus to trade with Europe. For centuries they had also competed for the lucrative positions as tax collectors and official accountants to the Ottoman and Egyptian governments. The periodic mutual animosities between the Jews and Christians were well known, a "two-edged sword," in the words of the British consul.[9]

In the spring of 1840 it appeared that the competition for administrative positions, which had shifted in favor of the Christians, especially the Greek Catholics, during the Egyptian occupation, might heat up again. By late 1839 the great powers—especially Britain and Austria but also Russia and Prussia—had become increasingly concerned that the expansion of an independent Egypt threatened the survival of the Ottoman Empire. The sultan's empire had been the "sick man of Europe" since the Greek revolt, and Ibrahim Pasha's surprising victories over the Ottoman armies, followed by the defection of the Ottoman navy to the Egyptians, suggested that the Sublime Porte might not be able to resist additional encroachments and dismemberments. With the Metternichian balance of powers and the role of the Ottoman Empire as a bulwark between Europe and Asia threatened, early in 1840 Lord Palmerston began negotiations with Alexandria, hinting that Britain would recognize Egypt's independence if Syria were restored to the sultan's empire.

Predictably, France continued the centuries-old diplomatic competition with Britain by taking the Egyptian side in the dispute, supplying an adviser to the Egyptian military and promising support to the Egyptians against England and the other great powers. France was a powerful ally, but memories were long in the Middle East, and there were many who remembered that Horatio Nelson, with a small squadron of Royal Navy ships, had put an end to Napoleon's Egyptian expedition. Two generations later eloquent but vague French assurances were unpersuasive alongside the sight of British fleets off Alexandria and Beirut and the scuttlebutt that, if necessary, the British were willing to land an army in Lebanon. Knowing wags in Alexandria and Damascus began talking about the restoration of Ottoman rule in Syria and asking what it would mean for the Christian and Jewish minorities.

In Constantinople the young new Ottoman sultan had promised reforms. His Gülhane Decree of 1839, the Noble Rescript of the Rose Chamber, granting the rights of citizenship to all of his subjects, including the Christian and Jewish minorities, was received enthusiastically when it was first read publicly in Syria. But the high-minded language of the decree—"The Muslim and non-Muslim subjects of our lofty Sultanate shall, without exception, enjoy our imperial concessions"— was too abstract to have much effect without specific implementation, and the Christians of Damascus had lived under Ottoman rule long enough to know the pace of the bureaucracy. The gap between the policies in a *firman* and changes in practice could span decades, perhaps generations. And even if the sultan's decree took effect immediately, for the Christian community and especially the Greek Catholics who dominated the commercial life of Damascus, the equality promised by the decree would mean a step *down* from the privileged positions they enjoyed under the Egyptian administration. The real impact of a restoration of Ottoman rule, as the Christian quarter of Damascus saw it, would be a return of the coveted administrative positions as sarrafs and tax collectors, and the commercial advantages that derived from the exercise of administrative authority and influence, to the Jews who had held those positions before the Egyptians arrived.[10]

Indeed, from the coffeehouses in the Christian quarter of Damascus, the diplomatic dance going on in Alexandria and in the foreign offices of the great powers looked like one more chapter in a vast Jewish conspiracy. The West might know little about the Jews of Damascus, but the Christian and Jewish quarters of Damascus were familiar with stories of the power and influence of the Jews in Europe. Like so much of the world of the early nineteenth century, the Christian quarter of Damascus had heard story after story of how the powerful, wealthy Jews of Europe, especially the Rothschild family, with their powerful banks in the capital of every great power, had used their money and power to influence monarchs, governments, investors, and commercial interests. That the much-publicized images of Nathan and Lionel Rothschild at their celebrated posts in the London stock market were cartoons from the newsweeklies, and the sarcastic descriptions of James de Rothschild in the Paris bourse were parodies by Heinrich Heine, did not diminish the influence of the myths they launched.

For the Damascus Christians even the Egyptian alliance with France could seem fraught with risks. France was officially the protector of the Catholic clergy in Syria, but the word "Catholic" had different meanings for the French and for the Damascus Christians. France had always been far more supportive of Roman (Latin-rite) Catholics and Maronites than of the Greek (Melchite) Catholics who were the largest Christian denomination in Damascus.[11] And from the perspective of the conservative Christian quarter, France was also the nation of the Revolution, the nation that had turned a powerful monarchy on its head with the Rights of Man, the nation that had granted full citizenship to the Jews. The Christian quarter saw the French Revolution as fundamentally anti-Christian. The realization that their status as the dominant minority in Damascus was dependent on the support of the French, and the suspicion that their putative ally was as vulnerable to the influence of the Jews as the British was galling. In the paranoid mentality of the Christian quarter, *everyone* knew that Jews *everywhere* stuck together. That made it easy to believe that the Jews of Damascus were secretly supported by a conspiracy of what the Christian quarter saw as the Jew-loving nations of Europe.

With rumors circulating everywhere, Damascus was ripe for intrigue. Hanna Bahri Bey, the chief adviser to the pasha, lost patience with the slow pace of the investigation and said to the chief of police, "How long are you going to let the case of Father Thomas drag on? Can't you find two or three reliable men . . . who could dig up a corpse and each take a limb and go into a Jewish home—Murad [Farhi's] or [Aaron] Stambouli's or someone else—and then create an uproar . . . saying 'Look here, we've found Father Thomas.' "[12]

Muhammad al-Talli, who recorded Bahri Bey's comments, had his own agenda. He had negotiated his release from the pasha's dungeons with the promise that he could lead Ratti-Menton and Beaudin to the parties responsible for the disappearance of Father Thomas. When he told Hanna Bahri Bey that he was being stopped in his "operations," Bahri told him to "keep calm, let them do what they are doing, and we'll see how it all ends."[13] It was good counsel, but al-Talli was impatient to see his own advice acted upon; his reputation as a police informant and spy and the effectiveness of his efforts at extortion rode on the outcome.

Al-Talli was also greedy. He knew David Harari from past dealings, and Harari's brother Aaron even described al-Talli as a "friend." It was known in the Jewish community that al-Talli had fingered the barber Solomon al-Hallaq, and he had been seen leading search parties in the quarter, so David Harari probably was not surprised when al-Talli visited him to present an ultimatum. "Make sure that the Jews give me money," al-Talli told Harari, "or I'll do them a bad turn." Harari agreed to pay al-Talli, but only after the case was satisfactorily settled. His motive, he later explained, was "fear that it would be said he [Harari] had bought him [al-Talli]."[14] Miffed by what he saw as a rebuff, al-Talli went to the serail to make good on his threat.

At al-Talli's urging, the pasha determined to jog Solomon al-Hallaq's memory. The barber was given a total of four sessions of the bastinado, hundreds of blows of the kurbash on the soles of his feet, the backs of his thighs, and his buttocks. In pauses between the floggings the interrogators put a tourniquet around his head, twisting it so hard the cord broke. The barber's chin turned "quite white," and "a convulsive trembling set every limb of his body in tremulous motion." After the torture sessions he was taken back to his cell. Muhammad al-Talli accompanied him.[15]

On the morning of Friday, February 28, three weeks after the disappearance of the monk, and shortly after Muhammad al-Talli had spent time in the cell of the barber, Ratti-Menton and Beaudin received an urgent summons to the serail. Sherif Pasha told them that after further sessions of the bastinado the previous night, the barber had corrected his earlier testimony and had now confessed to participation in the murder of Father Thomas.

The barber's new testimony was that he had gone to David Harari's house, as he had said in his earlier testimony, and found the Harari brothers, their uncle Joseph Leniado, and two other rabbis, Moses Abulafia and Moses Salonicli there. The barber now said he had in fact not left the house but had stayed and had assisted in the murder of the father. He said he had pulled the monk's head up by the beard in order to facilitate the flow of blood into a copper basin and later had helped strip off the monk's clothes. Then they had burned the clothes and carried the body into an adjoining room. Later that evening, when Harari's servant Murad al-Fatal returned to the house, he and the barber cut the body up, smashed the skull on the marble and stone floor of the courtyard, and under cover of darkness dragged what remained of the corpse to one of the sewers of the Jewish quarter.[16]

The barber suddenly remembered every detail of the night of the murder. He said that David Harari had started to cut the throat of the monk but that his hand began to tremble and his brother Aaron Harari finished the job.[17] He remembered that the room they dragged the corpse to for dismemberment had walls of wood. He said the Harari brothers promised him money and that they had said they would pay for the servant al-Fatal to marry at their expense.

The final statement of the barber's testimony is written as though it were a transcript of the interrogation. It was actually put together later, a summary statement in the form of questions and answers, similar to the Inquisition procedure of requiring every confession obtained under torture to be repeated later under "normal" conditions.[18] The interrogation in Damascus was in Arabic and Turkish; Beaudin translated the testimony into French for the dossier the consul was preparing on the case. The details the barber now claimed to remember were compelling:

Q. What about the sack [used to carry the remains of the monk to the sewer]? Was there one or two, if one did you carry it by yourself, and what color was it?

A. It was like a coffee sack, of packing cloth, grey. There was only one sack, and we [the barber and al-Fatal] both carried it, sometimes one of us or the other, sometimes together.

Q. What did you do with it when you were finished?

A. We left it at David Harari's.

Q. You said that when you slit the priest's throat and collected the blood, not a drop was spilled. What about the blood after the cadaver was dragged to the other room?[19]

A. I didn't pay attention.

Q. What about the room where you dismembered [the corpse]?

A. It wasn't finished; there was earthen and wood debris; he was dismembered on the dirt floor.

Q. What about the entrails?

A. We didn't cut up the bowels; we took them in the same sack and threw them in the sewer.

Q. The sack didn't allow the material contained in the entrails to drip?

A. A coffee sack is solid, there was no question of letting it drip.

Q. When you dismembered the father, how many of you were involved, how did you cut him up, and what kind of knives did you use?

A. The servant and I did it, while the others indicated how it should be done. We traded off when we got tired; it was the same kind of knife as used in a butcher shop, the same one that was used for the murder.

Q. What happened to the knife?

A. We left it at the house?

Q. After you cut up the father, on what floor did you smash him up?

A. On the floor between the two rooms.

Q. It is of course sheltered?

A. It is covered.

Q. When you broke up the head, the brain came out. What happened to it?

A. We took the brain with the bones.[20]

Murad al-Fatal, David Harari's servant, was interrogated again after the barber's confession. The pasha offered al-Fatal a complete pardon if he told the truth. He was then given another session of the bastinado and confronted with the barber's testimony. Still, he denied any role in the murder.

Then he met with al-Talli and the barber. The barber said, "Don't be afraid to talk; I have confessed everything." The coaching and encouragement of al-Talli again proved decisive. Murad al-Fatal confessed that he had assisted the barber in dismembering and disposing of the body of the monk. On the smallest details of events that had taken place three weeks before, the servant's story, even his language, agreed almost exactly with the barber's testimony:

Q. What about the intestines?
A. We cut them and what was inside them, put them into the sack, and threw it into the sewer.
Q. Nothing escaped?
A. The sack was good and solid; nothing escaped.

. . .

Q. After he was dismembered, on what kind of floor did you break the bones.
A. On the floor between the two rooms and in front of the doors of the rooms, a space which is covered.
Q. The brain, what happened to it?
A. We gathered bones and the brain together, and carried everything.[21]

Al-Fatal was emphatic that he was not present during the killing of Father Thomas. He said that after the body had been disposed of and the barber went home, he stayed at David Harari's house for an hour and a half, filling nargilehs with tumback so David Harari and the other men who were there could sit around and smoke.

It was exactly the testimony the pasha and French consul had been waiting for.

7

Confessions

VISITORS TO DAMASCUS could not help noticing that most of the city lacked sewers. Open swales cluttered with sewage, refuse, and dead animals ran down the sides or center of the rutted alleyways that passed for streets, and during the rainy season debris would course down the streets and through gaps under the city walls. In the dry season the fetid stench of festering garbage and rotting flesh in the streets drove anyone who could afford the luxury to the refuge of enclosed courtyards with their fragrant fruit trees and blossoms.

Ironically, the glory of its cities had been one of the prides of early Islamic culture. In Cordoba in the year 1000 there were miles of lighted streets and aqueducts and sewers that rivaled the triumphs of Roman engineering. There is no evidence that Jews from Spain brought city planning and engineering skills to Damascus after the expulsion from Spain, but whether through wealth, hygienic concerns, or aesthetic and olfactory priorities, many streets of the Jewish quarter of Damascus, unlike much of the rest of the city, were built over covered sewers. Some houses in the Jewish quarter were constructed with drainpipes that ran from washrooms and latrines directly into the sewers, welcome luxuries in a culture in which so much family life and entertaining took place outside in the courtyards or in open-air cafes.

After their testimony at the serail, the barber and David Harari's servant were taken to the Jewish quarter to identify the room in David Harari's house on the Street of Stones where the murder they described in their testimony had taken place. They rode there on donkeys, supported on either side by soldiers, their backsides and feet too lacerated from the bastinado for them to sit upright or walk unassisted.

The two men identified a small room in Harari's house as the site of the murder. The room was to the left of the divan, with windows in front looking onto the interior courtyard and high windows in back looking out onto the street. The barber had testified that no one in the neighboring houses would know what was going on inside. A visitor to Damascus months later thought it was "scarcely possible that any person would submit quietly to the pains of death without cries, which would have certainly been heard in the street behind." The official notes of the search did not comment on the windows in the room.[1]

The French consul and his party focused on the search for blood stains and other direct evidence of a murder. They found a burn mark on the white marble floor, which they assumed was from when the conspirators had burned the clothes of the monk. The marble and inlaid stone floors also appeared to be freshly washed, and the searchers identified faint red stains low on a wall alongside the door. Ratti-Menton wrote in his journal that the freshly washed floor and the stains on the wall were definitive evidence that a murder and the draining of blood from a corpse had taken place there.[2]

The French consul had not yet spent a full year in Syria. Perhaps he did not realize that early March, when his search took place, was the beginning of spring, when the relentless cold rain and wind of the Damascus winter finally give away to a month of pleasant weather before the onslaught of the summer heat. March was the month when households in Damascus underwent the traditional spring cleaning, including sweeping and washing the floors to remove the sand and dust motes blown in by the winter winds. There was nothing especially suspicious about the floor being washed in March, and there was no indication that the stains on the wall were human blood; later visitors thought they almost certainly were not blood.[3]

The search party of the French consul, Colonel of the Artillery Hazik Bey, Beaudin, Dr. Massari, a squadron of soldiers, and a crowd of Christian bystanders went from David Harari's house to the edge of the Friday or chicken suq, outside the home of Rabbi Abulafia on the corner of School Street, and close to the gate where the deceased night guard had monitored the street. There, the two witnesses identified a stone sewer cover as the place where they had disposed of the body.[4]

Soldiers lifted the stone cover and climbed down into the mud. The city water had been turned off to allow the sewer to drain, but a stream of water suddenly coursed down the channel. The French consul ran into the adjoining house, demanding to know why they had flooded the channel. The young woman there did not answer quickly enough, and with his usual quick temper, Ratti-Menton struck her, shouting that her actions proved that she and her family were co-conspirators in hiding vital evidence.[5]

When the water in the sewer finally drained, the soldiers threw up broken bones, a fragment of scalp, and a shapeless rag made of the material normally used for a fez. The bones appeared to be human, the fragment of scalp looked like a monk's tonsure, and the rag was black with a red stripe—the colors of the distinctive European-style skullcap the monk usually wore. The crowd accompanying the search was sure of what the soldiers had found.[6]

The French consul filed his first report to Paris the next day. Ratti-Menton dated his letter to Marshall Soult, the premier of France, February 28, as if he had begun writing the report *before* the decisive revelations at the serail and the dramatic discovery of evidence in the sewer of the Jewish quarter. It is clear from the first sentence—"An appalling drama has just painted the city of Damascus in blood"—that the consul expected his artfully constructed narrative to have an impact. In fifteen pages of often dramatic prose, he chronicled the disappearance of the monk, his own role in the investigation, and the careful progress of narrowing the search to the Jewish quarter and the ultimately successful interrogations of the barber and David Harari's servant. The report sidestepped mention of the torture used to persuade the confessions at the serail and did not mention the deaths by bastinado of Isaac Yavo and the night watchman, allowing only that an "appropriate" degree of severity had been used to extract the confessions. The report of the climactic breakthrough in the interrogation and the discovery of the bones and other objects in the sewer while he was writing his dispatch not only lent dramatic shape to the narrative but effectively preempted criticism of the search procedure and the pace of the investigation. The consul's report triumphantly concluded that on the basis of the confessions and the discovery of the evidence in the sewer, the case had been solved: "In the many criminal cases which I have come across" (he didn't have to remind his audience that he had studied law in Paris before joining the diplomatic corps) "I do not recall any that exhibited so precise a match of the details provided by the perpetrators of the crime."[7]

But Ratti-Menton was not content to accuse the wealthiest and most powerful Jews in Damascus of murder. The charge he wanted to make was far more serious, indeed venal. To convince Paris that the accused Jews were guilty of ritual murder, he had to confront the realities of 1840, when many in France no longer believed that Jews had horns. The legacies of the Enlightenment, the grant of citizenship to the Jews of France during the Revolution and the Napoleonic era, and the ascent of prominent Jews in the commercial and cultural life of the capital had changed French attitudes toward the Jews among all but the ultramontane factions. Ratti-Menton, whose own previous comments on the Jews, at least the Jews of France, were as enlightened as the views of the audience he found himself addressing, knew that a rehash of ancient myths and exaggerated charges against the Jews would meet widespread skepticism in Paris.

To make his sensational charge Ratti-Menton employed clever and subtle rhetorical tricks. In his narration of the night the monk disappeared, when he reported that the crowds in the street were shouting that the monk had been "sacrificed" by the Jews, the word he used was *immolé*, which has the same meaning and connotation in French as in English: to sacrifice, usually by fire.[8] The term is used in the Vulgate Bible for animal sacrifices by burning—"When you sacrifice a thanksgiving offering to the Lord, sacrifice [immolate] it so it may be acceptable in your favor"[9]—but seems an odd choice for what the crowds allegedly thought was the fate of the monk. Ironically, the usual punishment given to Jews accused of ritual murder in early modern Europe was immolation. Whether the term was Beaudin's translation of actual shouts or Ratti-Menton's modification of the translation, or whether the whole report of the shouts was a rhetorical construct, a phantom memory as Ratti-Menton fabricated or imagined the case against the Jews, it was a word well-chosen to evoke a horrific reaction in his audience.

The consul then raised the "social" question of "whether it is true that the Jews, as the public accused, employ human blood in the celebration of their religious mysteries" and demonstrated his own enlightenment by admitting that he was himself initially skeptical of the charge of ritual murder. But, he allowed, as he followed the case, "with real distress, bit by bit," he had to discard his skepticism in "the face of the mounting evidence." He was finally convinced, he wrote, when, "questioned by me on the matter, Harari's servant replied that he had heard talk of a custom among his coreligionists which involves taking human blood to mix with the flour for the Passover dough. The initiates distribute it among themselves. [The servant, Murad al-Fatal] added that ordinary people are not admitted into the initiation of this terrible mystery."

Ratti-Menton's technique was clever. By proclaiming his initial skepticism, attributing the horrifying charge to a Jewish servant, and adding the qualification that "ordinary people" are not initiates into the "terrible mystery," he had effectively preempted a skeptical response to his report. The long letter concluded with Ratti-Menton's observation that the pasha was soon expected to pronounce judgment on the guilty parties and to impose a penalty "which I believe to be exemplary"—in other words, the death sentence.[10] His justification of the sentence invoked the majesty of King Louis-Philippe and a telling phrase from recent French political debate: "Three months after the arrival here of one of His Majesty's consuls, the Jews have dared to attack people under the direct protection of the consulate. This is a challenge thrown down against the titular powers of His Majesty's government, and for this reason—as well as for the outrageous assault on humanity represented by these diabolical sacrifices—it is essential to subject these sectarians of the Jewish religion to a salutary terror. It is the prejudice of wild beasts which produced the crime, and it is essential to strike them by striking at those hideous prejudices."

The phrase "sectarians of the Jewish religion" was code language in French political discourse, a reference to the long-running debate over whether the Jews of France were French citizens of the Jewish faith as Napoleon and other advocates of citizenship for the Jews maintained or a separate nation within France as anti-Semitic groups charged. As a deputy of the National Assembly dramatically put the choice, "To the Jew as an individual—everything; to the Jews as a nation—nothing."[11] For those who believed the latter view, it was an easy transition from identifying the Jews as "sectarians" and a "separate nation" to the less genteel but more effective rabble-rousing terms like "wild beasts," "hideous prejudices," and "diabolical sacrifices."

Sherif Pasha was also emboldened by the new confessions. He quietly released the Jewish boys and the other men who had been held hostage, while ordering the arrest of the men named in the confessions of the barber and the servant: David Harari, his brothers Aaron and Isaac, their uncle Joseph Harari, their other uncle Rabbi Joseph Leniado, and rabbis Moses Salonicli and Moses Abulafia. No one in Damascus was surprised when poor men like the barber, David Harari's servant, the tumbak seller, or the night watchman were subjected to the bastinado. Now some of the wealthiest and most respected merchants in the city would be at the mercy of the pasha's interrogators in the barracks behind the palace.

From the Inquisition until the abolition of the procedure in France in the eighteenth century, judicial torture in Europe was construed, or at least rationalized, as a contest between the interrogators and the accused. The severity and duration of torture administered to the accused was strictly regulated, and the tortures employed in interrogations were often carefully matched to the alleged crimes. Typical for crimes of murder and dismemberment was the *strapada*, a rope thrown over a high beam and tied to the suspect's hands behind the back so that pulling the rope twisted the arms backward from their sockets; to increase the effectiveness, weights were attached to the suspect's feet and the rope was jerked instead of pulled slowly. A suspect who lost the contest, who broke down and confessed, was considered guilty. A suspect who resisted the pain of the torture and refused to confess was at least partially exonerated. French and other European legal systems attributed guilt on a sliding scale—unlike the absolute guilt or innocence of British or American legal proceedings—which allowed them to rationalize the torture that had been administered to an accused who did not confess as appropriate punishment for the limited measure of guilt that attached itself to anyone even suspected of a serious crime. The rationale did not make the tortures any less painful, and the public that was sometimes allowed to witness the tortures was as craven as the mobs at public hangings, but there was at least lip service to a theoretical basis for the application of tortures.[12]

At the pasha's barracks in Damascus in the spring of 1840, there was no subtle rationale for the use of torture on the arrested men. The purpose of the tortures administered to the accused Jews in Damascus was not to determine whether they were guilty—in the Christian quarter and at the serail they were already assumed to be guilty—but to force the accused men to confess so their testimony would complete the legal investigation and trial. Their interrogations served the same function as the Communist show trials of the 1950s in Czechoslovakia and the USSR, where confessions, degradations, and executions of the accused ultimately validated what initially seemed bizarre and arbitrary prosecutions and confirmed the new orthodoxy of the party. With no legal strictures limiting the interrogation procedures in Damascus, the pasha was free to assign arbitrary tortures, many of which seem to have been selected as much to humiliate the accused men, or perhaps to entertain the audiences at the interrogation sessions, as to force confessions.

Isaac Harari, a merchant of fifty, was flogged, slapped, boxed, and had his ears pulled. He was plunged into a tank of freezing water and held there for fifteen minutes. A candle was held under his chin, close enough to singe his beard, then under his nostrils, so he breathed in the flames and the hot wax dripped onto his bare chest. His genitals were crushed in the hand of an official.

David Harari, forty years old, was subjected to three or four sessions of the bastinado. His arms were pinched with the iron nippers normally used to place burning charcoal in the tobacco bowl of a nargileh. His genitals were crushed. His ears were pulled so violently that the outer portion of his right ear had to be removed by a surgeon.

Aaron Harari, aged fifty-five, was beaten on the bastinado, both on the soles and the upper part of his feet. His genitals were crushed three times, hard enough to cause exudation. He was thrown down so that his eye bled. His beard was burned with a candle.

Rabbi Joseph Leniado, aged fifty, and Joseph Harari, aged eighty, were flogged.

Rabbi Moses Salonicli, aged fifty, was subjected to the bastinado twice, two hundred to three hundred strokes with the kurbash each time. When the sole of his left foot was too lacerated to continue, they shifted to his buttocks. Interrogators pulled his ears. The soldiers inserted reeds between the flesh and fingernails of four fingers on his right hand and three fingers on his left hand.

Rabbi Moses Abulafia, aged forty, was bastinadoed twice, once on the soles of his feet, until they were so lacerated that he could not walk, and then on his buttocks. Twice, each time for as long as three days, he was forced to stand without sleeping. Interrogators twice crushed his genitals.[13]

The trial records are silent on how the tortures for each subject were chosen. We do not know whether reeds were driven under Rabbi Salonicli's nails because his fingers were symbols of the pages of the sacred texts they turned or whether the men whose genitals were crushed—a singularly symbolic torture in a culture obsessed with manhood—were considered exceptionally threatening or otherwise deserving of humiliation. In the confines of the dungeons of the serail and the adjoining barracks, the interrogators could take advantage of the situation to settle old scores: the men who had once dominated commerce in the markets and whose fortunes had been the focus of envy would now be watched by an audience while they were flogged or forcibly held under the surface of a pool of icy water.

The arrested men were not young and strong like the barber, David Harari's servant, or the tumbak merchant Isaac Yavo. The ages they gave in their interrogations were rounded—forty, forty-five, fifty, eighty—apparently either they or the scribes recording the testimony did not think precise ages important. By the life expectancy standards of the mid-nineteenth century in the Middle East, they were middle-aged or old. If they had once worked with their hands and backs, those days were long behind them. As merchants they spent their days in the suqs and evenings on divans or in the cafes. Their feet were not calloused but accustomed to soft, yellow leather slippers.

Even when the flesh is weak, faith or an adherence to a code can harden the spirit against pain. The arrested men knew what had happened to Isaac Yavo and the night watchman. They had heard that Yavo had recited the Sh'ma even as he was flogged to death, and they knew that it was a mitzvah for a man to die with those words on his lips. They had read every year in the Yom Kippur liturgy about Rabbi Akiva, the second-century sage who was tortured to death by the Romans, flayed with iron combs that lacerated the flesh like the strands of a kurbash. According to legend, when he was tortured Akiva had smiled as he recited the Sh'ma, and a Roman officer asked him if he was a sorcerer because he seemed oblivious to the pain. The rabbi answered that all his life when he said the words "You shall love the Lord your God with all your heart, with all your soul, and with all your might," he had wondered if he would ever be able to fulfill that commandment. "Now that I am giving my life, and the hour for reciting the Sh'ma has come, and my resolution remains firm, should I not smile?"[14] Like Rabbi Akiva and Isaac Yavo, the incarcerated men might have derived strength and the will to resist by repeating that concise credo, a shorthand for all that they believed as Jews. In the Jewish quarter some had already referred to Yavo's death in the dungeons as a *kiddush Hashem*, literally a "sanctification of the name of God," the term reserved for those considered martyrs for the faith.

But for those who faced torture and interrogation after the barber and David Harari's servant had given their confessions and after the discovery of what the French consul and pasha claimed was evidence of the murder of Father Thomas, martyrdom held little hope. What had Yavo's death accomplished? The pasha and Ratti-Menton and Beaudin still focused their investigation exclusively on the Jewish community. In the Jewish quarter men were still being arrested and women and children were still in hiding, afraid to go out lest they be included in the accusations or subjected to random violence on the streets. What had Yavo's martyrdom done to stop that?[15]

Defiance is the privilege of the young and independent, of men without obligations or family. The men being tortured were wealthy merchants with families and businesses that depended on them. Joseph Leniado was typical. His wife said he was responsible for "feeding twenty mouths."[16] As merchants they knew how to assess the risk and return on a venture. Facing interrogation and torture, they had to make the same assessments. If they died as martyrs they would leave behind families that had been dependent on them and businesses vulnerable to the predations of competitors. They could hope that the community would take care of their families, but the Jewish community was under siege. The complete destruction of the community no longer seemed impossible—if not through the persecution of the pasha and his allies, then from dispersion as more Jews left, hid, or even converted to Islam. Who would take care of their families then?

The pasha and the French consul made a show of keeping the prisoners isolated from one another in order to claim that there was no cross-pollution of the testimony. Because of the isolation, each prisoner faced the Prisoner's Dilemma, the challenge of balancing self-interest against the common interest.[17] If the prisoners all refused to confess or testify against the others, the pasha's case would have had only the testimony of the barber and David Harari's servant, which probably would not have been enough to convict the accused Jews. At the same time every prisoner was made to believe that if he confessed and testified against the others, he would spare himself additional torture. We can only imagine the pain of that choice in the face of the hideous tortures the pasha promised.

Isaac Harari was the first to be questioned. Despite the grueling tortures he had undergone, he maintained his innocence, repeating his earlier testimony: he knew nothing of the monk and had not seen him in a long time, certainly not the afternoon or evening when he supposedly disappeared. He had no idea what might have happened to the father. After the pasha repeated the questions and Harari again gave the same answers, the interrogators brought the barber into the room. Solomon al-Hallaq repeated his early deposition, including the accusation that Harari had helped to kill the monk. To further jog Harari's memory, the pasha's official scribe, Mansour Tayan, read the statements of the servant Murad al-Fatal and the barber, with their detailed accounts of the role each of the accused men had played. Harari was then thrown into the pool of freezing water again, and his head was held under.[18] In mid-winter in Damascus, no one could hold out for long in the freezing water.

When he was finally pulled out of the freezing water, Harari assented to the barber's confession. Before he gave his formal statement, which would become part of the trial protocol, he was confined in a cell with the barber—just as the barber had shared a cell with Muhammad al-Talli before his own confession. The next day Isaac Harari agreed to every detail of his role in the murder as it had been described in the confessions of the barber and David Harari's servant.

The other accused men were then questioned one at a time in the presence of Isaac Harari and the barber. Confronted with two confessions, one from the barber, and the other from a brother, cousin, nephew, or friend, and threatened with more torture if they did not confess, the accused men faced overwhelming pressure to accede to the story the barber had told. Harari's brother David and Rabbi Moses Abulafia assented to the depositions, giving statements that confirmed the details in those accounts, including their own roles in the murder. Aaron Harari gave some conflicting information but assented to much of the barber's testimony.

Joseph Harari, variously described as between sixty-five and eighty years old, and Joseph Leniado, fifty years old but with a "delicate

constitution and timid," were too weak after their sessions of the bastinado to be interrogated. Leniado's feet were heavily lacerated from the
kurbash and became infected. Both men died within ten days of their
flogging.

Only one of this group of accused men insisted on his innocence.
Rabbi Moses Salonicli, a merchant and part-time rabbi, maintained, as
he had in his previous interrogation, that he had nothing to do with the
alleged crime and that he had no knowledge of Father Thomas's disappearance. He was confronted with the accumulated testimony, first
from the barber and then from others, that he had been entrusted with
Father Thomas's watch on the night of the murder. The rabbi answered
that he had seen nothing of the monk that night and that since the
Festival of the Tabernacles (the Jewish holiday of Sukkot, which fell in
September 1839) he had not been in David Harari's house. He added
that he did not go around with the Hararis and that he knew "nothing
about this affair."[19]

In the face of the rabbi's adamance, the pasha ordered David Harari
brought into the interrogation room. Confronting an accused man with
one of the men who had already confessed and with threats of further
torture had worked to elicit confessions from the others. David Harari
said to the rabbi, "Didn't you take the watch and the blood? Didn't you
take the blood to [Rabbi] Abulafia and don't you have the watch?"

Salonicli was in pain. The flogging had left the sole of one foot
horribly lacerated. His fingers were crippled from the reeds that had
been thrust under his nails. He said, "I never saw anything, absolutely
nothing."

The pasha was determined. "Moses!" he said to the rabbi. "Many witnesses have testified. Your own accomplices testified that you were with
them, and yet you persist in your denials. Give me just two witnesses
who say where you were at the time of the murder of Father Thomas."

Salonicli answered, "I was at home, as my family can attest. I do not
have other witnesses."

In fact, two guests had been at Salonicli's home that evening.
Salonicli refused to name them for fear that they too would be subjected
to the bastinado or other tortures.[20]

When the rabbi's interrogation resumed the next day, David and
Isaac Harari were again brought in to testify that Salonicli had taken the
monk's watch. Salonicli still denied any knowledge of the events. He
said his two accusers were lying.

The pasha had David and Isaac Harari swear on a Bible and on the
name of Moses that their own testimony was truthful. The pasha asked
Salonicli, "They bear witness against their religion?"

Salonicli answered, "They are beyond the religion."[21]

Ratti-Menton admitted in his letters to Paris that "Turkish justice" was used to obtain the confessions but insisted that he had excused himself and left the serail whenever the bastinado or other tortures were used.[22] This insistence allowed him to divorce himself from the use of torture in his reports to Paris and even to suggest that he had opposed the torture and urged that it not be used. Others in Damascus did not share the French consul's qualms. Damascus was a small enough city, and the investigation of the disappearance of the monk was sufficiently sensational, that the torture sessions at the serail were no secret. The pasha, Beaudin, and some of Ratti-Menton's aides often personally witnessed the sessions. Others from the Christian quarter, including the dragoman of the British consul, also attended interrogation sessions. Some who attended claimed that the pasha was so obsessed with the case that there was no other opportunity to secure an audience with him.[23] It seems more likely that the torture sessions had become a spectacle for a privileged few, the sort of event that would later get talked about over nargilehs and cups of sweetened coffee, where the forbearance or weakness of the accused members of the Jewish community under torture could be dissected and criticized as the Romans had once reviewed the performances of gladiators.

Although he was careful to dissociate himself from the torture, and hence insisted that he had not been present for some of the interrogation sessions, Ratti-Menton had his own agenda that required him to ask many sharply directed questions of the accused men. To prove the charge of ritual murder he had made in his report to Paris, he needed to establish both a conscious motive on the part of the leading Jews of the community and a chain of possession of the blood they had supposedly taken from the monk. His first effort was with the barber.

During the interrogation of Isaac Harari, while the barber Solomon al-Hallaq was present, Ratti-Menton asked the barber, "What did they [the Jews] do with the blood?"

The barber said, "It's for bread used for festivals."

"How do you know that?" the consul asked.

The barber answered, "I heard the accused say that the blood was for sanctified bread."

Hanna Bahri Bey, the pasha's chief adviser, was at the session as an observer. He asked the barber, "But you have not seen the blood, how did you know that the blood was for consecrated bread?"

It was a good question and was never answered in the interrogation. Sanctified or consecrated bread is not a Jewish concept.[24] There is a blessing, Hamotzi, said before eating bread; observant Jews say a special blessing for everything one would eat and every act. There is a lengthy prayer said at the end of a meal at which bread is eaten, different from the short prayer at the end of meals that do not include bread, because the sages regarded bread as the staff of life. Jews are encouraged to eat *matzot* (unleavened bread) at Passover in memory of the Exodus when there was not enough time to make leavened bread. But there is never an act of consecrating or sanctifying bread in Jewish liturgy. In Damascus, with its strong Greek Catholic presence, consecrated bread probably meant the *kurban*, the six- to eight-inch round, flat loaves stamped on top with the Greek letters IC XC NIKA, which were used as the Host in Greek Catholic Masses. Those loaves could hardly be confused with the matzos that Jews baked in communal ovens at Passover. It seems likely that the whole idea of consecrated bread was suggested to the barber, probably by al-Talli or Beaudin.[25]

Bahri Bey followed up the questions about consecrated bread by asking the barber, "Why did they kill Father Thomas? Was it for a principle of religion? Was there an enmity between them? Or was it for his money?"

The barber answered, "I don't know."[26]

The French consul got a more useful answer when he asked Aaron Harari, "But why did you kill Father Thomas?"

Aaron Harari said, "It was for the blood that we followed the principles of our religion."

This was the answer the French consul wanted. But when Ratti-Menton tried to track what had happened to the blood that supposedly had been drained from the monk, the answers he got kept changing. One day Aaron Harari said the blood was at Rabbi Abulafia's house; a few days later he said it was at Rabbi Antabi's house. Rabbi Abulafia first said it was at David Harari's house, then that it was at his own house, and later that it was at Rabbi Antabi's house.

Asked to explain why the accused men gave such contradictory answers, Isaac Harari said, "Because they are afraid of being flogged or killed."

Answers like that muddied the official protocols of the trial. The pasha brought the Harari brothers back for further interrogation, assuring them that all he wanted in their testimony was "the truth."

Imagine the thoughts of these men. They had been tortured for days. Two of their close friends or relatives, Joseph Harari and Joseph Leniado, had been flogged to death. Before that a young, strong man whose only crime was telling the truth about what he had seen and a night watchman who had been on duty in the Jewish quarter on the night in question had also been flogged to death. Now, after admitting that their own testimony was not truthful, that they had only acceded to the barber's confession to fend off more torture, suddenly the chief interrogator and judge tells them that all he wants is "the truth."

The Harari brothers answered the pasha by revoking their earlier confessions, admitting that they had only confessed in the hope of receiving a speedy execution, which at least would end the tortures: "The truth is that we know of no murder; but if you will torture us again, we shall make our former deposition."

As if to test their latest statement, the pasha ordered them tortured again, until they once again confessed themselves guilty.[27] As far as the pasha was concerned, the disappearance of Father Thomas was solved.

With the case of the disappearance of the monk solved, the pasha turned to the disappearance of the father's servant. A missing servant would normally not have attracted much attention in a society as stratified as Damascus. Servants frequently fled after they had been beaten or otherwise abused; some were slaves or feared that they would become slaves or be sold. Life was cheap in Damascus. It was usually easier to purchase or hire a new servant than to pursue a runaway.

But Ibrahim Amara was no ordinary servant. He had lived at the Capuchin monastery since childhood and was closer to a companion and assistant to the father than a servant. As the city became obsessed with the investigation of the disappearance of Father Thomas, even the British consul—whose diplomatic reports were usually confined to commercial matters, Egyptian troop movements, and provisions for British outposts in places like Acre—thought it significant to report to London that so far "no discovery has taken place respecting the . . . Padre's servant who disappeared with him in the Jew quarter of the City."[28]

Except for Isaac Yavo's testimony, which the pasha had rejected, the only testimony about the servant had been from the two Greek men who claimed they had seen him in the Jewish quarter on the night the monk disappeared.

The pasha pressed the barber Salomon al-Hallaq for information about the disappearance of the servant. The barber testified that he had no part in what happened to Amara but that he had heard the others talking and that Murad al-Fatal had told him that the servant was also "sacrificed" and that his body was later cut up into pieces and tossed into a latrine that led into the sewers.[29]

Al-Fatal was brought back for more questioning. The barber could account for his own whereabouts throughout the evening Father Thomas was allegedly murdered, but there were lacunae in the alibi of al-Fatal, specifically his whereabouts between the time he had gone to fetch the barber and the point later in the evening when he claimed he had returned to David Harari's house to assist in dismembering and disposing of the corpse of the Father Thomas. Everyone—the barber, al-Fatal, and the others who had admitted to the barber's versions of events in their own confessions—agreed that al-Fatal was not at David Harari's house for those hours. The pasha demanded that al-Fatal explain where he was.

On February 29, in response to persistent questioning from the pasha and the incentive of another session of the bastinado, Murad al-Fatal finally said, "The truth is that my master [David Harari] sent me to find Meir Farhi, Murad Farhi, and Aaron Stambouli to ask them to keep a watch for Father Thomas's servant. If the servant came looking for the father, they were to make sure he didn't raise an alarm and have the whole affair discovered." Instead, they were to tell the monk's servant that the monk had come to the Jewish quarter to vaccinate a child. Al-Fatal said that when he brought this message to the intended recipients at Farhi's house, he also found Isaac Picciotto, Joseph Farhi, Aslan Farhi, and Rabbi Abulafia waiting there.[30]

Ibrahim Amara, unlike Father Thomas, was an Egyptian subject. But as the legal servant of a French protégé he too fell under French jurisdiction.[31] Ratti-Menton and Beaudin were allowed to continue the questioning of al-Fatal until he described the murder of the servant in graphic detail. He said he found the group waiting in the smaller courtyard of Farhi's house, where the latrines were located. Isaac Picciotto and Aaron Stambouli were holding the servant, whose mouth had been bound with a white linen strap. The door was barricaded with a beam. A copper basin was under the servant's throat. Murad Farhi slit the servant's throat, while al-Fatal and Meir Farhi held his head, Isaac Picciotto held his feet, Aaron Stambouli pressed on the servant's chest, and the others held the body straight to aide the drainage of the blood. They all waited the quarter of an hour until the servant was dead and the blood had drained. Then al-Fatal had to go back to his master's house. The others who remained behind disposed of the bones and flesh of Father Thomas's servant in one of the latrines.[32]

The people named in al-Fatal's new testimony included every wealthy and influential member of the Damascus Jewish community who was not already incarcerated for the murder of Father Thomas. The Farhi family was even wealthier and more influential than the Hararis and had a longer and broader tradition of service as tax collectors and accountants under the Ottomans. Aaron Stambouli and Isaac Picciotto were well-to-do merchants. Stambouli was also trained as a rabbi. Picciotto had business connections in Europe, and his family in Aleppo had a long history of service as consuls for various European states. Aslan Farhi was married to the daughter of the current chief rabbi. Many of the men named had been members of the delegation that had come to the French consulate to offer a reward for information on the disappearance of Father Thomas. If the accusations in this new testimony could also be confirmed by confessions, the entire leadership of the Jewish community would be convicted of ritual murder.

8

Evidence

ON MARCH 2, just two days after the pasha and the consul declared that they had solved the crime of the murder of Father Thomas, the crowds from the Christian quarter took to the streets again—this time for Father Thomas's funeral. With the confessions and the evidence from the sewer fresh on minds and lips, the funeral was an opportunity for the Christian community of Damascus to again forget their sectarian differences and show their united feelings toward those who had been accused of the murders.

The funeral was presided over by Father Francis of Ploaghe, another Sardinian, who had been sent from Beirut to replace Father Thomas at the Capuchin monastery. The bone fragments that had been recovered from the sewer were placed inside a double coffin covered with black velvet and carried in solemn procession from the French consulate to the Terra Sancta church by Greek Catholic priests. The entire Christian clergy of Damascus, and the English, French, and Austrian consuls, accompanied the coffin through streets so thronged that the police and troops could hardly clear the way for the cortege. At the church Father Francis led a mass, and a Maronite curate delivered a funeral oration. The coffin was then carried in procession to the Capuchin monastery, where the remains were interred near the altar of St. Elias. The French consul announced that a suitable tombstone would be commissioned. The text of the epitaph, in Italian, had already been decided:

Here lie the bones of
Father Thomas of Sardinia
Apostolic Capuchin Missionary
assassinated by the Jews
the 5th of February of the year 1840[1]

Outside the church the crowd shouted for the execution of the Jews who had "assassinated" Father Thomas.

Once news of the confessions and the discovery of the bones and other evidence in the sewer became public, Damascus was a changed town. The suqs, counting houses, and once-lively street life of the Jewish quarter were quiet, as even merchants who had not been mentioned in the testimony were reluctant to venture to their stalls or the cafes.[2] In the poorer sections of the Christian and Jewish quarters there were ugly incidents as Jews were accosted by Christian crowds while the police stood by or turned their backs.

Leisure had always been the mark of a man in Damascus. Before the disappearance of Father Thomas, evenings in the Jewish quarter had been devoted to languorous visits to the homes of friends or to coffee-houses where men could smoke nargilehs and sip endless tiny cups of sweetened coffee as they talked about business, news, and rumors. Now, with the pasha's soldiers searching the Jewish quarter daily, trying to ferret out the hiding places of the men the pasha had ordered arrested as suspects in the murder of the servant Ibrahim Amara, it was only behind bolted doors, or in the secrecy of their hiding places, that the Jews of Damascus could speculate about what had happened.

The horrible developments of the last month were almost too fantastic to believe. To many in the Jewish community the accusations and the investigation were an obvious plot, a scheme by Beaudin, the French consul, and the pasha, with much of the Christian community as co-conspirators. The confessions and accusations of the barber and Murad al-Fatal, poor men who were easily coerced with offers of money and pardons, followed by the just-in-time discovery of evidence in the sewers of the Jewish quarter were like manufactured stage props of an elaborately staged drama.

But why would the pasha, the French consul, and Beaudin put such a plot together? The most compelling explanation was that they were setting the stage for the extortion of a bribe. With the leadership of the Jewish community held hostage in the pasha's dungeons, the pasha could demand a huge payment from the community in return for releasing the accused Jews and letting the accusations quietly fade away. It would not have been the first time; there had been extortions from the Jewish community in the past, demands of extralegal payments for the privilege of continuing to do business or keeping a synagogue open. Before the Egyptians came to power, the sultan once ordered the imprisonment of the "high priest" of the Jews (chief rabbi Abulafia) and the "prime minister" to the pasha (Raphael Farhi), along with twelve other respected Jews in the Damascus community. He gave them the choice of paying a bribe of 40,000 purses of piastres or losing their heads. The local population, whipped into a fervor by the propaganda that accompanied the charges, had shouted, "Praise be to the Lord! A curse upon Raphael their *ḥakham*! A curse upon all the Jews, their fathers, their mothers, grandfathers, grandmothers, their children, and their children's children."[3]

More recently, Beaudin had periodically threatened to ruin Jewish merchants if they did not pay the settlements he demanded on behalf of his European clients. He would produce documents and witnesses to alleged transactions, knowing that the merchant he was pursuing could not read the French or Italian of the documents and that most of the merchants would conclude that it was cheaper to yield to the extortion than to force a case into the local courts, where the restrictions on a Jew testifying and the demands for baksheesh might prove more onerous than the extortion Beaudin demanded. It was also a common swindle for men of uncertain occupation, like al-Talli, to make false accusations, find witnesses to corroborate their testimony, and rely on the Ottoman courts, where the Jewish victim had no legal standing, to pressure the accused party to settle the matter. The only difference between these petty extortions and what the pasha might be doing with his allies, the French consul and Beaudin, was scale and the pasha's liberal abuse of the dungeon cells and torture engines.

Another theory was that the arrests were not for extortion but only a deliberate scheme to discredit, isolate, and humiliate the Jewish community. By framing the prominent Jewish merchants for a hideously repulsive crime, the pasha, Ratti-Menton, and Beaudin would succeed in branding the chief competitors of the Christian merchants and administrators with these abominable charges, marking them as outcasts. With enough false evidence and coerced testimony, they could even hope to sway world opinion outside Syria against the Jews.

The coffeehouse explanations were creative and appealing, but many in the Jewish community were convinced that the pasha and the French consul were doing exactly what they intended, that they were not only going to humiliate the Jewish community but would actually go ahead with their sham investigation until they had convicted and executed the accused Jews. There was no secret about the talk of British pressure on Muhammad Ali in Alexandria to abandon Syria back to Ottoman rule, and it was easy to assume that an Ottoman restoration would result in the reappointment of Jews to the coveted administrative and fiscal positions. The preemptive conviction and execution of the leading Jewish merchants would in one swoop eliminate the potential rivals and decapitate the leading Jewish merchant families. The pasha would then be able to expropriate the funds of those families,

71

enriching his own treasury and making certain that the Jewish families would never again compete with the Christian merchants. The executions would also cast such fear in the Jewish community that the pasha and his allies could assume that the remaining families would flee Damascus or convert to Islam or Christianity—effectively completing the destruction of the Jewish community.

While the Jewish community debated, the pasha had a public crier announce a reward of 5,000 piastres for information leading to the arrest of those named as the murderers of Father Thomas's servant. The crier also read a decree promising a sentence of death to anyone guilty of hiding the fugitives who had been accused of the murder of the servant—members of the Farhi family, Aaron Stambouli, and Jacob Abulafia, the brother of the rabbi.[4]

The pasha's troops and police began another round of searches in the Jewish quarter, affording the soldiers more opportunities to satisfy their curiosity about the fabled wealth of the Jewish merchant families and giving the French consul renewed opportunities to proposition the Jewish women. From the Jewish quarter the search fanned out, following the street rumors that said the Jews had paid Muslims to hide them in other quarters of the city. It was in one of the Muslim quarters that the troops finally found one of the accused men, Aslan Farhi, the twenty-year-old son of Raphael Farhi.

Aslan Farhi was a good candidate for interrogation. Despite his father's prestige and wealth and his own marriage to the daughter of the chief rabbi, the young Farhi was widely thought of as "weak and sickly in constitution." He was also the target of ridicule and jibes because he continued to live in his father's house where it was rumored that he refused to sleep alone with his wife and made someone else in the household sleep in the same room. Sherif Pasha had a different explanation for Aslan Farhi's behavior; he said that Aslan was still young and had "not imbibed the Jewish tricks."[5]

After he was arrested Aslan was held in the French consulate where al-Talli, who had been so effective with the other witnesses, may have coached him. Aslan was apparently not a good pupil, and his initial interrogation at the consulate proved as unproductive as the consul's previous efforts. Like the other suspects the French consul had tried to interrogate, Aslan was then delivered to the pasha for further interrogation. At the serail he was put into a cell with Murad al-Fatal, who had implicated him and the others in the murder of the servant Ibrahim Amara, presumably so al-Fatal could coach his testimony. But when Aslan was again interrogated in the morning, he still denied all knowledge of the murder.

The pasha then ordered Aslan flogged on the bastinado, suggesting that an extended session of four hours ought to be enough to change his testimony. Aslan began to tremble, and the pasha repeated the order, this time allowing that if Aslan would confess to his role in the murder he could be spared torture and be given a safe conduct. As if to make the choice graphically clear, the pasha held a piece of paper in one hand, representing the safe conduct, and a kurbash in the other. He told Aslan to choose.

Aslan chose to confess. He repeated a few details from al-Fatal's testimony and was then brought to the pasha's divan, where a large group was in attendance. For the benefit of the audience, Aslan and al-Fatal were examined separately, to demonstrate that they independently gave the same testimony. When it was al-Fatal's turn he repeated the details to which he had testified earlier, exactly where the head and feet of the monk's servant Ibrahim Amara were, who stood to his right and who to his left, and which task each man had performed. When Aslan testified on his own, his story meandered, contradicting the details of al-Fatal's testimony. The scribe was transcribing Aslan's declarations when the pasha stopped him. "We need not write down this nonsense," he said. "We have evidence enough."[6]

A week later the troops discovered a sickly young son of Meir Farhi hiding in the house of a Muslim washerwoman. Meir Farhi was a fifty-five-year-old merchant with three children, a fortune estimated at 500,000 piastres, and a reputation for fairness in his business dealings. He had been the organizer of the original group that had offered a reward for information about the disappearance of Father Thomas. The pasha ordered Meir's young son flogged until he revealed his father's whereabouts. After twenty to thirty lashes the boy said his mother might know where the father was.

The boy's mother was arrested, but she refused to betray her husband. The pasha then ordered that she be forced to watch while her son was given another three hundred lashes. At that point, according to an observer, "the maternal feelings at last prevail over the conjugal, and she betrays her husband."[7]

Meir Farhi was arrested and brought to the serail. The pasha began his interrogation by asking Farhi how many pots of gold he had. Then he demanded that Farhi confess to complicity in the murder of Father Thomas's servant.

Farhi answered, "If Your Excellency's object is only to know the truth, then I tell Your Excellency that neither I nor my fellow accused know anything of murder; if the object, however, be simply to force us to confessions, then Your Excellency only need tell me what confession will suffice, and I am ready to make it without torture."[8]

Farhi gave the required testimony. The pasha then ordered him imprisoned and insisted that he pay the 5,000 piastres reward for his own capture.

With confessions from the two Farhis to corroborate the testimony of the servant Murad al-Fatal, the pasha and Ratti-Menton could consider the murder of the servant Ibrahim Amara solved. With the exception of two members who died in the dungeons of the serail after the bastinado, Isaac Picciotto (who as an Austrian protégé was exempt from prosecution by the French consul), and the fugitives who had eluded arrest, most of the members of the original delegation of prominent Damascus Jews and all three senior rabbis of the community were now incarcerated in the serail.

To complete the collection of evidence, on March 7 Ratti-Menton led a search party to a location al-Fatal had identified on a branch of the sewer system that connected to a latrine in one of the Farhi family houses. Soldiers went down into the sewer and found more fragments of bones, a scrap of a cap, and part of a shoe. The brother of Ibrahim Amara promptly identified the shoe—a fragment of one of the soft yellow slippers worn by most men in Damascus—as indisputably belonging to his brother.

Lest there be any question about the validity of the evidence found in the sewers, the bones found at both sites were submitted for identification to a panel of seven native physicians, one Christian and the rest Muslim, and also to a second panel of European physicians, including the pasha's personal physician, the head of the city quarantine, and the head of the hospital. The individual bone fragments were quite small, a few kilograms in total, parts of femurs, tibia, a patella, and fragments of fractured skull. There was no collarbone, hip, fingers, foot bones, or other obviously human remains despite the testimony of the barber and David Harari's servant that they had put all of the bones into the sewers.[9]

The examining physicians were unanimous in declaring the bones to be human. The Austrian consul, Caspar Merlato, added his own certification of the identification based on the opinion of an Austrian physician.[10] One independent European physician, Dr. Lograsso, was allowed to examine the bones. He concluded that they were not human and were most probably the bones of a goat or sheep. (His identification is not surprising; ovine and caprine limb bones are so similar to human limb bones in dimensions and strength that they are frequently used for testing of orthopedic procedures and devices.) Dr. Lograsso's dissenting opinion was ignored in the official prosecution of the case.[11]

The other evidence from the sewers was also reviewed by experts. Father Thomas's regular barber, the Austrian consul Caspar Merlato, and Father Francis, the new Capuchin monk who had replaced Father Thomas at the convent, all identified the fragment of black and red fabric that had been found in the sewer as part of the Father Thomas's customary skullcap.[12] Although the cloth and the fragment of Ibrahim Amara's slipper had supposedly been in the sewers with decaying animals, rubbish, and sewage for four or five weeks, none of those called upon to make identifications voiced any doubt that the cap and slipper belonged to the monk and his servant.

As news of the new confessions and the validation of the evidence by experts spread through the city, the accusations and catcalls that had been heard on the streets since the father disappeared changed to demands for the execution of the convicted Jews. Even among the consular community, any traces of skepticism seemed to melt away in the face of the evidence and testimony. Nathaniel Werry, the British consul, summed up the consensus in the European community when he wrote that it had always been the opinion of the Christian population of Turkey that the Jews "scattered throughout the Country immolated clandestinely Christians to obtain their blood, to celebrate their feasts therewith, in their religious ceremonies—this fact has been proved here. The Padre Tomasso, chief of the Capuchin Convent, under the French protection and his servant, were immolated in the houses of two of the most influential Jews of this city."[13]

It would take three weeks for his report to reach London, and at least as long for a reply to come back. By then, many in Damascus assumed, the accused men would already be hanged.

9

The Rabbis

IN 1803 an Orthodox Christian monk in Moldavia (Bessarabia) published a book in which he promised to reveal the "mystery of the blood," the supposed secrets of Jewish uses of Christian blood. The author claimed that he was the son of a rabbi and that his own father had told him the secrets before he converted to Christianity, threatening him with a horrible fate if he should reveal them to anyone, even his own brothers or, if he got married, his wife. His father had instructed him to convey the secrets only to his most intelligent son and explained that through this process the secrets had been guarded so closely over the centuries that even most Jews were unaware of the details. The monk wrote that he realized he was putting himself in the gravest danger by writing the book but that he was not afraid because "my hope is in the Father, my refuge is the Son, and my shield is the Holy Spirit."

Despite the sensational premise of the book, the original edition in Moldavian, a dialect of Romanian, remained obscure. Then in 1834 a new edition was published in Greek, which had long been a lingua franca from the Black Sea to the Balkans and throughout much of the Middle East. Copies of the Greek translation, entitled *Ruin of the Jewish Religion*, found their way to cities like Alexandria and Damascus. The Greek Catholic patriarch of Alexandria noted on the front page of his own copy that "this work is extremely rare, because it seems that Jewish gold has made it disappear from the face of the earth." In Damascus Beaudin translated excerpts of the book to include in the trial protocols of the men accused of murdering Father Thomas and his servant.[1]

The Moldavian monk's book is a remarkable compilation of preposterous fabrications and distortions of Jewish rituals supposedly based on what the monk claims is the power and authority of rabbis, learned

Jewish scholars, and the "Pharisees, whom they call Hasidim," who he claims have for centuries acted as a cabal controlling the Jewish use of Christian blood. As examples of the alleged Jewish use of blood, the monk claims that when a Jewish boy is circumcised the rabbi mixes the blood of a Christian and that of the circumcised boy in a glass with wine, dips his little finger into the wine and says, "I say unto you, your life is in the blood"; that rabbis treat illnesses by rubbing Christian blood on lesions or symbolic areas of the body as a quasi-baptism; that before a Jewish marriage the bride and groom fast and then after the ceremony eat an egg sprinkled with ashes from burning a handkerchief that has been dipped in Christian blood; that at Purim Jews celebrate their liberation from the hated Haman by killing a Christian and that the rabbis make little three-cornered honey pastries, dabbing blood from the martyred Christian on each, and then send them to their friends as deliberate mockeries of the Christian trinity; that at Passover, most of the matzos are prepared without Christian blood, but the rabbis make a special piece of matzo, the *afikomen,* by mixing in ashes from a cloth that has been soaked in the blood of a martyred Christian and burned, and at the Passover meal, at which everyone gets drunk, "it is obligatory for every Jew, even the youngest, to eat a little piece of that matzo"; that on Christmas Eve Jews stay up all night playing cards and "cursing Christ, His Mother, and all the saints"; that Jewish children are taught to hate and curse Christians and are instructed never to go within ten paces of a Christian church without reciting a special curse; and that all Jews are under divine curses of Egyptian plague, hemorrhoids, boils, itch, madness, blindness, depression, and inflammation of the joints, which explains why all European Jews have scabies, those of Asia suffer from ringworm, those of Africa have ulcers of the feet, and those of America suffer extraordinary weakness of the eyes, which gives them a stupid appearance.[2]

Many of the monk's fabrications are clever propaganda; they include enough recognizable references to Jewish ritual practices and miscitations of the Bible and the Talmud to seem rooted in Jewish liturgy and theology. His story of how his father had conveyed the secret truths to him and the instruction that he was to pass the secrets along only to his most intelligent son appears to be a parody of Exodus 13:8 ("And you shall explain to your son") and the patrilineal identification of Kohanim, the descendants of the ancient priestly tribe. The other fabrications draw on misinterpreted or twisted fragments of Jewish ritual practice to establish their pseudo-authenticity. At a circumcision it is traditional for the *mohel* to encourage the infant boy to suck on a finger that has been dipped in wine, both as a symbol of joy on the occasion that brings a boy into the Jewish covenant and because the child imbibes enough wine to deaden the brief pain of the circumcision. At Purim it is traditional to eat triangular fruit pastries called *Hamantaschen* (Haman's pockets) or *orecchie di Haman* (Haman's ears) and to give gifts of food to others. Jewish couples traditionally fast on the day of their wedding in recognition of the importance of the act of marriage; and before the fast of Tisha be'Av, which mourns the destructions of the Temples in Jerusalem and the expulsions from England and Spain, it is traditional to eat an egg that has been dipped in ash. It is an old tradition that Jews stay home on Christmas Eve and Christmas Day, and while rabbis and scholars have offered mystical or scholarly reasons why Jews should not go to their houses of prayer or study that day, the compelling practical reason was that where Jewish minorities lived among a Christian majority, like Moldavia, Jews who ventured out at Christmas ran the risk of being accosted and beaten on the streets by Christian hooligans.

The fabrications in the Moldavian monk's book were familiar folk myths in Europe and greater Russia, where the blood libel had a long history. The origin of the idea that Jews murder Christians and use their blood for ritual purposes is obscure and is probably traceable to pre-Christian Greek authors, possibly to a propaganda stunt by agents of a half-demented early king of Syria to excuse his own profanation of the temple in Jerusalem. The ancient accusation resurfaced in Norwich, England, in 1144 and eleven years later, in Lincoln, nineteen Jews were hanged without trial after the body of a Christian boy named Hugh was found. Geoffrey Chaucer wrote of the supposed murder of Hugh in "The Prioress's Tale," and six centuries later Charles Lamb wrote that he would not step into a synagogue because he could not shake the "old prejudice." From England the myth of the blood libel spread east on the broadsheets of peddlers and in the sermons of itinerant preachers and Franciscan friars to France, where, in 1171, between thirty-one and thirty-five Jews were burned to death for an alleged ritual murder in Blois, and then to the German states and greater Russia. In periodic eruptions Jews would be blamed for the disappearance of Christian children and tortured until they confessed to the imagined accusations of their torturers, including embellishments with the language of Christian martyrdom, supposed revelations of secret Jewish rituals, or imagined tales of purchasing Christian blood from travelers on the roads. As the myth and accusations were repeated, the details became codified so that the accusations in different towns and regions read as though they were copied from the same template. The predictable forms the myth assumed in turn lent support to the allegations in pamphlets, broadsides, and books like the work of the Moldavian monk that the use of Christian blood by Jews was a vast conspiracy run by a secret cabal of rabbis. While there is no instance of a documented crime that matched the myth, and many faked accusations were exposed, the myth persisted even in the face of repeated denials by popes and kings.[3]

But Europe and Russia are far from Damascus, and before 1840 there was no tradition of blood libel charges against specific Jews or trials for ritual murder in Damascus. There had always been the Easter sermons and whispered rumors, just as Christian parents had long told their children tales of the Jewish bogeyman. The Jews and Christians lived in adjacent quarters in Damascus and met daily in the suqs and on the streets. The Christians were aware of Purim and other Jewish holidays, which sometimes spilled into the streets. Christian youth shouted taunts and threw stones at Jewish funeral processions and the *sukkot* at the Festival of Tabernacles. Christians were aware of Jewish ritual butcher shops and perhaps had been guests at Jewish weddings or circumcision ceremonies, which in the Sephardic tradition were especially elaborate, with much visiting the night before, a special chair where the grandfather sat to hold the baby boy who was to be circumcised, and celebrations after the ceremony.[4] But the precise details of the ritual murder accusations that were so well known in Europe seem to have arrived in Syria only with the translations of the Moldavian monk's book, which served Ratti-Menton and the pasha as a convenient chapbook for the cases they were building against the leading members of the Jewish community.

By tying the Damascus accusations to a long tradition of charges of blood libel, the Moldavian monk's book also provided a rationale for Ratti-Menton and the pasha to continue their dogged pursuit of the case. What might have appeared another episode of exotic Oriental barbarism, especially when it was coupled with reports of the torture used in the investigation, could instead be presented as an extension of a phenomenon familiar in Europe. The French consul and the pasha could pretend, and perhaps had come to believe, that their prosecution would prove the truth of the myth that by the nineteenth century seemed to have been dismissed by post-Enlightenment skepticism in European capitals. The British consul Nathaniel Werry, a supporter of the prosecution, encouraged them by telling the pasha "that he was now in the way to render his name immortal as H[is] E[xcellency]—*viz*, the fact that the Jews periodically kill Christians, to make a religious use of their blood."[5]

A modern court might consider the failure to find the bodies of Father Thomas or his servant a hindrance in the prosecution of murder cases, but for Ratti-Menton and the pasha the lack of bodies—other than the bones found in the sewers and attributed to the monk and his servant—

was an advantage, as there was no physical evidence that would contradict even the wildest accusations against the Jews. The prosecutors had only to allege a method of murder and a disposition of the blood of the victims that matched the pattern in the Moldavian monk's book to have the outlines of a case of ritual murder, with a printed text to "document" the crime. Indeed, without the inconvenient physical evidence a body might present, there was no limit to the details that could be introduced into the confessions coerced from the accused men.

But a few details in the Moldavian monk's account of Jewish ritual murders inconveniently contradicted the facts of the alleged crimes in Damascus. In the blood libel allegations that spread across Europe and Russia, and in the Moldavian monk's account of the alleged Jewish ritual murders, the victims were invariably prepubescent Christian boys, killed at or near Passover. The monk explains that the Passover murders were meant as a substitute for "tormenting Christ" and that only a Christian child could imitate Christ's suffering, because as a virgin the child would possess the purity of Jesus. The one exception to the allegedly mandated sacrifice of children, according to the Moldavian monk, was Purim, when any Christian was a satisfactory victim. Also, in the tales of blood libel from Europe and Russia Christian imagery was heavily emphasized. To symbolize a Christ recrucified, the alleged child victim would have to be circumcised, as Christ was, so most of the stories and trials claimed that the child victims were mutilated, often with claims of prick marks on the penis as well as puncture wounds through which the blood was supposedly drained. In another invocation of Christian imagery, the marks were sometimes claimed to be from thorns. The perversions of the crown of thorns and the penis, the organ of Christ's sensual nature, which according to Christian theology had been overcome in his sacrifice, added to the revulsion toward the alleged crime.[6]

The accusations in Damascus did not fit the traditional allegations. Father Thomas and his servant were not children; when they disappeared, the father was an old man and his servant Ibrahim Amara was middle-aged. And they had not disappeared at Easter or Passover, which fell in mid-April 1840, but in early February. Purim in 1840 was on March 18, six weeks after the alleged murder of Father Thomas and his servant. Before anticoagulants and serum preservatives, there was no way the blood of victims killed in February could be used to make Passover matzos as the Moldavian monk had described in his handbook. And while there were no bodies to affirm or contradict allegations of mutilation, the testimony had included no descriptions of circumcision or other wounds like those described in the Moldavian monk's account.

To get around the mismatch between the pattern of ritual murder supposedly documented in the Moldavian monk's book and the available evidence and testimony on the disappearance of Father Thomas and his servant, Ratti-Menton and the pasha created a new mythology, inventing or emphasizing selected details to try to create a pattern of connections to Jewish thought or ritual practices that would prove that Father Thomas and his servant had been murdered as part of a "religious scheme worked out in accord with the regulations of the chief rabbi."[7]

"One thing is essential to note," Ratti-Menton wrote in a report to Paris. "In both homicides there were *seven* principal murderers; in both homicides, *three* rabbis were present." He made sure the interrogations of the accused men included questions designed to solicit confirmations of those numbers, and he apparently repeated the numbers often enough in his conversations in the Christian quarter that the reports of other consuls mentioned the three rabbis and the seven alleged murderers with the same emphasis—as if they somehow explained the crime.[8]

Ratti-Menton seemed to believe, or to want his audiences to believe, that there was some special significance in the numbers, that the *three* rabbis and *seven* murderers had a theological or ritual significance like the Christian trinity. Perhaps he or one of his advisers had been studying the Bible, where the number seven appears in the days of the creation, the seven circuits the Israelites took around Jericho before it fell, and the seventh year of the farming cycle when land is left fallow. Or maybe they were aware of details of Jewish rituals like the seven days of Passover or Sukkot, the seven circlings of the bride around the groom in a Jewish marriage ceremony, or the seven blessings that are said for the bride and groom.

Three rabbis sit as judges on a *beit din,* or rabbinical court, which gave Ratti-Menton's repeated mention of the three rabbis allegedly present for each murder the tone of quasi-authenticity that was used so effectively in the Moldavian monk's book.[9] The number seven applied to a group of men has no more significance in Judaism than the seven-year intervals on which most universities award sabbatical leaves. The significant number for a group of men is the ten required for a *minyan,* the minimum number of adults who must be present to recite certain prayers or to read the Torah.

In the testimony the pasha and Beaudin had coerced from the barber and the other accused men, the victims' throats were slit in a manner similar to the technique a Jewish ritual butcher (*shoḥet*) uses to kill a chicken or lamb. The regulations governing kosher slaughter require that an animal be killed with a single, painless stroke of the knife across the throat below the large ring of the windpipe and that the blood be drained from the animal within a prescribed interval of time, to minimize the suffering experienced by the animal. To Christians the precise regulations may have made kosher slaughter seem a form of ritual sacrifice. Indeed, there had been a tradition in the middle ages of regulations forbidding the Jews from ritual slaughter of animals on Good Friday, lest their act contaminate the spiritual sacrifice of Christ which Christians believed supplanted the carnal Jewish sacrifice.[10] Ratti-Menton and Beaudin could count on their local audience, living in close proximity to the Jewish quarter, having seen the Jewish butcher shops, and probably being familiar with the kosher slaughter regulations and procedures.

The magic numbers, the invented parallels to Jewish ritual practices, even the patterned accusations from the Moldavian monk's book were not necessary to convict the accused Jews. The confessions and the supposed evidence from the sewers had effectively closed the cases before the pasha. The multiple confessions corroborated one another, and the expert testimony had certified the validity of the evidence. By the legal standards of the pasha's court, the accused Jews had been convicted of the murders of Father Thomas and his servant Ibrahim Amara.

Ratti-Menton's invented myths also were not necessary to convince the crowds in Damascus. In the Christian quarter, and even among the Europeans of the consular corps, there was widespread acceptance of the charges against the Jews. The crowds were already demanding public executions.

But Ratti-Menton was preparing to plead before a different court, and public and official opinion in Paris and the other capitals of Europe and the world were not as receptive a tribunal as Sherif Pasha and the Christian quarter crowds. The Paris press and public loved criminal investigations. The famed first head of the Sûreté, Eugène-François Vidocq, and the character Vautrin in *La comédie humaine* that Balzac modeled after Vidocq, solved crimes with panache and carefully orchestrated publicity. The murders they solved were for the usual reasons—a love dispute, an insult, jealousy, a grudge, or a business deal gone awry—and they solved crimes by brilliance and insight, not judicial torture. The coerced confessions in Damascus and the consul's exercises in numerology and invented ritual practices might persuade his fellow consuls and the street crowds in the Christian community of Damascus, but in enlightened France the combination of ritual murder accusations and the use of the bastinado and other tortures were sure to be greeted with considerable skepticism.

To make his case to the Quai d'Orsay and the French public and press, Ratti-Menton needed to prove a crime more abominable even than the brutal details of the evidence from the sewers and the confessions. The alleged dismemberment of the bodies of the father and his servant, the crushing of the remains, and their removal in sacks to the sewers made for horrendous reading, but Parisian newspaper readers were inured to violence. Ratti-Menton needed to prove a crime so heinous and barbaric that even those who were quick to apply the Rights of Man to the Jews would shudder in horror, a crime that would make sophisticated Parisians reconsider their views of the Jews, or at least of the Jews of the Middle East. For Damascus and for Ratti-Menton the stakes were high. If the charges could be made to stick, it would make the Jews of Damascus pariahs, destroying the status of the Jewish community forever. It would also catapult Ratti-Menton from a flagging career as a consul in a remote corner of the Ottoman Empire.

But even with translations of the Moldavian monk's book introduced into the trial protocols, there was no evidence of the alleged ritual aspects of the murder except the coerced confessions. To make his case the French consul needed to trace the custody and whereabouts of the blood of the murder victims. If he could produce the blood of Father Thomas and his servant and show that it had been handed by the murderers to a rabbi and then up through a hierarchy of rabbis, it would prove his case even to the most skeptical Paris audience.

Yet no matter how many times he asked, and how often the pasha threatened the accused Jews with additional tortures, the answers Ratti-Menton got to his questions about the blood remained ambiguous or inconsistent. The barber and David Harari's servant Murad al-Fatal claimed that they knew nothing of the blood except that it had been collected into a basin and then put into a bottle. They both could describe the white bottle, called a *khalabièh*, that was supposedly used to collect the blood, and the copper pan similar to those used for oil in the suqs, into which it had been drained, but no one seemed to know the whereabouts of the alleged bottles of blood.[11] The other accused men, who after sufficient coercion by the bastinado had agreed with the initial testimony on almost every detail of the alleged murders, were also contradictory and unsure when asked the whereabouts of the blood. Aaron Harari testified one day that the blood was at Rabbi Abulafia's house, and then a few days later he testified that the blood had been taken to Rabbi Antabi's house. Rabbi Abulafia said at various times that the blood was at Harari's house, his own house, or at Rabbi Antabi's house. It was as if they had not been properly coached on this one point.

Ratti-Menton preferred to believe the explanation in the Moldavian monk's book: that the ordinary Jews did not know about the so-called "mystery of the blood," that only the rabbis knew these secrets. With the help of the pasha the French consul focused his investigation on the

Damascus rabbis, hoping that they could be persuaded to confess and that their confessions would be sufficient proof to stanch even the skepticism he anticipated from Paris over the charge of ritual murder.

According to the confessions of the barber and the Hararis, Rabbi Moses Salonicli had not only assisted with the murders and the bleeding of the victims but had also taken the monk's watch and, later, had received the blood and passed it along to Rabbi Moses Abulafia for safekeeping. Even when he was confronted with the substantial and multiple testimonies accusing him, Rabbi Salonicli refused to confess. He adamantly denied handling the blood, denied any knowledge of the monk's watch or other possessions, and denied any complicity in or knowledge of the murders. The pasha had him tortured: repeated sessions of the bastinado crippled one of his feet so he was unable to walk, and the reeds thrust under his fingernails left his fingers twisted and knotted. Still, the rabbi maintained that he knew nothing of the affair and that he had been home that evening with his wife and family.

When the combination of threats, torture, and confrontation with the testimony against him—which had been so successful when others were interrogated—failed to elicit a confession from the rabbi, the pasha tried charm. During a pause in the interrogation he spoke "affectionately" to Salonicli, who like the pasha himself was born not in Damascus but in the Balkans: "Moses, look, we are compatriots, and for that reason I have special regard for you: tell me the truth and I swear on the Qur'an that nothing will be done to you."

Salonicli answered, "Your Excellency, I would rather die in the bosom of my own religion."[12]

Even the pasha, who had great confidence in the efficacy of torture in persuading uncooperative witnesses, seemed to realize that Salonicli would not cooperate. He and Ratti-Menton turned their attention to the chief rabbi, Jacob Antabi. Antabi's election as chief rabbi had been controversial. His predecessor, Haim Nissim Abulafia, was a wealthy man who had close contacts with the local government and officials. Abulafia's wealth and influence had been resented in the Jewish community, where many preferred to rely on their own connections, and in a controversial election he had been succeeded by Jacob Antabi, who was neither wealthy nor especially well connected, except for his marriage to a daughter of Raphael Farhi. The new chief rabbi was on poor terms with the Harari family, who were commercial and social rivals of the Farhis. He had repeatedly reprimanded David Harari for having local dancing women and "bad company" at his house, and on at least one occasion he had threatened Harari with excommunication. The Hararis had retaliated by withholding a portion of their contribution toward the chief rabbi's salary and by threatening to complain about the chief rabbi to the government.[13] The splits and antagonisms in the community must have seemed a promising background for the interrogation of the rabbi.

On March 1, a Sunday, the pasha had Rabbi Antabi arrested and brought from the Jewish quarter to the serail on a donkey. Hostile crowds on the streets cursed and jeered the rabbi and gathered at the palace to watch his interrogation. When Sherif Pasha ordered the rabbi to produce the bottle containing Father Thomas's blood, the rabbi said that he could not do so. At the pasha's orders, soldiers with drawn swords and the pasha's cook armed with a butcher's knife surrounded the rabbi and prepared to decapitate him.

At the last minute the pasha granted the rabbi a reprieve. The rabbi was then thrown into a tank of freezing water. When he came up for air, soldiers hit him with heavy sticks until he submerged himself to avoid the beating. Before long the rabbi was suffering from hypothermia and exhaustion. He tried to end his agony by staying at the bottom of the tank. Word was sent to the pasha, who came running and ordered the rabbi pulled out of the water. The rabbi was then beaten unconscious. When he woke up he was beaten unconscious again.

As he had done so successfully with other recalcitrant prisoners, the pasha offered the chief rabbi a pardon and a life pension in the Holy Land if he would only confess. The rabbi refused. The pasha ordered a tourniquet put around the rabbi's head. Soldiers tightened the tourniquet until the rope broke, and the rabbi "dropped like a corpse before the whole crowd." The soldiers then tied a rope to the rabbi's penis and used it to drag him around the courtyard of the palace. Soldiers crushed his genitals until he lost consciousness. He was bound to two poles, tossed into the air and allowed to come crashing down onto the stone pavement. The rabbi lost track of how long the ordeal lasted.[14] He never confessed.

The two rabbis were roughly the same age as the other accused Jews and in comparable physical condition. Indeed, Rabbi Salonicli was a part-time rabbi who, like the other accused men, was also a merchant in the suqs. The rabbis were confronted with the same confessions of the barber and servant naming them as accomplices in the murders and subjected to the same or worse tortures. Joseph Leniado, another rabbi, had also remained silent while he was flogged, and ended up so lacerated from the bastinado that he died in his cell. The silence of these rabbis under torture is even more impressive when we consider that under the twisted logic of the Moldavian monk's book that so captivated Ratti-Menton and the pasha, the rabbis were caught in a trap. If they confessed they would be judged guilty of the murder of the monk and his servant; if they refused to confess they would be accused of hiding the truth of ritual murders, which according to the Moldavian monk's book was the sworn secret of the rabbis, especially the chief rabbi. With that logic the rabbis could only lose in their contest with Ratti-Menton and the pasha.

Why did the rabbis hold out when others yielded to the torture and threats? Psychologists and some former victims of torture have speculated that faith or a strong political conviction can provide the victim of torture with the self-confidence or a reserve of inner strength that enables them to resist the pain and psychological pressure. Their religious studies may have provided the rabbis with powers of concentration or experience in mental exercises that could help to resist or ignore the pain. Men who chose to become rabbis, passing up the temptations of the marketplace, might be men of such inner security that they were somehow less vulnerable to pain and pressure. Or as spiritual leaders they may have felt a sense of duty, a determination to set an example for their community.

Whatever their reasons, eventually even the pasha and the French consul seemed to conclude that no amount of torture would elicit confessions from these men, that the rabbis would die first. They kept both incarcerated and alive, perhaps aware that if the rabbis died as martyrs their deaths might have strengthened resistance to the investigation and to the French consul's goal of proving that the Jews had committed a ritual murder.

The pasha and the French consul finally turned to a fourth rabbi, Moses Abulafia, the son of the former chief rabbi of Damascus. The son's career was not as illustrious as that of his father, who had gone from Damascus to a highly respected position in Jerusalem, and from the moment when Jacob Antabi had been chosen to replace the senior Abulafia as chief rabbi, there had been bad blood between the junior Abulafia and the chief rabbi.[15] It must have seemed another ideal opportunity for interrogators to exploit a tear in the social fabric of the Damascus Jewish community.

The younger Abulafia, who was a merchant as well as a rabbi, also had his differences with the Hararis. He knew them well enough to say "Good day!" or "Good evening!" but saw them socially only on formal occasions and resented that he had never been invited to their frequent "parties for fun, soirées, or business dealings." The reason, the rabbi believed, was not a difference of social rank but of wealth. "We are of the same rank," Abulafia said, "but he [David Harari] is rich."[16] The pasha and the French consul may have suspected that these resentments and antagonisms in the community would provide an opportunity for a skilled interrogator to drive a wedge between the factions.

Rabbi Abulafia was around forty years old—like the others, his age was recorded as a round number—and a heavyset man. After he was arrested and accused of participating in the murder of Father Thomas, he was deprived of sleep, flogged on the bastinado until he could no longer walk, and dragged around by his genitals. He did not bear up well under the torture, and when confronted with the confessions of the barber and the Hararis he confessed to his own complicity in the murder, including the Hararis' charges that after the murder of the monk he had received the bottle of blood for safekeeping from Rabbi Moses Salonicli.

On this last point the rabbi's confession was unsure. When Ratti-Menton asked him where the blood was, Abulafia kept changing his story, saying sometimes that it was at David Harari's house, at other times that it was with Rabbi Antabi, and finally that it was in his own house "in a chest of drawers."

When the interrogations of the other rabbis reached dead ends, Rabbi Abulafia, who could no longer walk unaided because of the lacerations to his feet from the bastinado, was carried to his house on the corner of School Street by four soldiers accompanied by Ratti-Menton, the consul's assistant dragoman Francis Salina, and the chief of police. The sewer drain where the evidence of the monk's murder had been found was just outside the rabbi's house. Once they were inside, the rabbi asked his wife, Ora, to fetch the blood. Ora, who was holding their infant child, had no idea what her husband was talking about. The rabbi began shouting at her. Frightened for herself and her child, Ora Abulafia insisted that she did not understand what her husband was talking about.

At that point the rabbi broke down. He said there was no blood, that he had only told the interrogators that the blood was in his house so he would have a chance to see his wife and child. He said that he could no longer bear the pain of the tortures and so he had lied "so I would be killed; so they would take my blood; so they could say 'Here is the blood of Father Thomas.' . . . even death would be better than these tortures."

Ratti-Menton had a quick temper when things did not go his way. Outraged that his search for the blood had ended in this pathetic confession, he began shouting at Ora Abulafia and hitting her. He ordered Frances Salina to hit her hard on the head and body. When the impromptu beating proved fruitless, Ratti-Menton and Salina tied a cord around the rabbi's neck and dragged him around the courtyard of the house while his wife watched in horror. As her husband's body bounced over the stones, Ora Abulafia could see the lacerations on the soles of his feet from the floggings in prison. The bones of his feet protruded through the open wounds.

Ratti-Menton and Salina then took the rabbi, his wife, and their infant child to the serail, where the consul sent a request to the pasha to have Ora Abulafia flogged. Only a last-minute appeal by an official, one of those sudden and unexplained changes of mind that has spawned the notion of the whimsy and authority of the Oriental potentate, spared Ora Abulafia. Instead, an order was issued for the rabbi to be given another two hundred lashes of the bastinado, with his wife and infant child watching.[17]

Even for a strong man, the stinging lashes of a kurbash are exquisitely painful. Strapped down, the subject is powerless. Men scream from the pain; some men soil themselves. Rabbi Abulafia's feet were already horribly lacerated. He had already shown himself weak in the face of torture. Now his wife and child would watch his humiliation, witness his weakness.

Abulafia had already burned his bridges with his earlier confession of complicity in the murder of Father Thomas. Even if he had only confessed to the accusations to spare himself more torture, he had set himself apart from the other rabbis. They had held out; he had not. They would be regarded with the highest admiration, as martyrs, examples of the principles of *kiddush Hashem*. Would anyone in the community ever again trust or respect Moses Abulafia as a rabbi?

The day after this humiliating beating, Rabbi Abulafia agreed to answer the French consul's questions. He signed a statement saying that he had delivered the blood to the chief rabbi and that the chief rabbi had organized the entire affair.

"What purpose does the blood serve?" Ratti-Menton asked. "Is it for making consecrated bread for your holidays? Does everyone eat it?"

Abulafia answered: "The blood used in the consecrated bread is not divided up among everyone; it is only given to the *ḥakhams* and zealots . . . before Passover, the other *ḥakhams* send [the chief rabbi] the flour and he makes the bread with his own hands. Nobody watches when he mixes the blood with the flour."

"Is the blood sent away?" the French consul asked. "Or is it only kept here for the Jews of Damascus?"

"The *Ḥakham* Jacob [Rabbi Antabi] told me he sends it to Baghdad as well."

"Was the plot specifically to seize a priest, or would any Christian have sufficed?"

"The goal of the plot was to capture a Christian," Abulafia answered. "But Father Thomas appeared, and he was taken and killed.

I told them they shouldn't murder him because someone would research [what happened to] him. They didn't want to hear [me] and they killed him."[18]

Rabbi Abulafia's new testimony matched perfectly with the allegations of the Moldavian monk's book. The news of the rabbi's testimony was a blow to the Jewish community, but it was not his last surprise. When he finished testifying, Rabbi Abulafia told the pasha that he wanted to become a Muslim.

10

The Talmud

TEN DAYS later Rabbi Abulafia appeared at the pasha's divan wearing the green caftan and white turban of a Muslim. His new name was Muhammad Effendi.

The rabbi's apostasy was even more shocking than his confession of complicity in the murder of Father Thomas and his servant. In Damascus people knew about the bastinado and the tourniquet; they had seen the crippling lacerations men received from the kurbash and had witnessed the agony of men held down in the tank of freezing water. Anyone who had felt or seen the bastinado knew how difficult it was to resist the demands for confessions.

But why would the rabbi convert to Islam? Abulafia's father, a distinguished rabbi in Jerusalem, thought his son's behavior owed to his being a disciple of those who taught "new ways." Abulafia's own explanation was that he had no choice; there was no other escape from the unbearable torment of the tortures. The rabbi did not cite it, but in his "Letter on Apostasy" Maimonides had written that if the choice was death or the Muhammadan confession, it was permissible to "Utter the formula and live!"[1] Abulafia did know Muhammad al-Talli, and it is possible that the idea for conversion was planted by al-Talli. Or perhaps after the many days of tortures and threats, culminating in the humiliation of the flogging with his wife watching, the rabbi began to identify with his tormentors, in a variation of the hostage syndrome that has been described in some modern terrorist events.

There may be another explanation of his conversion in the new name he took. Muhammad, the name of the prophet, was a typical name for a convert to Islam as a sign of respect and faith and was also a good match with the rabbi's given name of Moses. Traditionally, a Christian converting to Islam was required to follow his new Arabic name with *ibn Abdullah* (slave of God), but the Egyptians in Syria, who had been known to use mosques as barracks and to permit wine shops in the suqs, were equally casual in their administration of conversions.[2] The second half of Abulafia's new name was not Arabic but Turkish: *Effendi* is a Turkish honorific that roughly means sir or gentleman and is typically a term used by a supplicant to address an official. The name Muhammad Effendi also has a historical connection that was almost certainly known to Abulafia and to the other members of the Jewish community.

In the seventeenth century the world of Sephardic Jewry was swept with a sudden and intense messianic fever focused on Shabbetai Zvi, a Turkish Jew whose followers included an adept publicist named Nathan of Gaza. In quick sequence Shabbetai Zvi proclaimed himself the messiah, conducted a symbolic marriage between himself and a Torah scroll, and pronounced the ineffable name of God, an act that Jewish tradition allowed only to the high priest in the Holy of Holies of the Temple in Jerusalem on Yom Kippur. Nathan of Gaza's bulletins proclaimed the deeds and plans of the new messiah, and Shabbetai Zvi's promise of redemption enticed thousands of followers from Egypt to Amsterdam to Sofia, rich and poor alike, including much of the Sephardic rabbinate, to sell their worldly goods and follow him. The Ottoman authorities, confronted with enormous marches and potential uprisings throughout the empire, summoned Shabbetai Zvi to Istanbul and offered him the choice of converting to Islam or facing trial and execution. Martyrdom seemed the obvious choice for the charismatic leader, but to the shock and disbelief of his followers, he chose to convert. The name he took was Muhammad Effendi.[3]

Many of his followers, concluding that his Muslim name was a signal that he had not really converted, waited for Shabbetai Zvi's return. One group, drawing from the Lurianic kabbalah notion of "breaking of the vessels" or "death of kings," claimed that his apostasy was not a betrayal of his beliefs but "a decisive and unique mission" that would allow him "to enter the realm of the *qelippah* in order to destroy it."[4] Shabbetai Zvi died in exile in Albania ten years after his conversion, but the myth of his return was so powerful that until the fall of the Ottoman Empire it was said that each morning a delegation of officials went to the gates of Salonica to see if he had come back. By a circuitous route the legend of Shabbetai Zvi even tied into the blood libel myth: Decades after Zvi's death another false messiah named Jacob Frank proclaimed himself Shabbetai Zvi's successor and announced that for himself and his followers the new messianic era had voided Jewish laws. When their wife-swapping orgies earned them ostracism by traditional Jewish communities, Frank's followers converted to Catholicism and charged their former co-religionists with murdering Christians to use their blood for ritual purposes.

Although he never announced a motive other than to end the torments of the bastinado, Abulafia may have had a message of false conversion or a "mission" of "breaking of the vessels" in mind when he took his new name with its heavy burden of associations. Or, just as the French consul, in the hothouse atmosphere of Damascus, seems to have begun to believe the accusations against the Jews, Abulafia may, in the isolation and pain of his torture and interrogation, have been convinced that his Judaism was the cause of his woes. He told the pasha and the French consul that he wanted to renounce the "Israelite faith" because the Israelite prophets, beginning with Abraham, who was prepared to sacrifice his son Isaac, were all brutal beasts. To expose them he agreed to translate the Hebrew holy books and reveal the precepts of the Jews "against all other peoples."[5]

It was exactly the evidence of motive that the pasha and the French consul needed to complete their case.

The Moldavian monk's book was not the only research the French consul, Beaudin, and the pasha put into their prosecution. Early in the investigation a Catholic in Damascus brought an eighteenth-century Latin text, *La prompta Bibliotheca* by Lucius Ferrari, to the attention of the French consul and the pasha. Ferrari's book purported to document a homicidal Jewish hatred for Christians, and before long many in the Christian quarter were talking about the book. Arabic and Italian translations were available in Alexandria, Tyre, and Beirut, but to meet the sudden local demand, Ratti-Menton had excerpts translated into French and Arabic.[6]

At his divan the pasha questioned Muhammad Effendi about the contents of the book. When the former rabbi explained that the damning passages in *La prompta Bibliotheca* were taken from the Talmud, he was put to work translating suspect passages of the Talmud from the original Aramaic, which no one in the pasha's circle could read, into Arabic. The pasha was so enthused by the prospect of documenting the motives for Jewish ritual murders from the Jewish texts that in a parody of King Ptolemy's employ of seventy-two Israelites to separately translate the Hebrew Bible into the Greek Septuagint in the second century BCE, he was said to have ordered three different rabbis in Damascus to translate the Talmud passages, keeping them apart while they worked and threatening them with death if a comparison of their translations showed they were responsible for the slightest fabrication.[7]

The Talmud is a remarkably misunderstood book. Variously thought of as a compendium of laws, theology, or mysterious secrets, it is actually a summarized sketch of the debates of sages on questions of law, legend, philosophy, logic, pragmatism, history, science, anecdote, and humor. It was written in Aramaic, the lingua franca of Palestine and Babylon in the early centuries of the common era, when the rabbis in Palestine and in exile in Babylon were rebuilding Judaism after the destruction of the Temple in Jerusalem. Portions of the text are also in Hebrew, and there are borrowings from Greek and Latin, reflecting the breadth of learning of the contributors and redactors.

While it has been meticulously edited, the Talmud remains an exploration of reason, argument, and evidence. The sages venture into an incredible range of subjects, from the sublime to the absurd. Alongside, or as part of, their discussions of religious, civil, and criminal law and religious observance, they discuss in detail what happens if a mouse comes into a house after the bread crumbs are cleaned up for Passover. They ponder the problem of a fetus transferred from one womb to another, an issue that did not arise in the real world until invitro fertilization and surrogate motherhood. They take up the question of whether the mythical *golem*, a man-made robot, could participate in a minyan, the quorum of ten needed for some prayers. As often as not the arguments surrounding an idea end not with a definitive ruling but with one of three recurrent phrases: "the question remains undecided," "still in controversy," or "needing further study." Whole threads of their discussions are based on free association, like a stream-of-consciousness novel, and the method of dialectical reasoning *(pilpul)* applied to these diversions and explorations can lead to interim statements that are extreme or absurd. Although the sages ultimately reject these absurd conclusions, the dead ends of rejected ideas remain in the text as evidence of the explorations. As a result, the Talmud can be conveniently mined for quotations that, when taken out of the dense context, express viewpoints at odds with conventional morality, ethics, reason, experience, and the conclusions of the sages.

Because the Talmud was composed in the centuries when Judaism and the early Christian sects were competing for followers, with each defining itself at least in part in contrast to the other, there are passages in the Talmud that refer to Christian beliefs and practices. Christian censors objected to many of these references as demeaning. For example, they objected to the word *goy*, which means "nation" in Hebrew and is frequently used in the Talmud to refer to gentiles, and even to the use of the word *Talmud* itself. References to Rome or Idumea had to be replaced with Babylon, Persia, or Syria, and an entire tractate, Avodah Zarah, which focuses on issues of avoiding idolatry and idolaters, was censored from many editions as anti-Christian. Over the centuries these passages prompted Christian censors to impose changes or deletions in the text and in Paris and other cities to order public burnings of the Talmud.[8] It was exactly these controversial passages reflecting on Jewish attitudes toward gentiles that were cited in Lucius Ferrari's book and drew the attention of the pasha.

In one of the more bizarre episodes of the investigation of the disappearance of Father Thomas, the pasha appointed himself to preside over a series of formal disputations between Muhammad Effendi and Chief Rabbi Antabi on the meaning of various passages from the Talmud. One debate was held at the pasha's divan, with Beaudin, Ayyub Shubli, and others from the European community in attendance. Muhammad Effendi, invited to present a disquisition on the attitudes of the Jews toward gentiles as reflected in the Talmud, claimed that Judaism considered non-Jews to be "brute beasts" and offered as evidence the biblical story of Abraham's binding of Isaac in Genesis 22, specifically the description that "Abraham saddled his ass and took with him two of his servants" and that when they reached Mount Moriah Abraham said to his servants, "You stay here with the ass. The boy and I will go up there; we will worship and we will return to you." Muhammad Effendi explained that the Talmud cited this passage to support the conclusion that non-Jews, "like the two servants, were comparable to asses."

Asked if this was correct, Rabbi Antabi agreed that it was the interpretation of the Talmud on this passage. Before he could explain the context of the discussion in the Talmud, the pasha's questioning moved to another point. Muhammad Effendi went through quote after quote from various tractates of the Talmud, citing instances where a phrase or line equated gentiles with beasts. He argued that just as a beast could be slaughtered, the meaning of the Talmudic passages was that a gentile too could be slaughtered. He cited rabbi Shimon Bar-Yohai, arguing that "even the best of the gentiles should be killed." He identified passages in the tractate Sanhedrin (which is devoted in part to capital punishment) as justifying the killing of a gentile who observed the Jewish sabbath and said that it was justified for Jews to kill a non-Jew because Moses killed an Egyptian he saw beating an Israelite. And he argued that according to the Talmud a gentile can be condemned by a single witness and a single judge, while it requires twenty-three judges and two witnesses to condemn a Jew.

Muhammad Effendi's translations of the Aramaic and Hebrew passages in the Talmud to Arabic were reasonably accurate, at least to judge by the French translations of his Arabic that have survived in the *procès-verbal* of the trial, but his out-of-context quotations wildly perverted the original intent of the passages he cited. The citation condemning a "heathen" on the testimony of one witness and the ruling of one judge is from a special law directed against the Roman practice of prenatal murder.[9] The quotation requiring a court of twenty-three judges to condemn a Jew is from a passage where the scholars are trying to dilute the harsh language of Deuteronomy which demands that "a wayward and defiant son, who does not heed his father and mother and does not obey them even after they discipline him" be taken to a public place where "the men of his town shall stone him to death."[10] The Talmud scholars deliberately placed checks and balances on the interpretation of that passage from Deuteronomy, including the court of twenty-three judges for a third offense, to make the harsh biblical penalty impossible.[11]

Chief rabbi Antabi was expected to answer each of Muhammad Effendi's points but was not allowed to explain the context or qualification of the isolated quotes or to argue that many of the passages were tentative arguments that were ultimately rejected by the Talmudic sages. Antabi was a reluctant participant in these debates. He was in pain, so crippled from the torture he had received at the serail that he had to be carried to each session by two soldiers. He considered the piecemeal dissection of selected passages from the Talmud so inappropriate and so humiliating that at one session he begged the pasha to decapitate him rather than proceed with the mockery of an inquiry.

"Don't do that!" Muhammad Effendi said to the pasha. "Be careful. He only wants to die a martyr. It is better to torture him."

The former rabbi then turned to Rabbi Antabi and said, "Tell the Pasha where you put the blood after I gave it to you. That's the way to put an end to your torments."[12]

The chief rabbi tried to offer arguments that the goal of the rabbis in these passages had been to prevent idolatry and assimilation and not to apply different moral standards to other people. He cited the Noahide commandments as the moral standard the Jews applied to other people and explained that the passages Muhammad Effendi had cited referred not to Christians but to "ancient peoples who did not recognize God."[13] Muhammad Effendi interrupted him, declaring that this was deliberate obfuscation, an attempt to hide the truth that the passages referred to all non-Jews.

It was, of course, impossible for the chief rabbi in a sentence or two to explain the context of complex arguments or to demonstrate the subtle dialectic method of the Talmud. The most the rabbi could do was to deflect a few of the charges. When Muhammad Effendi suggested that there was a sinister meaning in the blank spaces in the Talmudic text, the chief rabbi pointed out that those omissions were passages that referred to Jesus which had been censored by the Christian authorities who regulated printing of the Talmud and that they had no other significance. Antabi was then asked to respond to the quotes from the Talmud "in his own hand," presumably so his written statements could later be used as evidence. He answered that he could not write in Arabic, only in Hebrew, and asked why he should write an approval "when the books are many and demonstrate the contradictions to those who would challenge [the interpretation]."[14]

The public debate at the pasha's divan was not the end of the Talmud inquiries. The pasha and Beaudin so enjoyed the humiliating debate that they held a series of late-night soirees where they would drink, comment, and joke until midnight or one in the morning while they listened to staged debates between the former rabbi and the chief rabbi. Muhammad Effendi would regale them with stories like the one recounted in the Moldavian monk's book, of how Jews dip a handkerchief in Christian blood, dry it, burn it to ashes, and then on the day after a Jewess is married strew the ashes on a hard-boiled egg that is eaten by the young couple.[15] The chief rabbi was then supposed to answer the charges.

As humiliating as these public and private disputations were for the chief rabbi and the Jewish community, Muhammad Effendi failed to identify a single passage in the Talmud that referred to ritual murder or human sacrifice. At one session one of Ratti-Menton's assistants, Ayyub Shubli, pressed the former rabbi, pointing out that given the biblical injunctions against the consumption of blood—"blood is the life and thou mayest not eat the life with the flesh"[16]—they needed an explanation of the apparent contradiction between the alleged need for blood for the matzos and the "notion of uncleanness" attached to blood that was so clear in Jewish law. Muhammad Effendi's answer could have been straight out of the Moldavian monk's book. "That is the secret of the chief rabbis," he said. "They are the only ones who know about this and about the way the blood is used."[17]

It was not the answer the pasha and the French consul had sought. But amidst the fervor that had been whipped up against the Jews, even an evasive and indirect explanation was sufficient evidence of motive for those who were convinced of the guilt of the Jews. After weeks of the bizarre disputations over the passages from the Talmud, the view in the Christian quarter, including among the official representatives of the supposedly enlightened nations, like the British consul, was that the extracts of the Talmud taken from the "Rabbin prisoners . . . authorize this immorality," and "the Secret which has been hitherto traditional and only imparted to the initiated, now has been revealed to the public."[18]

11

A Brief for the Defense

L EGEND says that when an anti-Semitic populace terrorized the Jews of sixteenth-century Prague with accusations of a blood libel, the great kabbalist Rabbi Judah Loewe fashioned the figure of a man out of clay, brought his creation to life with special prayers that invoked the Hebrew words used by God to create the universe, and assigned the golem he had created with the task of protecting the Jews. Until he became too bold and independent, the golem is supposed to have dutifully caught anti-Semites who were planting false evidence.

The Jews of Damascus had no golem to protect them from false evidence. Indeed, the legal procedures the Egyptians had inherited from the Ottoman Empire did not even allow the accused men to mount a defense. They were not represented by lawyers in their judicial proceedings before the pasha and the French consul, and they were never given the opportunity to raise challenges to the lack of physical evidence, to the use of torture to coerce confessions, to the coaching of witnesses, or to the suspicious match between the list of those accused of the murder and the ad hoc group of wealthy Jewish merchants who had offered a reward for information on the disappearance of the monk.

Indeed, as the prosecution picked up momentum and as information about the prosecution spread to Aleppo, Beirut, and Alexandria, so that flight to a nearby city was no longer an escape from the widening prosecution, the only defense left for those in the Jewish quarter was to hide and hope for a miracle. Those accused of the murder of the monk were all in custody or dead, but despite the ardor of the French consul and the pasha's troops in their repeated searches, a few of the Jews who had been named as murderers of the servant Ibrahim Amara were still successfully hiding.

The fugitives were not the only loose ends in the investigation. Despite the searches of homes and the sewers and the repeated torture and interrogation of the incarcerated Jews, no trace had been found of the monk's watch, cross, or keys or of the most important evidence of all: the blood that had allegedly been drained from the victims and put into bottles. Chief Rabbi Antabi, despite weeks of torture, interrogation, and staged disputations, still refused to admit that human sacrifice is prescribed in the Talmud or other Jewish texts. The consul and the pasha could argue, on the basis of the Moldavian monk's supposed revelations of the "mystery of the blood," that the rabbi's silence was an example of the secret oaths the rabbis swore and hence proved his guilt. But especially if the case was ever to be scrutinized by Western legal standards, that argument was not likely to hold up. With the exception of the barber and David Harari's servant, both of whom had been promised substantial rewards for their confessions, and the rabbis who had confessed to nothing, the accused men were all wealthy merchants. The pasha and the French consul never answered the obvious question of why men of wealth, men who had servants in their businesses and their homes, who could ring a bell to have a servant to fill their water pipes and bring them cups of sweet coffee and tea, would personally participate in a crime as coarse and repulsive as the alleged murder of a monk and his servant.[1]

Ratti-Menton and the pasha brushed away the lacunae in the case. With the arrival of spring Damascus was in the midst of another contagion of plague, which slowed the search for evidence and the fugitives. Ayyub Shubli quarantined himself in the French consulate to edit the judicial protocols that Beaudin had translated from the Arabic originals. The case against the murderers of Father Thomas was effectively complete, and everyone seemed to assume that it was only a matter of time before the remaining fugitives accused of the murder of the monk's servant—including various Farhi family members, Aaron Stambouli, and Moses Abulafia's brother Jacob—would be found and forced to confess to participation in the murder of Ibrahim Amara.

By the end of March the talk in the streets and coffeehouses of the Christian quarter had turned from if to when the Jews would be executed. Street crowds sang newly composed ballads praising Father Thomas and explaining the disappearance of other individuals as nefarious acts at the hands of the Jews.[2] There was no formal announcement of an execution date, but one day a number of the Jewish prisoners were dragged out into a public square and a gallows was erected. A cheering crowd gathered, but at the last moment the convicted men were taken back to cells in the military barracks next to the serail. Street gossip said that Ratti-Menton had intervened to spare the condemned men because he needed further testimony for his investigation.[3] It seems more likely that the pasha had staged a mock execution to persuade further confessions from the other incarcerated prisoners, or perhaps to placate the street crowds who were demanding a final resolution to the case.

The pasha offered no explanation for the aborted execution or the delays in carrying out the executions. Although he was the chief judicial officer as well as the governor of greater Syria, the protocols establishing his authority required that any execution would only be carried out with the specific authorization of his father, Viceroy Muhammad Ali in Alexandria.[4] Sherif Pasha had written to Alexandria as early as February 29 to report that the accused assassins would be dealt with "to the orders of your Highness," but the combination of slow camel trains, the higher priority Muhammad Ali assigned to his diplomatic negotiations with the great powers, and the infuriating inertia of the court in Alexandria delayed the answer to Sherif Pasha's requests. By the end of March Muhammad Ali had not even hinted about when he would grant permission to hang the Jews. Like the crowds in the street, the pasha and the French consul could only wait.

One reason Ratti-Menton and the pasha were eager to see the executions carried out was because a chink had developed in the case.

One of the men Murad al-Fatal's confession had named as a murderer of the servant Ibrahim Amara was Isaac Picciotto, the young merchant of twenty-five who had negotiated the deposition of Isaac Yavo. The Picciotto name was well known in Syria, both from the prowess of the family as merchants and because they had long served as consuls representing Austria, Holland, the Kingdom of the Two Sicilies, Sweden, Russia, and Prussia in Aleppo. Isaac Picciotto lived and married well: his beautiful young wife Rebecca was the niece of Rabbi Abulafia.

There had been bad blood between Picciotto and Ratti-Menton from the beginning of the investigation. Ratti-Menton flagrantly ignored the personal assurances he had given Picciotto and had sent Yavo to the serail for interrogation by the pasha, which, as everyone in the Christian and Jewish quarters knew, had resulted in Yavo being flogged to death in the pasha's dungeons. Picciotto also had long-simmering disputes with Beaudin and Muhammad al-Talli. Beaudin had subpoenaed Picciotto in connection with alleged claims of nonpayment of debts to European suppliers, which Picciotto vigorously denied. Picciotto claimed he had no business dealings with al-Talli but that after seeing the man's lewd behavior at the homes of other Jews, he had refused to let him into his own home: "From that moment," Picciotto said, "he swore unabated hatred against me."[5]

With three enemies among the principal investigators, a marriage to the niece of one of the Damascus rabbis, and his status as one of the more successful merchants in the Jewish quarter, it was not surprising that Picciotto was named as a suspect early in the investigation. By mid-February stories were circulating that Picciotto had bribed the barber to not testify against other members of the Jewish community. One rumor said Picciotto offered the barber five francs for every blow of the bastinado he suffered in silence. Another rumor claimed that some of the blood from the alleged ritual murders had been sent to Picciotto's uncle, Chevalier Elias de Picciotto, the Austrian consul-general at Aleppo.

Because of their long history of diplomatic service to Austria from Aleppo, the Picciottos were Austrian protégés. For many in Syria, protégé status was nothing more than a commodity to be bought and sold. Merchants bribed the Damascus consuls of European powers and their dragomans to obtain the coveted status that would protect them from the legal authority of the pasha, and in the tradition of corruption inherited from the Ottomans, the Egyptian administration accepted baksheesh to approve requests for protégé status. The sudden expansion in the number of protected individuals and the questionable qualifications of many who had bought their protégé status led to challenges of some of the claims by individuals and consuls. But Picciotto's own bona fides, based on the long record of service of his family as Austrian consuls, were beyond challenge. Austria had long exercised a role as the protector of Catholics, and ancient treaties granted Austria the right to protect Catholics in the Ottoman Empire. While the French claim as protector of the Catholic clergy, and especially the Capuchins, trumped the Austrian claim in the case of Father Thomas, the ancient capitulation treaties had given the Austrian emperor and his agents strong standing in the Ottoman lands. And Picciotto had a convincing argument that the very same tangles and twists of Ottoman law and custom that had granted the French consul the right to investigate the disappearance of Father Thomas accorded Isaac Picciotto an exemption from the legal authority of the French consul and the pasha.

Despite Picciotto's legal status as an Austrian protégé, Caspar Merlato, the Austrian consul in Damascus, was an unlikely protector. Merlato, an insurance agent from Trieste, had been appointed to the unpaid Damascus post in 1836. The business he had assumed his diplomatic position would attract never developed, and by 1840 Merlato was having a hard time making ends meet.[6] Along with most of the other foreign consuls he had taken an early and strong stand on the disappearance of Father Thomas. On February 21, only two weeks after the disappearance of the monk and his servant, Merlato assured the pasha that he would not interfere with the arrests of Jews who were Austrian protégés, even if they were only suspected of complicity, and that he had personally warned the Jews under Austrian protection that "the secret guarded by the Jewish nation would serve no purpose and would prove prejudicial to the innocent." A week later he wrote that "these villains . . . murdered the poor old man and collected his blood."[7]

When the first physical evidence was found in the sewer, it was Merlato who confirmed the identification of the monk's cap. He also certified the identification of the bones as human by an Austrian physician and took credit for the role that members of his consular staff had played in eliciting the initial confession from the barber Solomon al-Hallaq. At one social gathering in the Christian quarter he said that in all probability it was not just "religious precepts" but a "commercial motive" that had inspired the murders of the monk and his servant. This last comment may have inspired Ratti-Menton, who was at the gathering, to ask during the interrogations of the accused men whether the blood was only used locally or sold in other cities, such as Baghdad. Early in the investigation Merlato ordered Picciotto and his house put under secret surveillance.[8]

Later in the investigation Ratti-Menton visited Merlato to discuss the investigation of the presumed murder of the servant Ibrahim Amara and followed up by sending his Austrian counterpart a formal letter reporting that the new confession by the servant Murad al-Fatal had "gravely compromised" Isaac Picciotto and asking permission to have him arrested. Merlato approved the request, and that afternoon Isaac Picciotto was arrested and interrogated at the serail by the pasha. When Ratti-Menton then announced that the discovery of the bones of Ibrahim Amara in the sewer confirmed the testimony naming Isaac Picciotto as one of the murderers, Picciotto was transferred to the French consulate for further interrogation.[9]

With his protégé status, powerful family connections in Aleppo, and business contacts in Europe, Picciotto could have avoided involvement in the investigation by fleeing Damascus. Electing to stay in Damascus and putting his trust in the protection of the Austrian consul Caspar Merlato seemed a foolish choice after the consul had repeatedly showed that his views on the disappearance of Father Thomas and his servant agreed with those of the pasha, the French consul, and the rest of the consular corps. But after his initial run-in with Ratti-Menton, Picciotto was an angry young man. Without a large family to protect, he could dare to be bold.

Ratti-Menton and the pasha had every reason to assume that Picciotto's interrogation would go like the others. Except for the two rabbis and the four men who had been flogged to death, none of the accused had resisted the combination of torture and confrontation with the confessions of the others. Once Picciotto confessed, it would implicate another important Jewish family and another member of the group of respected citizens who had first offered a reward for information on the disappearance of Father Thomas.

Just before he began his interrogation of Picciotto, Ratti-Menton received an unexpected hand-delivered letter from his Austrian counterpart. Despite his earlier support of the investigation and his harsh comments against the accused Jews, Caspar Merlato now demanded that the French consul communicate "officially . . . the chief articles of the charges against M. de Picciotto" so that the Austrian consul could himself proceed "without delay to the preparation of judicial protocols."[10]

Merlato's insistence that he, and only he, had the right to prosecute any charges against Isaac Picciotto was a serious challenge to the French consul. Ratti-Menton was eager not to lose any authority over the investigation, and particularly not to allow potentially maverick testimony. He also knew that the rivalry between France and Austria over the representation of Catholics in the former Ottoman Empire mirrored larger diplomatic issues, which added to the potential ramifications of the case. Ratti-Menton promptly answered Merlato's message, claiming that because Father Thomas was only a French protégé rather than a citizen, the primary responsibility for prosecution—even in the instance of a capital murder case—rested with the Egyptian government, and for that reason he had transferred the entire prosecution of the murder of Father Thomas into the hands of Sherif Pasha, "who undoubtedly can employ more numerous and decisive methods of investigation than any foreign agent."

This was of course a reversal of the French consul's previous position; it also potentially undermined the entire tradition of foreign protection in the Ottoman Empire. But there was a measure of truth in what Ratti-Menton wrote: anyone who had followed the investigation would agree that the pasha had employed more decisive means of interrogation than the French consul. Indeed, Ratti-Menton's own interrogations had in every instance failed until the pasha had applied his more persuasive techniques. Even during the house searches, when the French consul had tried to seduce the wives and daughters of the accused men and offered them favors in return for their cooperation, he had failed to get any of the women to suborn the testimony of their husbands and fathers.

"From this moment," the French consul's note concluded, "I shall have no choice but to protest against any separate procedure which you might pursue in the question of the murder of Father Thomas or that of his servant."[11] It was strong language, but there was no one to whom Ratti-Menton could usefully protest; even if a dispatch to Europe were to arouse interest on the Quai d'Orsay, the resulting exchange of diplomatic notes would take months. With no possibility of intervention from their respective foreign offices, the two consuls—already too angry with one another for face-to-face diplomacy—battled on in a formal exchange of hand-delivered letters. Merlato answered Ratti-Menton with a flat riposte: "I have the honor to inform you that the procedure taking place at the Austrian consulate will not vary from the existing treaties between the Austrian court and the Ottoman Porte nor from the legal rights accorded to Austrian subjects."[12]

The stakes in the dispute were high. If Picciotto were to testify under Austrian protection, without the threats of the bastinado, he might undermine the case against the Jews. But the law was also clear: Picciotto was an Austrian protégé, and the same tangled treaties that granted the right to prosecute the murder of Father Thomas to the French consul also granted the Austrian consul the right to prosecute any crimes charged against Isaac Picciotto. What was not clear was why Caspar Merlato, who until only a few days before had supported the case against the Jews and volunteered independent testimony supporting the accusations, was suddenly defending Picciotto's right to be examined at the Austrian consulate, free from the pressures and tortures that the other witnesses had endured at the serail.

Ratti-Menton accused Merlato of having been bought off by the Jews, pointing out that in the last few weeks, after so many years of a failing insurance business, the Austrian consul had suddenly closed his business, had moved from an unremarkable small house to an elegant and spacious new house, and had declared himself a full-time consul. A colleague of Ratti-Menton also suggested that a dispatch from Isaac Picciotto's uncle in Aleppo, the Austrian consul-general Elias de Picciotto, might have changed Merlato's mind.

Merlato answered that he changed his position solely on the basis of "moral considerations deduced from the standing and the position of the accused; and also from the savage treatment to which they were subjected."[13] What neither the French nor the Austrian consul mentioned was that the great powers were in the first moves of a struggle over spheres of influence and the balance of powers in the Middle East, a parallel contest to the Great Game that would be played out in central Asia. Metternich's Austria sided with England in support of the Ottoman sultan and against France and her Egyptian ally. The rules of the game put Austria and France on the opposite sides of any issue that could have diplomatic repercussions in the area. Even if Caspar Merlato had been inclined by personal values or opinion to agree with the charges against the Jews, diplomatic duty called for him to stand up to the French consul. Ratti-Menton warned the Quai d'Orsay that the Austrian consul in Damascus was concealing guilty parties that were under his protection and that they should not be surprised to receive a representation from Vienna about the matter.[14]

The feisty exchange with Ratti-Menton was still in progress when Merlato and his staff began the formal examination of Picciotto at the Austrian consulate. Picciotto flatly denied all of the charges against him as "absolutely false," railed against the "audacity" of the servant Murad al-Fatal who "invented such lies," and pointed out that from early evening on the day the murders were supposed to have taken place, he and his wife had been at a party at the home of Georgios Mahsud, an employee of the East India Company who was well known in the Christian quarter. Picciotto named Muslim and Christian guests who were at the party and who could vouch that he had been there, including Francis Salina, the assistant dragoman of the French consulate. At the end of his interrogation he remained in protective custody at the Austrian consulate, safe from the bastinado, the tourniquet, and the pool of ice water that had been so effective in eliciting confessions from the other accused men.

Georgios Mahsud was questioned about Picciotto's testimony and confirmed that Picciotto and his young wife had arrived at his home a half-hour after sunset on the night of the alleged murders and had been there for much of the party. Mahsud also testified that in his opinion the Jews were guilty of the murders of Father Thomas and Ibrahim Amara. This last statement made his confirmation of Picciotto's alibi even more effective.[15]

Ratti-Menton and the pasha were not willing to drop the matter. The pasha summoned Isaac Picciotto to appear before him at his divan. Four times over a period spanning ten days, Picciotto was escorted to the serail by an Austrian official who remained there during the interrogation to assure that Picciotto would not be tortured or badgered. Emboldened by the protection he enjoyed, Picciotto not only refused to cooperate with the pasha's leading questions but took advantage of his immunity to challenge the entire investigation, raising the defense that none of the other accused men had been allowed to make. He called the testimony of Murad al-Fatal "slander," pointed out that statements made after the bastinado and torture should not be admissible, and argued that the "slanderers" who had testified against him were all "coached." He was especially scathing toward Aslan Farhi, who had confessed to a role in the murder of Father Thomas's servant and had named Picciotto as an accomplice. Aslan's confession, Picciotto said, could be forgiven since he had been promised that his life would be spared: "If I were [in his situation] I too would have resorted to lies in order to save myself. May God save me for the sake of my honor and conscience from doing anything like that."[16]

Picciotto grew bolder as the interrogation continued. During one session Hanna Bahri Bey, the pasha's chief adviser, translated the pasha's remarks from Turkish to Arabic for the record. Picciotto protested: "Who is doing the interrogation, you or the pasha?" In response Ratti-Menton called Picciotto "impudent" and "insolent" and said that his manner and defiance were all a conscious policy—which was undoubtedly true.

On another occasion Ratti-Menton referred to Picciotto as a "murderer." Picciotto, his face red with rage, shouted that the consul's accusation was an outrageous insult and that he would not listen to or respond to another question. Ratti-Menton left the session in a huff, and Picciotto, true to his word, refused to answer any more questions. In an exchange of letters afterward, Caspar Merlato protested that by any standard of Western justice Picciotto was innocent until proved guilty, which made Ratti-Menton's remark slanderous, and that if the case was in the hands of the pasha, as Ratti-Menton had argued in an earlier letter, the French consul had no right even to attend the questioning of Picciotto. The French consul answered that while the term he had used might be formally inappropriate, he should surely be permitted to use a harsh expression in response to Picciotto's "arrogant tone and ridiculous threats."[17]

Picciotto was undaunted by the exchanges of threats and so confident of his status and safety that his beautiful young wife Rebecca began talking of a ball to celebrate the expected release of her husband. She even promised the first dance to a visiting German traveler who had expressed sympathy for the family.[18]

The pasha and Ratti-Menton knew that Picciotto's testimony could shatter the prosecution of the accused Jews. The case against those charged with the murder of Father Thomas was not directly affected, but the case against the accused murderers of the servant Ibrahim Amara—especially the members of the prominent Farhi family—depended on the confessions of Murad al-Fatal and Aslan Farhi, who had both testified that Isaac Picciotto was with them and that he had helped murder the servant. If Picciotto's alibi was left standing, it called those confessions, and hence the entire case, into question. And if the case against the accused murderers of Father Thomas's servant collapsed, it would undermine the entire judicial proceedings against the Damascus Jews.

As a rebuttal the pasha and the French consul brought in two Christian men, Hanna-Boulad and Ibrahim-Gorrah, who testified that during the hours when Picciotto claimed to be at the party at Mahsud's house, they had seen him in the rue de Keukassiai with two women and a servant. Confronted with this testimony, Picciotto said, "The intentions of certain people for the complete destruction of the Jewish nation are well known."[19] Finally, the pasha recalled Georgios Mahsud to testify that he had not been wearing a watch the evening of the party and hence could not be precisely sure when Isaac Picciotto had appeared at his house. Sherif Pasha was then able to announce that in fact Picciotto had not made an appearance at the party until two hours after sunset and that until then he had been with the other murderers.

This last testimony—that Mahsud was not wearing a watch and could not be sure of the exact time when Picciotto had arrived at his party—was desperate and fragile in a culture in which public clocks did not exist and in which Muslims, Christians, and Jews all routinely told time not by clocks or watches but in relation to the calls for Muslim prayers that were announced by the *muezzins* from minarets in every corner of the city. In the trial protocols the witnesses invariably give the time of events as "one half hour after the sunset prayer" or "one hour before the noon prayer." The various confessions all said that the father was killed "between the *maghrib* and the *isha*" (the sunset and evening prayers). Even a rabbi testifying about when he went to the synagogue gave the time as "after *asr*" (the afternoon prayer). George Mahsud's original testimony was that Picciotto arrived at his party "one half-hour after *maghrib*."[20] Mahsud did not need to wear a watch to know when Picciotto arrived at his house; the call of the muezzins was his watch.

The old walled city of Damascus is compact. Rumors and news quickly became the subject of the day in the coffeehouses and suqs. For the citizens of Damascus, who eagerly followed every detail of the case, the contest between the French and Austrian consuls and Isaac Picciotto's feisty defiance of the pasha and French consul were good theater, a prolongation of the excitement of the investigation with those unexpected twists, repeated encounters between the characters, and a counterpoint of accusations and counter-accusations that invited endless discussion.

But the analysis of the cafe critics, and even the twists of plot they watched so closely, did not matter. By the time Picciotto testified, belief in the guilt of the Jews was so universal in the Christian community that the prosecution had acquired an inertia of its own. The Christian quarter of Damascus had become a chorus for the drama that played out at the French and Austrian consulates, the pasha's divan, and the dungeons of the serail. Like the actors who spoke out in the interrogations, the bystanders were swept up in a script that seemed to write itself. Crowds that had first stood on the streets shouting fulsome accusations, and later gawked and cheered at the humiliation and public torture of the chief rabbi, now demanded executions. The widening chasm between victim and spectator, overlaying a legacy of centuries of mutual fears and misapprehensions, had transformed the choreography of the city from the subtle social truce of the ritualized greetings that had once masked fundamental conflicts into a *danse macabre*.

When the drama reached that fever pitch, even the contradictory testimony of Isaac Picciotto did little to halt the inevitable. Fear—of embarrassment, humiliation, defeat—can magnify the inertia of a conviction. A child or even an adult caught in a mistake, especially if they are confronted in a manner that makes them feel belittled or threatened, will often persist, denying even an egregious mistake, insisting that the accuser refuses to see the whole truth or that a conspiracy has only made it seem that they were mistaken. The niceties of legal proceedings, which by Western standards were discounted in the Ottoman Empire under the best of circumstances, had already fallen by the wayside. The players in the drama had taken their positions on the stages of the city and spoken the lines that set them against one another; their roles, and the outcome of the play, were scripted by age-old attitudes and fears. Contradictory testimony, loose ends in the plot, missing evidence, confirmed alibis, the obvious excesses of the investigation, including deaths from the bastinado and the blatant coaching of the coerced confessions, even the inexplicable deviations from the patterns of ritual murder that the French consul and the pasha had "discovered" in the Moldavian monk's book, could not stem the momentum of the drama playing itself out in the streets of the city.

Damascus waited impatiently, expecting that any day a camel train would arrive from Alexandria with the news that the death sentences had been affirmed. So eagerly did they await the inevitable final act that no one seemed to notice that there was another audience for the drama playing itself out in Damascus.

12

The Geography of
Information

T HE WORLD was eager for rapid communications even before
Samuel Morse sent his famous "What hath God wrought?"
message in 1844. The French army relayed semaphore signals
between towers on hilltops to make certain they could send troops to
suppress a rebellion in a distant department before the revolutionaries
could summon help. The Rothschild banks routinely and secretly paid
ship captains to carry their private mail and cultivated shipping offices
and navies to provide their agents with advance notice of ship movements so that when ships arrived at ports ahead of schedule to find no
one ready to unload their cargo, a Rothschild agent would still be waiting at the dock to accept a sealed pouch of private mail. When Nathan
Rothschild died in Paris in 1836, the news was so important it was dispatched to the London office of the bank by carrier pigeon.[1] By 1840
even ordinary travelers could take advantage of the flurry of road, railroad, and ship building that had begun to shift transport and commerce
from the pace of animal carts and the whimsy of the wind to the era of
powered speed. Steamships made scheduled runs across the Channel
and the Mediterranean, and the railroads had become so reliable that
Britain adopted the penny stamp, good for a letter anywhere in the
United Kingdom.

But even the burgeoning demand for speed could do little about the
transport available across the deserts and mountains of the Levant.
There was no railroad yet in Syria; the Hijaz Station and the line leading
south would be built at the turn of the century to carry hajj pilgrims to
Mecca. The fastest route between Damascus and Europe in 1840 was via

camel train to Alexandria or Beirut, then by the new packet steamers to Marseilles, Genoa, or Trieste, and from there to Paris or London by stage. If all of the connections worked, a message took twenty days to travel from Damascus to Europe. The connections rarely worked perfectly, and diplomats and others who needed reliable communications sometimes had to hire their own Tartar camel drivers and purchase their own strings of dromedaries. Even private camel trains didn't help when water supplies at the desert oases were short or when marauders and bandits were especially active. And while the steamers to French Mediterranean ports were faster than direct routes to British ports, they incurred both the potential insecurity and the increased charges of French mail.[2]

The foreign consuls in Damascus were a close-knit community. They lived as neighbors in the European quarter, attended the same Roman Catholic or Protestant churches, and with the exception of occasional official functions at the serail or when they entertained local residents for commercial or political reasons, they were social friends primarily with one another and with other resident Europeans. The foreign consuls spoke and wrote to one another in Italian or French, the diplomatic languages of the Middle East, instead of the Arabic, Turkish, and Greek of the local population, and despite diplomatic and commercial differences between the countries they represented, they shared a common background and values as educated, privileged, European Christians who saw Syria and Damascus in terms of the contrast of what they would call the civilization of the West with the barbarism of the East.[3] From that perspective, the consuls, with few exceptions, did not question the charges that had been brought against the Damascus Jews. From their education and social rank, the foreign consuls probably would have accepted—at least publicly—the notion that the Jews in their home countries, at least in France and the United Kingdom, were upstanding citizens and entitled to the rights of citizenship. They were certainly aware of Jews who had distinguished themselves in letters, science, commerce, and politics. But those Jews, any one of the consuls would have been quick to note, were from the civilized West. The Jews of Damascus, in their eyes, were an entirely different people, an isolated tribe tainted with the barbarism of the East and capable of crimes that were unimaginable to an enlightened European.

The common values and outlooks of the consuls cut across diplomatic differences. Although France and England were in the midst of diplomatic sparring over the future of Syria, in his reports Nathaniel Werry, the British consul and a longtime resident of the region, approvingly repeated the details of Ratti-Menton's case, including the spurious allegations that Ratti-Menton had added to bolster his charges of ritual murder. In each instance of ritual murder, Werry reported, "seven of these influential persons performed the sacrifice, being in each four laymen and three rabbins." He also echoed the claim that the extracts from the Talmud which the rabbi-prisoners had translated revealed the "secret which has been hitherto traditional and only imported to the initiated . . . to the public."[4]

The Austrian consul, Caspar Merlato (he was called Giovanni in the Italian the Austrians used as their lingua franca in the Near East), initially agreed with Ratti-Menton and Werry about the disappearance of Father Thomas and his servant and had offered assistance in identifying the evidence and providing surveillance of the suspects. The American consul also subscribed to the prevailing opinion in the Christian quarter, writing to the secretary of state that "a most barbarous secret for a long time suspected in the Jewish nation . . . at last came to light in the city of Damascus, that of serving themselves of Christian blood in their unleavened bread at Easter, a secret which in these 1840 years must have made many unfortunate victims. . . . In the place where the servant's remains were found, a quantity of human bones . . . have been discovered which proves that they were accustomed in that house to such like human sacrifices."[5]

The consuls were in no hurry to send the details of the prosecution to their foreign offices, perhaps because they were unsure of the reception their reports would receive. Ratti-Menton had waited three weeks, until he considered the case solved, before he sent his first report to the Quai d'Orsay and to his superiors in Alexandria and Constantinople. The other consuls were equally circumspect. Werry first mentioned the disappearance of the monk on the ninth page of a long summary report he sent to Foreign Minister Palmerston on March 23. Even within the region, Werry consigned Father Thomas to the third item of a report he sent to Viscount Ponsonby, the British ambassador in Constantinople, at the end of February.[6]

When the consuls did send off their dispatches on the disappearance of Father Thomas and his servant and on the investigation and accusations against the Damascus Jews, they wrote their reports as if everyone who read the dispatches would share their convictions and opinions. They seem to have been so accustomed to the reinforcement of shared values and prejudices in their tight consular community that they forgot that there were cities and whole nations where official and popular views of the Jews did not subscribe to the assumptions that underlay their own views. The consuls seemed not to realize that the notion of the sharp division between the "civilization" of the West and the "barbarism" of the East which they used to define themselves as

110

foreigners in an exotic land was not universally accepted and that in cities of Europe or America, and even for the sophisticated diplomats in Alexandria or Constantinople, the idea of accusing anyone of the crimes they attributed to the Jews of Damascus was so preposterous as to be a sign that the accuser was himself tainted with barbarism.

The consuls also were not prepared for the possibility that the episode that loomed so immense through the magnifying lens of proximity and immediacy might be viewed in the capitals of Europe through a reversed telescope. The geography of information worked both ways in 1840: diplomats in faraway posts suffered the time lag in news about political events and changing priorities and perspectives in their capitals, just as the capitals were behind about daily events abroad. At the very moment that Count Ratti-Menton was flooding the Foreign Office on the Quai d'Orsay with reports from Damascus, the office was in the midst of dealing with a tentative Anglo-Russian alliance, the pressing Russian threat at the Bosporus, the reassertion of the new young sultan in Constantinople against Muhammad-Ali, and renascent Austro-Prussian cooperation bolstered by the young Friedrich-Wilhelm's ambitions toward a revival of the Holy Roman Empire.[7] Indeed, the time lag for communications between Damascus and Europe was long enough that Ratti-Menton's first official report on the disappearance of Father Thomas was addressed to a government that had fallen from power by the time his message reached Paris.

At the end of February 1840, when Ratti-Menton was penning his report, the government of Marshall Soult, who had only been in power since May 1839, faced an adverse parliamentary vote. On March 1 King Louis-Philippe, in yet another round of the ministerial musical chairs that had characterized his reign, replaced Soult with Adolphe Thiers.

The new premier was forty-two years old and already famous as a journalist, lawyer, politician, and historian of the French Revolution. A strong supporter of the conquest of Algiers in 1830, Thiers was convinced that the stability and effectiveness of his government depended on its achievements in foreign policy. Syria, where France was in a direct confrontation with the other great powers over the future shape of the Middle East, was a cornerstone of that policy. Against the background of that preoccupation, Ratti-Menton's reports of events in Damascus, and the French role in the investigation of the disappearance of Father Thomas, was not necessarily the diplomatic triumph Ratti-Menton thought he had presented to Paris.

And, as is so often the case in diplomatic matters, scattered drops of rain can begin to look like a storm. Werry and the other consuls in Damascus gratuitously amplified their reports of the incidents in Damascus with general observations about the Jews, adding, for example, that it has always been the opinion of the Christian population of Turkey that the Jews "immolated clandestinely Christians to obtain their blood."[8] With alerts like that floating about in the diplomatic correspondence between capitals, it was not surprising that other incidents involving Jews began to appear in diplomatic dispatches from the Middle East.

From Constantinople there were reports that a few days before the disappearance of Father Thomas a Muslim man left his child for safe-keeping with a Jewish shopkeeper. The child wandered off and was not in the shop when his father returned. The shopkeeper laughed the matter off, telling the father not to worry and joking, "I murdered him for Passover!" The shocked father furiously attacked the shopkeeper, who was arrested. The Greek and Armenian Catholics of the city demanded that he be lynched. Luckily, the child was found safe and sound. The chief rabbi of Constantinople ordered the Jewish shopkeeper subjected to two hundred blows of the bastinado.[9] At roughly the same time in Smyrna reports surfaced of the disappearance of a boy of ten or twelve who had been employed by a druggist. In the vocal consternation and apprehension about the fate of the boy, the words "Jew" and "sacrifice" were heard, until the missing boy, who had run away from his master, was discovered on a road leading out of town.[10]

The most serious other incident occurred on the island of Rhodes, where a young boy living in Tirianda was sent on an errand and failed to return home. A report later said that two Greek women had seen the boy headed toward Rhodes in the company of four Jews, and rumors quickly circulated that "the child in question was doomed to be sacrificed [by the Jews]." One man, Eliakim Stambouli, was arrested and tortured until he incriminated himself and other Jews. Those he named were in turn tortured, and a blockade was imposed on the Jewish quarter of Rhodes. The local European consuls joined cause with the governor and the Greek Orthodox archbishop, even participating in the interrogations of the arrested Jews. The Jewish community reported that "the consuls stated openly their purpose of exterminating the Jews on Rhodes or to compel them to change their religion."[11]

A single report of an incident of an alleged Jewish ritual murder might have fallen on deaf ears in the foreign offices, where the diplomatic professionals and foreign ministers were accustomed to reading daily barrages of reports from consuls and ambassadors around the world. For the consuls in Damascus, the conjunction of reports of alleged Jewish atrocities in Middle Eastern cities were a welcome reinforcement of their convictions. What no one could predict was how the more experienced diplomats in Alexandria and the officials at the home foreign offices would react. Would the sudden flood of reports of alleged atrocities trigger a dramatic response or profound skepticism? The geography of information in 1840 meant that the consuls would have a long wait to hear responses to their reports.

Because of the steamer schedules, mail from Damascus and other cities of the Levant arrived in Europe in batches. The same packet steamer that landed in Marseilles or Genoa with diplomatic dispatches from Damascus also brought newspapers from the larger Middle East cities like Alexandria and Smyrna, commercial and private mail, and casual reports from the merchants, travelers, and low-level diplomats who served as irregular stringers for European newspapers. Some of these casual correspondents wrote their newspaper reports as a public service, to try to persuade opinion in Europe or to focus attention on the corner of the world where they were temporary or long-term expatriates. Others wrote for vanity or token payments. They all wrote anonymously, and none made much of an effort to verify the street rumors that formed the basis of their reports. Because Marseilles was the home port for the packet steamers that crossed to the eastern Mediterranean ports, the Marseilles newspapers, especially the *Sémaphore de Marseille* and the *Sud,* carried the earliest and most frequent coverage of events in the Near East.[12]

The first newspaper reports of the disappearance of Father Thomas appeared in Marseilles in mid-March. Written the third week of February, before the pasha and the French consul had "solved" the case, the stories reported Father Thomas's disappearance and noted that "a number of Jewish families" were suspected. The *Sémaphore* reported that "the Jews are subjected non-stop to torture in order to force them to name the authors of a crime which revolts everyone" but justified the harsh methods of interrogation by the horror of the suspected crime.[13]

In an era before news services, major newspapers routinely reprinted stories from other newspapers without acknowledging the source of the material or making any effort to verify the story. The early stories from the Marseilles papers were widely reprinted in major European cities, often by newspapers that were regarded as the journals of record. The article from the *Sémaphore* appeared in the *Times* of London, the *Journal des Débats* in Paris, and the *Leipziger Allgemeine Zeitung.* The stature of those newspapers lent authority to the casual reports from anonymous stringers, so that in many European capitals what had been street rumors in Damascus or Beirut was elevated overnight to the status of serious news reporting.

These early stories of the disappearance of Father Thomas were sporadic and at least three weeks behind the events in Damascus because of the time-lag of the camel trains and packet steamers. It was a full three weeks after the "confession" by the barber Solomon al-Hallaq that the *Presse* in Paris, relying on a story from the *Gazette de Languedo*, brought the charges of ritual murder out in the open for the Paris public. "Rightly or wrongly," the paper reported, "the Jews in this city [Damascus] have the terrifying and inconceivable reputation of sacrificing a Christian on their Passover and of distributing the blood to their coreligionists in the region."[14]

With that sensational report, the French newspapers and others that picked up their stories began to report regularly on the events in Damascus. Some stories dwelled on minute details of the alleged ritual murder. The *Leipziger Allgemeine Zeitung* reported from Constantinople that Father Thomas had been "locked up in the cellar of a rich Jew, David Harari, and there ceremonially slaughtered by a Jewish butcher; his blood was secretly divided up among the fanatical Jews."[15] A few of the stories made an effort to balance mention of the "atrocious fanaticism" and the "bloody form of sacrifice" with indignant statements that the Jewish suspects in Damascus "are flogged, their foreheads are skinned by the tourniquet, they are despoiled . . . all this is happening in 1840." Many papers carried a report from Father Francis of Ploaghe, the Capuchin who had been sent to replace Father Thomas in Damascus, which regurgitated the details of Ratti-Menton's and the pasha's prosecution of the Jews.[16]

At least one early notice was skeptical of the charges against the Jews. A report from Beirut suggested that Ibrahim Pasha and Sherif Pasha were trying to expropriate the wealth of the Jews. "Nobody here sympathizes with the Jews," the anonymous article in Augsburg's *Allgemeine Zeitung* reported. "That is the way things are in Syria; hatred here is not between the national groups, but between the religions, and one sect will happily give up half its possessions if that ensures that the other sect loses everything. All the Turkish pashas who used to rule in Syria knew how to exploit this hatred to the utmost and . . . Ibrahim [Pasha] does so no less."[17]

That early article proved an exception to what became a consistent pattern in the reports from the anonymous stringers. As the pasha and Ratti-Menton continued their interrogations, the *Sud* and the *Sémaphore de Marseille* chronicled each new story with such sensational headlines as "New Details on the Disappearance of Father Thomas: The Discovery of the Murderers" or with gruesome details of the alleged crimes. They reported that David Harari's servant had "sat on the victim's stomach," that the barber had "held him by his beard," that the two rabbis had "pinned him to the ground," and that David Harari "cut deep into his throat" with a "large knife" and his brother and the two rabbis "finished him off" while the others held the body head down, held a basin to collect the blood, and applied pressure to facilitate the draining of the blood. When the blood had been drained, they all "threw themselves on the corpse, cutting it to bits."[18]

A few leftist papers in France, Belgium, and some of the German states refused to print the stories, but the center and rightist newspapers in France, Belgium, Italy, the German states, Austria, and the Scandinavian states eagerly reprinted the lurid stories from Damascus. Two exceptions to the tabloid stories were Russia, where the news was either too remote or was effectively censored, and Rome, where the Vatican-controlled newspapers were notably silent on the matter. The few leftist papers that refused to print the story probably did so less from sympathy for the accused Jews or a sense of justice than to avoid the appearance of supporting ultramontane positions by making a martyr of the father. The Vatican had more deliberate and subtle reasons for the noticeable silence of their press on the issue.

Editorial comments on these early stories ranged from silence to wholesale condemnation of the alleged perpetrators. The Catholic Church, normally a dominant voice in many newspapers, was notably silent in the press and in public comment, but behind the scenes it had begun an extensive campaign to publicize the murder of the monk in the ultramontane press.[19] The conspicuous silence of the papers in Rome, it appears, was a deliberate and calculated move by the Vatican to avoid being identified as the promoter of the story and rumors from Damascus. Between the silence on the left, the uncritical reprinting of stories by papers in the center and on the right, and the machinations in the Vatican, few newspaper editorials asked whether the stories of ritual murder were actually true or whether anyone in Damascus may have had motives to falsely accuse and frame the Jews.

By April, after the first flurry of sensational articles about the case, the reports from Damascus had to compete with other news. Quiet directives from the Vatican tried to keep the Damascus story alive in the Catholic press, but in March 1840 France was focused on the politics of a new government and the preparations and pomp attending the return of the remains of Napoleon from St. Helena for entombment in the Invalides. The outburst of nationalism attending the return of the emperor made the events in Damascus seem very small by comparison. Across the Channel Britain was caught up in wars in the Hindu Kush and the Opium War in China, dealing with a collapse of the Jamaican economy after the emancipation of the slaves there, reeling from the deadly ending of Chartist agitation, and, just five days after Father Thomas disappeared in Damascus, celebrating the marriage of Queen Victoria to Prince Albert. In addition to the pomp of a royal wedding, the press and public were absorbed in testimonies of the queen's devotion to the prince consort and a barrage of editorials about her unconcealed efforts to elevate him to the status of co-ruler of the realm.

Even the most sensational stories from Damascus could not compete with an emperor or a queen.

13

Seeking Help

A N ANCIENT concept of Jewish law called *pidyon shvuyim* requires that everything possible be done to raise the money necessary to ransom Jews who are being held hostage. Even money that had been contributed to build a synagogue is supposed to be offered to ransom hostages.[1] The notion was so firmly established in Jewish doctrine and practice that in the Middle Ages extortionists would kidnap rabbis and other famous Jews and demand enormous ransoms for their release, confident that the ransoms would be paid.

But invoking pidyon shvuyim for the incarcerated and fugitive Jews of Damascus depended on getting information about their plight out to the world. And in the spring of 1840 the packet steamers arriving in Marseilles and Genoa from Beirut and Alexandria carried few messages from the Jewish quarter in Damascus. With the leaders of the Jewish community incarcerated and awaiting execution, two of the rabbis imprisoned in the serail, another rabbi converted to Islam and aiding the prosecution, and the pasha's troops systematically searching Jewish and Muslim quarters for fugitives accused of the murder of Father Thomas's servant, even those who had not been named in the arrest warrants were lying low, understandably reluctant to attract the attention of Ratti-Menton, Beaudin, or the pasha and his troops.

The first report from Damascus to find its way to Jewish authorities outside the city was from a British banker and businessman named E. Kilbee, who for many years served as an intermediary for donations collected in Europe on behalf of the Jewish communities in Jerusalem and Safed. On February 20, two weeks after the reported disappearance of the Father Thomas, Kilbee sent a report on the situation in Damascus to Hirsch Lehren, the director of the Jewish Holy Land Fund in Amsterdam. "I only hope and pray that Father Thomas will be found," he wrote. Around the same time P. Laurella, a vice-consul in Damascus representing Tuscan, Dutch, and Austrian interests, also wrote to Lehren suggesting that the pasha or his agents might have set up the disappearance of Father Thomas to "extort money from the Jews."[2]

As the situation in Damascus became more threatening, the Jewish community sent their own appeal to the only place they could expect help, writing to two prominent Jews in Constantinople and voicing hope that a peaceful settlement of the matter would soon be reached without outside intervention.[3] It was an old tradition for communities in the Ottoman Empire to mimic the hierarchical bureaucracy of the empire by sending requests and complaints to the leaders of their own community in Constantinople in the hope that their brethren in the Sublime Porte would have access to the sultan and his ministers. In 1835 a chief rabbi for the entire Ottoman Empire had been established, the Gülhane of 1839 had shown the sultan's sympathies for the minorities in the empire, and Abraham de Camondo, who had once been sarraf in Constantinople, had begun to assume the more sophisticated role of financier and adviser to the Ottoman sultans, comparable in many ways to the role the Rothschilds played in the European nations. Camondo functioned as an intercessor for Jewish interests at the Sublime Porte.[4]

Camondo was willing to help, but by 1840 Damascus was no longer under the sultan's effective rule. As long as Muhammad Ali in Alexandria refused to surrender greater Syria back to the sultan's rule and Ibrahim Pasha and his Egyptian armies remained in occupation, Damascus was effectively enemy territory to the Ottomans. That left Camondo and the other Jewish leaders in Constantinople powerless to intervene on behalf of their coreligionists in Damascus.[5]

Another hope for help was that diplomacy and a regular traffic of missionaries kept the Holy Land in the news in European capitals. Ever since the French Revolution, Christian millennialist movements had been scrutinizing the New Testament for clues to when the thousand-year reign of Christ on Earth would begin. Napoleon's invasion of Palestine in 1798 and his summoning of a Sanhedrin in Paris in 1807 refocused evangelical attention on the belief that the reign of Christ would begin in Palestine with the ingathering of the Jews, and the Protestant scriptural studies found support in Jewish millennialist interpretations from the Talmud and the Zohar, which identified the year 5600 in the Hebrew calendar—September 1839 to September 1840—as the time when the Messiah would arrive. Evangelical Protestants, who believed that the Jews, as heirs to the Israelites of the Bible, would be the direct beneficiaries of the biblical prophecies, and even Protestant denominations who were not strict millennialists, sent missions to the Holy Land to proselytize and conduct archaeological research. The British government encouraged the efforts and reminded newly appointed British diplomats in the area that "it will be a part of your duty as British vice-consul at Jerusalem to afford protection to the Jews generally."[6]

One of the more aggressive proselytizing groups was the London Society for Promoting Christianity Amongst the Jews, which set up an office in Jerusalem and determined to erect their own church there where they would hold simple Protestant services in Hebrew, avoiding the Greek and Latin of the "idolatrous" denominations while they prepared the way for the conversion of the Jews. By 1840 John Nicolayson, the leader of the London Society mission, had recruited four missionaries, all converted Jews, for the society's mission of providing direct aide to the impoverished Jewish communities of Jerusalem and Safed, and had set up a hospital with two of the missionaries as medical officers. The Jerusalem rabbis were understandably equivocal in their attitudes toward the London Society. The Ashkenazi and Sephardi rabbis firmly opposed the conversionist policies of the London Society but were desperate for medical and other aide for their communities and knew that the London Society had provided much-needed support to the impoverished Jewish communities of the Holy Land during epidemics and after the 1837 earthquake in Safed.[7]

In March 1840 Nicolayson began hearing disturbing rumors of blood libel accusations against the Jews of Damascus. The Jewish community of Jerusalem heard the same rumors and sent a delegation to George Pieritz, a medical officer at the London Society hospital and former rabbi at Yarmouth before he converted, "to beg he would do what he could to rid them of this calumny" and asking that he "go with them to Damascus for this purpose." The London Society missionaries agreed that the ritual murder accusations were absurd but advised the Jerusalem rabbis "to keep perfectly quiet lest they should draw the . . . calumny upon themselves."[8]

After further investigation and confirmations of the rumors by the governor of Jerusalem, the Grand Mufti, and local Roman Catholic monks, the London Society decided to send Pieritz to Damascus to make an appraisal of the situation there. He was highly qualified for the mission: as a Jewish convert he knew Hebrew and was familiar with Jewish ritual practices, he had been in the Middle East long enough to know his way around the suqs and the unspoken rules of social conduct, and as a physician he could evaluate the consequences of the rumored torture of the accused Jews. Several Jerusalem rabbis gathered at Pieritz's house on the day of his scheduled departure and offered to accompany him, until representatives of the London Society advised the rabbis that they would be wise not to attract attention to themselves. The rabbis followed the advice but agreed to pray for the success of Pieritz's mission, the first time they had ever offered prayers for a convert and missionary. As another gesture of respect for his mission, the rabbis decided that they would no longer impose a boycott on the London Society.[9]

Pieritz boarded a ship from Jaffa to Beirut on March 18—it was easier to take the ship and cross Mount Lebanon than to travel overland to Damascus—and arrived in Damascus late in March. He brought an introduction from the British vice-consul in Jerusalem and was graciously received by British consul Nathaniel Werry until Pieritz made it clear that he thought the whole case against the Jews was fabricated. Pieritz declined Werry's offer to introduce him to Ratti-Menton and the pasha, and instead of staying in the British consulate he moved in with a sympathetic European in the Christian quarter. A French diplomat called Pieritz's Damascus host "a renegade."[10]

When Pieritz began questioning the relatives and friends of the accused Jews, he learned that the Christian quarter of Damascus, except for the Austrian consulate, was openly hostile to the Jews. Pieritz "has taken quite a different view of the assassination committed here by the Jews than the French consul and local government did," the British consul wrote to the Foreign Office. "And strange to say looks upon the perpetrators as innocent victims. . . . [Pieritz was] wroth against me because he could not persuade me to be a convert to his opinions, when he was wholly ignorant of the evidence obtained . . . and relied solely on information . . . from the Jew brethren here."[11]

Pieritz stayed in Damascus until April 6, when he left for Alexandria. By then he had concluded from the gulf between what he learned from his queries and interviews and the official position of the French consul, the pasha, and their supporters in the European quarter that the ultimate resolution of the case would be decided not in Damascus but in Alexandria, where the future of the Egyptian empire was being debated. Before his report from Damascus was published in London, he forwarded notes to the Foreign Office on what he had discovered about the investigation procedures and the torture to which the accused Jews had been subjected, including some harsh comments on the British consul and others in the European quarter who enthusiastically supported the convictions of the Jews. Pieritz's reports were widely read in the Foreign Office and ultimately came to the attention of Lord Palmerston himself. The official response to those reports was not what the confident British consul in Damascus expected.

The Jerusalem rabbis who had set out with their own mission to Damascus, and were ultimately dissuaded from the dangerous initiative, had been following an old tradition of envoys venturing abroad to seek support for the Jewish community in the Holy Land. With their unconcealed poverty and the aura of holiness and studiousness of their dress, language, and manner, the emissaries were frequently successful in their appeals, especially among those who enjoyed the wealth and comfort of Europe or America and were willing to contribute to the impoverished Jewish communities of the Holy Land, supporting those who devoted their lives to study and prayer in Jerusalem and Safed.

As the rumors of the blood libel persecution in Damascus were confirmed by more reports that filtered to Jerusalem, the Jewish community there determined to draw on the traditional prestige their envoys enjoyed to protest and appeal the events in Damascus. In March 1840 Rabbi Haim Nissim Abulafia, a respected Jerusalem rabbi, former chief rabbi of Damascus, and the father of Rabbi Moses Abulafia, set out for Constantinople with Isaac Farhi, who was related to the Farhi family in Damascus. Their intention was to represent "the leaders of the Holy Land to seek help and protection" for the Damascus Jews. Another Jerusalem rabbi, Isaac Fakh, set off for Alexandria to lobby the European consuls-general there. He carried a statement from the head of the London Society declaring the ritual murder accusations in Damascus an "utter absurdity."[12]

News of the various efforts on their behalf seemed to rally the Jewish community in Damascus. There were reports that the community tried to negotiate with Muhammad Ali in Alexandria through an unnamed Jewish intermediary, offering to pay 500,000 piastres if he would cease the "humiliating" translations of the Jewish texts and not include the translations in the procès-verbal of the trials, free Raphael Farhi from his preventive detention, commute the death sentences, and guarantee better treatment of the imprisoned men. The community was supposed to pay 150,000 piastres upon "clarification and agreement" on the terms and the balance when the proceedings against the accused men were terminated. The enormous sum supposedly would come from an appeal at the synagogues of the community.[13] The improbable sums, and the emphasis on the excision of mentions of Jewish texts in the trial protocols, suggests that the rumors may have been spread by Ratti-Menton, Beaudin, or their supporters to further discredit the Jewish community.

The Jewish community seems in reality to have eschewed negotiations with the pasha or the viceroy in favor of reviving their campaign to reach help abroad. On the day Pieritz left Jerusalem, the Jewish community of Damascus sent a report and appeal for help to Raphael Alfandari, a key contact of Hirsch Lehren's Jewish Holy Land Fund in

Amsterdam, who had established an office in Beirut. The situation in Damascus had changed dramatically since the community had sent their earlier report to Constantinople. In the letters to Alfandari they reported the death of Isaac Yavo, the forced confessions of leading members of the community, and the sorry news that other members of the community, including men who had not even been incarcerated or accused of complicity in the alleged murders, had chosen to convert to Islam to avoid prosecution. One of the converts was Negri Behor, a prominent Damascus banker who had been close to Sherif Pasha and might have been in a position to put in a good word for his coreligionists.

These new reports from Damascus were written in Hebrew. Because most Jews regarded the language of the Bible as appropriate only for prayer or study, the choice of Hebrew underlined the gravity of their appeal. It also avoided the complexity of having to send appeals in multiple secular languages. The reports were laced with age-old, meaning-laden terms, referring to the kiddush Hashem of those who had died under torture in the pasha's dungeons, invoking the traditional curse of *yimah shemo* ("May his name be obliterated!") for Beaudin, and reporting somberly that Isaac Yavo had recited the *sh'ma* ("Hear, O Israel, the Lord our God, the Lord is One") before his martyrdom on the bastinado.[14]

Beyond the communications lags of the slow camel trains and packet steamers and the difficulty of sending and receiving messages from their besieged community, the Jews of Damascus faced a formidable challenge in communicating their dire situation across the gap of custom, practice, and self-image that separated them from the semi-assimilated Jewish communities of the West. By the nineteenth century the notions of loyalties that underlay pidyon shvuyim had been compromised and sometimes obliterated for many Jews in Western nations by the new boundaries of nationhood and citizenship, increased roles and responsibilities in modern economies and secular societies, and a reaction to the exclusiveness implied by the ancient Jewish concept. In states where the rights of citizenship and the social and economic gains of integration into modern secular society were seen as hard-won and fragile privileges, many Jews in Europe and America struggled to respond to a claim on their loyalty from Jews of a distant corner of the world whose customs and image might by association represent a threat to those achievements.

The messages arriving directly and indirectly from the Damascus Jews, with their reports of interrogations, public humiliation, torture, coerced confessions, and death sentences, were dramatic and arresting, but anyone who undertook to make appeals on their behalf faced the question of where to seek help. The fundamental and inescapable characteristic of Jewish life since the diaspora had been its fragmentation and dispersal. There was no world hierarchy of Judaism like the Holy See, the College of Cardinals, or the bishops and archbishops of the Roman Catholic Church. Other than societies that collected and directed funds for the Jews of the Holy Land, there was no international Jewish organization. There were no associations or lobbying groups that could mobilize aide or lobby officials in Damascus or Alexandria. The only names that Jews recognized universally were those of the great scholars, whose commentaries and compilations were studied by learned Jews everywhere.

There was one exception. The expensive European wars and the dramatic commercial and industrial expansion of the eighteenth and early nineteenth centuries had dramatically transformed the world of finance as nations and investors raised the funds to wage war and build railroads and steamships. By 1840 one family stood out in that world of finance: the Rothschilds, with their powerful investment banks in London, Paris, Frankfurt, Vienna, and Naples. The Rothschild banks made enormous loans and floated stock issues for commercial and government ventures. Their uncanny access to information and news, their celebrated business acumen, and their sudden and extraordinary wealth brought the Rothschilds untold fame and in turn unleashed volumes of satire and criticism in the newspapers, pamphlets, and scurrilous ditties. In the capitals where they had their banks, the Rothschilds had been presented to kings and sultans; in turn, they received envious kings at their country estates. Rothschild loans and financial instruments supported thrones from the northern reaches of Europe to Muhammad Ali in Alexandria. Cartoonists, satirists, and the daily press multiplied their fame, chronicling their every move and blaming or crediting the Rothschilds for every phenomenon short of the weather. The Rothschild name was imbued with such magic power that Heinrich Heine once saw a stockbroker tip his hat as he watched a servant carry Baron James de Rothschild's chamber pot across the floor of the Paris bank on the rue Laffitte.[15]

By 1840 the Rothschilds—Lionel in London, Baron James in Paris, Karl in Naples, Solomon in Vienna—were the most famous Jews in the world, renowned for the spectacular rise in their families' fortunes, their wealth, and their economic and political influence. They were also substantial contributors to Jewish appeals and were known to offer their names and influence to Jewish causes. For Jews in desperate need of help, eager to invoke the concept of pidyon shvuyim, the Rothschilds were the obvious target for an appeal.

When Raphael Alfandari in Beirut forwarded the reports he had received from Damascus to Hirsch Lehren in Amsterdam, he enclosed his own appeal, also in Hebrew, urging that Lehren write directly to the Rothschilds in Vienna, Paris, and London: "Let them [the Rothschilds] sanctify themselves by sanctifying the name of God; let them speak to the kings and to their ministers to persuade them to write to [Muhammad] Ali Pasha to have the proceedings heard by him and by the consul-general."[16] The last reference is to Austrian consul-general von Laurin in Alexandria, who as the legal protector of Isaac Picciotto could seek standing in Muhammad Ali's court.

In Amsterdam, Hirsch Lehren received the materials Alfandari sent from Beirut, the appeals from Kilbee, and the reports that had been sent directly from Damascus and sent an appeal on behalf of the Damascus Jews directly to Baron James de Rothschild in Paris. "The Jews will never be free of persecution until the Messiah comes," he wrote. "But the good Lord . . . has always given us men of eminence with sufficient influence to ameliorate their misfortunes. And in our times, He has given us the renowned Rothschild family which has the power to save their brethren suffering persecution. . . . Here is a chance to prove yourself the guardian angel of the oppressed and for you to open the doors of Paradise."[17]

A week later Lehren sent a second, more insistent appeal along with new letters he had received from the Middle East. This time he pressed Rothschild for an immediate reply, warning that "the life of many thousands of our co-religionists is at stake."[18]

The Jewish community in Constantinople did not respond to the appeals they had received from Damascus and Beirut for almost a month. Whether the delay was because of their lack of administrative jurisdiction over Damascus, or perhaps in unconscious imitation of the inefficiency and procrastination of the Ottoman bureaucracy, it was late March when they sent the documents they had received from Damascus along with a letter of their own in Italian to the heads of the Rothschild banks in Naples, Vienna, and London, appealing to the Rothschilds in the name of "the tie which so strongly binds together the whole Jewish community."[19]

Even the Rothschilds could not speed up the pace of the camel trains and packet steamers. The men nursing their wounds in the pasha's dungeons and the Jews hiding from the angry Christian mobs and the relentless searches and arrests of the pasha's troops through the streets of Damascus would have to wait months to find out whether the famed Rothschild wealth and influence could help an obscure community of Jews in an almost forgotten corner of the Middle East.

14

The Powers That Be

A LEXANDRIA, with its modern architecture, cafes, salons, and busy commercial and diplomatic activity, seemed more a European city than the capital of Egypt. The city looked to the sea, turning its back on the desert. The celebrated harbor, ringed by grand hotels and apartment buildings, attracted not only the steady stream of diplomats and financiers who sought the divan of the viceroy but painters, poets, and tourists enthralled with the beaches and the views. In 1840 a visitor looking out from the balcony of one of the hotels that ringed the waterfront could see not only the picturesque lateen-rigged fishing boats and the steamers that plied routes to Marseilles, Genoa, and Constantinople but a substantial fleet of warships—frigates and ships of the line—anchored in the harbor.

The fleet was the former Ottoman navy. The Ottomans rationalized the catastrophic defection of the fleet to the Egyptians in 1839 with the story that a traitorous grand vizier was about to surrender the fleet to the feared Russians. The French attachés in Alexandria, no doubt remembering the defeats Lord Nelson's squadron of ships had handed to Napoleon in Egypt, carefully inventoried their ally's captured fleet.[1] For Muhammad Ali, whose divan overlooked the Alexandria harbor, the warships were a bargaining chip in his long negotiation to try to hold on to his empire.

Even a fleet, the symbol of imperial might in 1840, was not enough to fulfill Muhammad Ali's aspirations. Despite his glorious capital and a realm that stretched from Egypt proper through Sinai, the Holy Land, and Syria to the edges of Anatolia and deep into the Arabian peninsula, Muhammad Ali aspired to the recognition and respect due the ruler of a great power. In the Arab culture of Egypt and the Ottoman Empire, where victory in battle was prized above all other virtues, he had

125

achieved that respect. He and his son Ibrahim had battled on behalf of the sultan when the Greek revolt threatened the Ottoman Empire; it was Ibrahim and an Egyptian army that had defeated the Wahhabis, a fanatical Arabian sect that threatened Ottoman rule in the Arabian peninsula; and Ibrahim had triumphed over vastly larger Ottoman armies in the battles for Syria. But those victories, Muhammad Ali discovered, did not bring the respect of the nations of Europe or America. To the great nations Muhammad Ali was still the governor of a breakaway province of the Ottoman Empire. The representatives they sent to Alexandria were not the ambassadors that would be sent to an independent power but consuls-general.

Muhammad Ali was convinced that he had to be accepted as a reformer. "When I came into Egypt," he told a visitor, "it was really barbarous; utterly barbarous. Barbarous it remains to this day. Still I hope that my labors have rendered its condition somewhat better than it was." The viceroy had already implemented many of the reforms in the young sultan's Gülhane Decree. He set up a printing press and ordered European books translated and printed in Turkish and Arabic; he even ordered Machiavelli's *The Prince* translated into Arabic, although it was ultimately not printed. When news of the events in Damascus reached Alexandria, he told visitors and foreign consuls-general, "You must not . . . be shocked if you do not find in these countries the civilization which prevails in Egypt." He eagerly defended his adopted son Sherif Pasha as a man of sound judgment and argued that if his son had done wrong in his prosecution of the Damascus affair, it was because he had been misled by others. "I am an illiterate man," the viceroy told a British visitor, "but still I do know a little of the history of your Nation and if I remember rightly the time is not so remote when England too was the scene of many an act as barbarous and cruel as those of Damascus."[2]

Yet if he took pride in the reforms he and his sons had introduced in the lands they conquered, Muhammad Ali did not abandon the manner of an Egyptian pasha. His was still a world that eschewed clocks and precise time. Diplomats who sought to present a petition or discuss negotiations still had to come to his divan, be received with the pomp and infuriating procrastinations of what was then called Oriental rule, and submit to the whimsy that would sometimes have them waiting days for a meeting or find themselves finally granted an audience only to discover that the viceroy's focus had waned or wandered to new interests. At his comfortable divan overlooking the harbor, the foreign consuls-general badgered the viceroy relentlessly.

Adrien-Louis Cochelet, the French consul-general, was old enough to have been assigned important administrative and diplomatic missions by Napoleon. In Egypt, where Napoleon's invasion and Nelson's victories were still sharp memories, Cochelet's long record of diplomatic service and high rank made him an ideal representative of French interests against the pressure of the British and Austrians. While he instinctively supported Ratti-Menton's charges from the earliest dispatch out of Damascus, Cochelet had enough diplomatic experience to be skeptical about the case the French consul was building, cautioning that any conviction of the Jews would "echo far and wide if, as asserted, although it is hard to believe, it [the alleged murder] was caused by a religious motive." He also warned Ratti-Menton that the use of torture could have negative repercussions. The camel trains delivered the advice too late to have any effect.[3]

In his dispatches to Paris Cochelet dutifully reported that on the basis of the statements of former rabbi Abulafia, it appeared "that human blood is required by the Jews for their Passover, that there was a shortage of it at Damascus," and that the "unexpected discovery" of these murders explained the previously inexplicable disappearance of various people who also "fell victim" to the Jews.[4]

Cochelet found himself opposed at the viceroy's divan by Anton von Laurin, the Austrian consul-general, who despite his staid background as a Jesuit-trained lawyer and career diplomat had proved himself capable of acting on the spur of a moment. Early in von Laurin's career, when he was an assistant consul in Palermo, a teen-age girl who had been forced into marriage fled her wedding and took refuge in the Austrian consulate. When her father arrived at the consulate, the girl turned to von Laurin. "They want me to marry a man I don't want," she said. "I love you; you should marry me yourself." Von Laurin, with scant hesitation, called a priest and married the girl.[5]

When he first heard about the arrests and convictions of the Jews in Damascus, von Laurin wrote to his superior Baron von Stürmer, the Austrian ambassador in Constantinople: "Early today I held a long discussion with Muhammad Ali about the case and learned from him that two of the defendants had given up the ghost under torture. When a Jew allows himself to be tortured even to death he must surely have a sense of his own innocence."[6] At the end of March von Laurin brought up the issue of the use of torture in the Damascus investigation at the viceroy's divan. With an Austrian protégé, Isaac Picciotto, accused of complicity in the alleged murders and held in protective custody in the Austrian consulate in Damascus, von Laurin's was not an abstract protest.

Muhammad Ali, eager to demonstrate the modernity and tolerance of his administration, either to advance his cause in the negotiations over his occupation of Syria or as a token of his own enlightenment, promptly responded to von Laurin's appeal, issuing an order forbidding the use of torture in the Damascus investigation. Von Laurin dispatched a copy of the order to Damascus, then had second thoughts that the decree might be too mild, went back to the viceroy, and persuaded him to issue a second, stronger order. Laurin sent the second order to Damascus on April 10 by camel train, the fastest service available.[7] The orders were dramatic, but with the investigation in Damascus effectively concluded and the accused Jews already convicted and sentenced, including those fugitives who were convicted in absentia, the order would have little or no practical effect.

Von Laurin was not alone in trying to defend the accused Jews. Colonel John Lloyd Hodges, the British consul-general, had been posted to Alexandria in 1839 with the task of taking a firm line against Muhammad Ali. When he first arrived in the Egyptian capital, Hodges was confident that he understood the rebellious viceroy. "Muhammad Ali will submit as soon as he sees a force able to compel him to do so at hand," he wrote in his first dispatch to Palmerston, "but not until then." A month later Hodges began to realize how desperate the viceroy was to hold onto his possessions: "His self-love might possibly lead him to risk a struggle. He counts much on . . . insurrection not only in Asia Minor, but also in Constantinople and Turkey in Europe." Muhammad Ali was riled by Colonel Hodge's warnings that the great powers and the sultan were nearing an accord on the future of Syria.[8]

When Hodges first read Nathaniel Werry's dispatches from Damascus, with their fulsome pronouncements of the guilt of the Jews, he cautioned the British consul to stay out of the matter. Werry cautiously backed off in his comments on the Damascus Jews in his next dispatch to Palmerston, reporting that "neither the detained accused nor the [Jewish] nation are now persecuted; the latter are generally in good spirits" and that "the Christians are somewhat depressed at the protection the Jews generally and apparently receive on this affair."[9] But even as he wrote the palliating note, Werry was unrepentant. On the same day he wrote to Palmerston he also wrote to John Bidwell, the official in charge of the consular matters at the Foreign Office, reporting that "the Jews are moving heaven and earth, both in Turkey, Egypt, and Europe, to gain over the governments, public authority and public opinion to their side, to establish their innocence"; that the French consul and the pasha could have made "immense sums of money" if they had been willing to accept bribes from the Jews; and that "tolerant as I am and moving in accord with the liberal and philosophic principles of the age," he considered the actions of the French consul "honorable and virtuous" in the face of the new attempts "to prove black white" and establish the innocence of the Jews and "thereby blacken the reputation of an honourable public functionary [Ratti-Menton] and destroy his career!" Werry argued that "any impartial and conscientious person will decide on reading the investigation that the Jews are guilty."[10]

When George Pieritz arrived in Alexandria from Damascus, Hodges presented him at the viceroy's divan. Later, on Palmerston's orders, Colonel Hodges wrote a lengthy appeal to Muhammad Ali citing Pieritz's reports of Jewish children deprived of food, Jewish adults tortured until they died, and others sentenced "to death—and it is believed executed—although the only evidences of their guilt were pretended confessions wrung by torture from their alleged accomplices." He noted that the treatment of the Jews in Damascus was the subject of protest meetings in London, cited a letter from the chief rabbi of London declaring that under no circumstance may blood be a food for Jews, and pointed out that the whole ritual murder charge was bizarre, since the murder of the father had taken place eleven weeks "prior to the commencement of the Passover, a space of time too considerable for the preservation of blood."[11]

Against the repeated appeals of von Laurin and Hodges, Cochelet had his hands full with the task of urging the viceroy to stand firm. By mid-April Cochelet was warning Thiers in Paris about the Austrian diplomatic efforts against the Damascus convictions, cautioning that the Austrian cabinet would probably make representations about the investigation and asking on behalf of his Damascus colleague that Paris delay any decisive response until Ratti-Menton had had an opportunity to defend himself.

If Cochelet was motivated primarily by diplomatic responsibility and loyalty to his colleague in Damascus, Hodges and von Laurin appear to have been motivated not only by the official policies of their governments and the strategic need to oppose France but by a strong personal sense of decency and personal outrage at the apparent miscarriage of justice and the vicious anti-Semitic campaign raging in Damascus. Whether Muhammad Ali was actually influenced by their arguments at his divan or only calculated that it would help his standing in the diplomatic negotiations over the independence of Egypt to appear to listen to their arguments and pay at least lip service to mitigating the prosecution of the Damascus Jews, the viceroy seemed to acknowledge their positions. As more details of the investigation and the legal proceedings arrived from Damascus, von Laurin escalated his requests, telling the viceroy that he wanted the case against the Jews reopened; the appointment of a commission of inquiry into the Damascus affair with the power to subpoena witnesses; and the naming of a special tribunal, composed of at least one European lawyer and two or three nonpartisan members familiar with criminal procedures, to hear the commission's evidence in Alexandria, free from the pressures of the Damascus crowds.

Like all negotiations at the divan, the discussions of von Laurin's requests proceeded by fits and starts. Hodges reminded the viceroy that the fleet of frigates and ships of the line in his harbor was sufficient justification for a British fleet and shipborne troops to take positions off the Alexandria harbor and the Lebanese coast. Muhammad Ali, no doubt remembering the effectiveness of Nelson's fleet in the same waters, and still eager to be accepted as a full-fledged ruler of a modern state, gradually acceded to von Laurin's requests for a separate inquiry and tribunal to investigate the prosecution of the Damascus Jews. He asked that he be given a memorandum setting forth the demands in detail and that von Laurin and his colleagues not only supervise the conduct of the inquiry but actually manage the proceedings.[12]

Von Laurin promptly sent letters to the Rothschilds, asking Solomon Rothschild in Vienna if he could find someone "experienced in the law who could advance this inquiry," reporting to Karl Rothschild in Naples that "the affair is going to be investigated on the spot by people, expert in criminal proceedings, who will be sent hither to us from Europe; and the judgment will be pronounced here," and advising Baron James de Rothschild in Paris that it appeared that they had succeeded in forcing the Damascus case to be reopened and heard before "unprejudiced, independent, and enlightened judges" and that he hoped the European press would expose the outrages of the Damascus investigation with "a cry of horror."[13]

The next day von Laurin drafted a petition to be circulated among the European diplomats in Alexandria. He had been in the Middle East long enough to know that it was one thing to exact agreement from the viceroy in a session at the serail and something else entirely to try to convert a verbal agreement into concrete actions. His petition circumspectly fawned and praised the viceroy, emphasizing that the consuls-general were offering their advice at the request of Muhammad Ali, that they recognized the right of the Egyptian judiciary to prosecute the Damascus case, and that they acknowledged that the viceroy was motivated "by the enlightened views which for centuries have led to the disappearance, or vigorous rejection, in Europe of the charge that the Jewish nation is guilty of human sacrifice." Diplomatic representatives of Austria, England, Prussia, Russia, Sweden, Norway, Denmark, Spain, and the United States signed the request that the accused Jews in Damascus be allowed to choose their own counsels who would be free to collect evidence for their defense.[14] It was an impressive show of unity, but the consuls-general of Greece, the Kingdom of the Two Sicilies, Belgium, Tuscany, the Netherlands, and of course France refused to sign the petition.

And even as von Laurin tried to organize his petition, others were campaigning to let the charges stand. The Maronite archbishop and Greek Catholic bishop of Aleppo and the Roman Catholic (Antioch) patriarch of Syria sent a joint letter to the pope, arguing that the Jews had indeed murdered Father Thomas and his servant and had committed similar crimes for years without prosecution, because "in addition to their craftiness, they are protected by Jewish consuls, who are to be found in Aleppo." The three prelates urged the pope to use his own influence to ensure that Catholic countries like Austria, Tuscany, and the Kingdom of the Two Sicilies removed their Jewish consuls at Aleppo and replaced them with Catholics.[15]

Rumors from Damascus and Alexandria crossed the desert with each camel train. Although the coffeehouses and divans of Damascus could keep busy reading the tea leaves of the occasional news of the diplomatic jostling in Alexandria, the prisoners, after surviving the bitter cold of winter in their unheated cells, now faced the searing heat of a Damascus summer. There was little to hope for. Muhammad Ali's orders forbidding torture had come too late to matter. No other decisive news arrived at Damascus. As the months went on the prisoners no doubt found it hard to convince themselves that they and their fates had not been forgotten.

There had been little progress finding the four accused murderers still in hiding, but nine of the sixteen accused murderers and Chief Rabbi Antabi were still being held in the pasha's dungeons, and Isaac Picciotto was still in protective custody at the Austrian consulate. Two of the accused men had died from the bastinado. Sherif Pasha quietly released Raphael Farhi and the others who had been held in protective custody but never charged, just as he had quietly released the imprisoned Jewish boys when their detention no longer served his purposes. Lest anyone misinterpret the releases as a gesture of conciliation, the pasha at the same time hardened the conditions of incarceration of those awaiting execution. The accused Jews were placed in strict military confinement in retaliation for the aggressive inquiries of George Pieritz and appeals written by two other outsiders, Herr Sasun of the Prussian consular service at Beirut and Samuel Briggs, an English banker and merchant from Alexandria. They were held in solitary confinement and were no longer allowed to change their clothes or bedding or to have regular contact with their families. They were infested with insects. Their feet, untreated after the bastinado, looked like they suffered from elephantiasis.[16]

The long standstill might have allowed heated passions to cool in Damascus, but it seemed to have the opposite effect of bolstering the adamance of the pasha, the French consul, Beaudin, and the hardening views in the Christian quarter. The divide between the Christian and Jewish minorities, once bridged by the veneer of politeness that hid tensions and disputes under the guise of a social truce, had widened into a chasm of open animosity. It was hard not to wonder whether the Jews could ever again live in peace in Damascus no matter what the viceroy's final decision.

By May it took considerable effort and courage for the Jews of the city to find a place for talk safe from the marauding searches of the pasha's troops and the unwelcome ridicule and attacks of Christian mobs on the streets. But talk was the chief industry of Damascus. Late afternoon and evening, the hour of soirees in the homes of friends or leisurely hours at the coffeehouses, was the time when scraps of gossip and news could be exchanged, pieced together, and analyzed. If much of the talk was idle speculation, an activity for which there was always time in Damascus, for the Jewish quarter there was also a need to answer the question of what had really happened to Father Thomas and his servant. Although nothing suggested that the accused Jews ever would have the opportunity to address a tribunal or present a defense, the implacable hostility of the Christian quarter increasingly made it apparent that no matter what the decision of the viceroy, whether the accused Jews were miraculously freed or publicly hanged, the survivors in the Jewish community would never be able to live at peace in Damascus if they could not explain the disappearance of the monk and his servant. The Christians would always accuse the Jews, demanding to know: if the Jews did not murder the father, what happened to him?

One explanation was that Father Thomas could have been secreted away to a monastery in Lebanon as part of a plot to allow Ratti-Menton, Beaudin, and the pasha to fabricate a case against the Jews. The scenario was popular not only in the Jewish quarter of Damascus but in Alexandria, where Colonel Hodges speculated that before he was beaten to death, Isaac Yavo had told the pasha that Father Thomas and his servant had been taken out of the city by Christians. It was certainly possible. There were dozens of monasteries tucked away in the mountains of Lebanon, and periodic Maronite and Druse rebellions disrupted travel in the remote valleys and hills of what was then called Mount Lebanon. The Egyptian armies that had been so effective against the Ottoman regulars proved themselves ineffective against the guerilla actions of the Christian rebels in the Lebanese mountains. If Father Thomas and Ibrahim Amara were hidden in one of the remote monasteries, it was unlikely that anyone would find them while the rebellion raged.[17]

Another popular theory was that Damascene Christians—most fingers pointed at the Greek Catholics—had themselves murdered the monk with the intention of framing the Jews. Street rumors had it that if Britain succeeded in forcing the Egyptians out of Syria and returning the area to Ottoman control, the Ottomans would return the administrative posts held by Greek Catholics and the commercial advantages that went along with those positions to the Jews. Framing the Jews for a heinous murder would eliminate them as rivals, ensuring the future of the Christian merchants and job holders.

Yet another suggestion was that the hot-tempered monk had made enough enemies to have become a target of the violence that made Syria dangerous for visitors and non-Muslim residents. Father Thomas's open insults of Muslims in the marketplaces were dangerous behavior in a culture where public encounters were by custom formal and mannered. As a Roman Catholic who lived ostentatiously in a community that had long despised the influence and foreign control of Roman Catholics, the father was resented. As a public figure who seemed not to back away from disputes and altercations, he had received threats on his life. In Damascus threats were not idle words. The Egyptian administration had ruled that no one, not even Muslims, could carry arms in the city, but many Damascus men were well trained swordsmen and marksmen and proud of their prowess. Men rarely traveled unarmed outside the city. The muleteer with whom the father had publicly argued, the muleteer's ally Kashar, or anyone else with a grudge over perceived slights or insults could have intercepted Father Thomas and his servant on a lonely road outside the city walls. Only the desert buzzards would ever know what had happened to them there.

There was also speculation that the monk, perhaps fearing for his own life after he had aroused the ire of Muslims in one of his altercations, might have voluntarily fled to a monastery in Lebanon or perhaps to one of the outlying villages that surrounded Damascus like suburbs. Some of the villages, like Salihiyeh, were well-known Muslim or Sufi religious centers, and others were predominantly or exclusively Christian. Many wealthy Damascenes had bought homes there as refuges. Although Beaudin's luxurious home in the Christian quarter was the scene of regular soirees that attracted the high Christian society of Damascus, he also owned a house in an outlying village—insurance in case the subtle truce between groups in the city ever broke down.

Isaac Yavo's testimony placed the father on the road to one of the outlying villages. That was the last time anyone had seen him alive.

There was still another possibility. Father Thomas lived well, with a luxurious residence in the convent, the frequent company of other prelates, doctors, and merchants in the European community, and a steady revenue from his medical practice. Except for his servant, he lived alone—the only clergyman in the Christian quarter other than the Greek Catholic diocesan officials who had taken an oath of celibacy. The Orthodox clergy, the Maronites, and the Greek Catholic parish priests were all permitted to marry. Thirty-two years of celibacy made for a lonely life in a city as voluptuous as Damascus, where temptations of the flesh were everywhere—in the lush, overripe fruits piled high in the suqs, the redolence of the perfume shops, the ripe meat hung out in the open in the suqs, the flashing glimpses of veiled women through open windows and doorways, or the back rooms of cafes and private parties where the laxity of the Egyptian administration overlooked the performances of women dancing in the Turkish style. With the wealth he had accumulated—given his long residence and many years of medical practice, the sums Beaudin and the French consul found at the convent might have been a fraction of the monk's wealth—Father Thomas and his servant could have started new lives, safely hidden away in a friendly village with their choice of wives and servants. They would not have had to go far to achieve anonymity. The Ottoman bureaucracy was infamous, and a few entrepreneurs like Muhammad al-Talli used tax-collection rights to exploit widespread "acquaintances," but an individual with the means to pay baksheesh could slip between the cracks in the bureaucracy. Father Thomas and his servant could have chosen safe and luxurious anonymity in a village outside the city.

All through the spring the cafes and soirees buzzed with speculation about what really happened to the Father and his servant and with endless analyses of when Muhammad Ali would finally issue an order permitting the execution of the accused Jews. It was early May when a special courier delivered a long-awaited decree from the viceroy in Alexandria addressed to his son Sherif Pasha. The message was not the execution order everyone had expected. Instead, the pasha's decree said: "The honorable consul-general of Austria, Herr von Laurin, informs me that certain uneducated people have been insulting the Jews in Damascus who, when they appeal to the government, have not received justice. Since the said insults, tolerated by you, are in contradiction to my will, you must ensure that this situation does not degenerate."[18]

The Jews of Damascus attributed the miraculous good news to Passover, which fell in late April that year.

Sherif Pasha did not share their joy. He wrote privately that the guilt of the Jews remained "as clear as the sun." His reaction was what British consul-general Hodges in Alexandria had privately predicted, even as he supported von Laurin in his petitions to the viceroy: "neither does it appear to me that the remonstrances of any other Power will have on his Highness the slightest influence." Torture, the consul-general wrote, always was and still remained the law of the land in Syria.[19]

The Christian quarter of Damascus took their cues from the pasha. The unexpected order from Alexandria, with its implied censure of the investigation and of the prevailing opinion in the Christian quarter, loosed a flood of pent-up anger. Mobs accosted Jews on the street and rampaged against Jewish property. They attacked synagogues, including the exquisite medieval synagogue at the village of Djobar to the east of the city, on the site where Elijah was supposed to have anointed Hazael as king.[20] Christian mobs took prayer shawls and phylacteries from the synagogues and put them on dogs. They desecrated the Jewish cemeteries, knocking over stones, digging up graves, strewing corpses and bones on the ground. As a special humiliation, Jews were seized off the streets and forced to labor on the construction of a church. Troops had to be brought into the city to forestall a massacre.[21]

News of the viceroy's order spread quickly. On Mount Lebanon, where the long-simmering Druse and Maronite revolt had erupted into open warfare, a band of Christian rebels stopped a party of travelers en route between Damascus and Saida. The seven Muslim and Christian travelers were allowed to go on their way. The eight Jews were murdered on the spot.[22]

15

The Richest Men in the World

LTHOUGH they were often referred to with a single reverential or
accusing name—as in Heine's formulation, "For money is the
God of our times, and Rothschild His prophet"—by 1840 the
Rothschilds were as distinct as the capitals where they had established
the branches of their bank. In Paris Baron James was constantly in the
newspapers and gossip sheets with his flamboyantly dandy-styled
curly red hair, his heavy German accent (which the French found comi-
cal), and his spectacular new residence on the rue Saint-Florentin at the
corner of the Place de la Concorde, the former residence of Talleyrand.
Baron James's wealth and impact on French society made his home and
his office on the rue Laffitte quasi-royal courts, with a court composer in
Gioacchino Rossini, a court painter in Ingres, a court chronicler in
Heine, and a court chef in Marie-Antoine Carème. "Men of all classes
and faiths, Gentiles as well as Jews, bow low and grovel before him,"
Heine wrote. "I have seen people who on approaching the great baron
shudder as if they had touched an electric current."[1]

By contrast, Solomon Meyer Rothschild, the head of the Austrian
branch of the family and the Vienna branch of the Rothschild bank, was
deliberately reserved in his manners and style. For decades the family
had allowed Austrian Chancellor Metternich, or as he was called by the
Rothschilds, "Uncle," to use their private courier service as an unofficial
diplomatic channel and had granted him and his friends favorable personal loans. In return Metternich saw to it that the Habsburgs favored
the Rothschilds for official banking; that the Rothschilds were made
hereditary barons, entitling them to use the aristocratic *von* or *de* in their
names; and that they were appointed honorary Austrian consuls-
general, which allowed them entrée to court functions and provided
splendid decorations for their formal attire. Solomon Rothschild was

also longtime friends with leading aristocratic families of the Habsburg empire, like the Esterhazys and the Zichys, with whom he had also made special banking arrangements. Yet even the influence of friends in high places was not enough to exempt the Rothschilds from the harsh regulations restricting the residence, education, and occupations of Jews in the Habsburg empire. Solomon Rothschild was not permitted to own a private residence in Vienna and lived at the Hotel Zum Römischen Kaiser.[2]

In the manner of a court Jew of the centuries before the French Revolution, Solomon Rothschild relied on his personal relationship with Metternich to discretely intercede and influence government action at the highest level. Rothschild was an effective *shtadlan*, using his connections abroad and the weighty influence of the bank to intervene on behalf of causes even as he privately advised the chancellor on economic and commercial matters. Metternich, the master diplomat, occasionally played Rothschild off against other banking interests, and they sometimes clashed, but for the most part their relationship was marked by extraordinary civility and mutual dependence. Metternich, though conservative in his political views, was a rationalist in his Catholicism and his personal beliefs, positions Solomon Rothschild found sympathetic. For his part, Rothschild recognized the limitations of the public roles of Jews in the Habsburg empire and was content with the private influence he could exercise by calling upon and bestowing personal favors. Discretion, deference, and attention to the impact of their actions on the part of both men made for a productive relationship.[3]

For differing reasons, Rothschild and Metternich agreed that the charges against the Damascus Jews were outrageous but perilous. Metternich, anxious to maintain Austrian influence in Syria, believed, as did his consul-general in Alexandria, that appealing to Muhammad Ali's sense of himself as a modern ruler was the best course of action to prevent the situation from going awry. Unaware that von Laurin had already intervened at Muhammad Ali's divan on his own authority, Metternich ordered his consul-general to urge the viceroy to issue orders that, "without interfering in the judicial process, would put a check on the cruel and stupid moves of the subordinate officials [in Damascus]." Metternich wrote that the accusation that Christians were deliberately murdered for "some blood-thirsty Passover festival" was "absurd," that the actions of Sherif Pasha in trying to prove the crime were "utterly inappropriate," and that given the viceroy's sense of himself it was important he realize that "the misuse of power, persecution, and the mistreatment of innocent people" would become known throughout Europe.[4] It was exactly what von Laurin had already done.

Perhaps from impatience or frustration with the slow post and the even slower pace of diplomatic intervention, or a suspicion that Metternich might not be energetic enough in opposing the prosecution of the Jews, von Laurin had sent copies of his reports on his negotiations with Muhammad Ali not only to his superior in Constantinople and to Metternich in Vienna but to the Austrian general-consul in Paris. Strictly speaking, this latter was an unnecessary correspondence. The Austrian ambassador in Paris was in charge of any diplomatic matters relating to France, and the office of general-consul in Paris was an unpaid, largely ceremonial post with no responsibility for matters in Damascus. But the appointee to the post was Baron James de Rothschild, which to von Laurin meant that his reports were likely to generate some response. In his letter von Laurin urged Baron James to work either directly or via the Austrian embassy to hold the French government responsible for what was happening in Damascus. He warned that the animosity of the non-Jewish population in Damascus could develop into an organized persecution of the Jews that could spread to the Holy Land, and suggested that the press was a force that could be mobilized in support of the beleaguered Jews.[5]

Von Laurin may not have realized that the Rothschilds in London, Paris, Naples, and Vienna exchanged frequent correspondence with one another via their speedy private international courier service. (They gained an extra measure of privacy for their correspondence by writing in *Judendeutsch*, German written in an odd Hebrew script, a family language that even outsiders fluent in Hebrew or Yiddish could not read.) Baron James de Rothschild interpreted von Laurin's suggestion of mobilizing the press as a license to turn documents that had been submitted to him over to the press and wrote privately to his brother Solomon in Vienna to urge that Solomon "do everything you possibly can in the defense of the just cause," meaning that Solomon should enlist Metternich in the press campaign. He added his opinion that "the gracious and humane goodwill which the Prince has shown in this sad affair gives grounds for the confident hope that this request will not go ungranted."[6]

Unwittingly, Baron James de Rothschild had triggered two of Metternich's pet peeves. While Metternich readily praised von Laurin for opposing the "absurd" accusations against the Damascus Jews, when he found that his consul-general in Alexandria had been communicating directly with Baron James de Rothschild in Paris and urging that Baron James use his influence to publicize the matter in the European press, Metternich sharply censured von Laurin. It was one thing to have Solomon Rothschild in Vienna voice his personal opinions in the quiet, dignified, and totally private communications that had characterized their partnership; it was something altogether different to involve the press. The public newspapers, Metternich wrote to von Laurin, "are not the authorities who have to deal with this case" and while the "affair may appear straightforward to you . . . because of the circumstances it has become much inflated and highly inflammatory."[7] Metternich had always been wary of a free press and its potential impact on the stability of regimes. He also seemed to take umbrage at the influence of the Rothschilds—especially when his own honorary consul in Paris took advantage of his social position and influence to act as if he were a real diplomat.

If the stable working relationship between Metternich and Solomon Rothschild substituted for a consultative mechanism on Jewish questions in Vienna, in London and Paris, where formal bodies existed to represent Jewish views on matters, every crisis was a new opportunity to work out the rules of the game for dealing with Jewish issues.

In Britain, a Board of Deputies representing the five major London synagogues had in 1760 taken upon itself the responsibility of advising and lobbying the government on Jewish issues. The board met regularly with all the formality and ceremony typical of a proper British committee and with an agenda consisting almost exclusively of ceremonial resolutions conveying congratulations or condolences to the royal family on appropriate occasions. The only controversial actions the board had undertaken were a 1766 appeal of a decision forbidding the Jews of Menorca, a Balearic Island where the British had established a presence, to open a prayer room in the city of Mahon, and an 1804 libel action against the printer of an anti-Jewish publication. With the semi-official board virtually moribund, the battle for Jewish emancipation in Britain was fought primarily by Whigs like Isaac Goldsmid, his son Francis, and David Salomons, while more conservative Jewish leaders like Lionel Rothschild cautioned against moving too fast.

The Board of Deputies had no precedents to rely on when it was confronted with the disturbing reports from Damascus in late March and early April 1840. The news from Damascus was a double-edged sword. As Englishmen and as the chief representative body of the Jews of England, the board was compelled to respond to the outrages perpetrated on their coreligionists in Syria and to the reported statements of the British consul in Damascus in support of the prosecution of the Jews. Many members reminded the others that the privileges the Jews of Britain enjoyed had been hard won, that the parliamentary battles and lobbying that had brought Jews into the social and commercial life of London and the nation had required considerable efforts, and that the status achieved by many British Jews might be jeopardized if they were somehow associated with the heinous accusations that had been made against the Jews of Damascus.

On April 21, 1840, the board called a meeting to discuss the Damascus situation, inviting not only the official members of the board but distinguished members of the British Jewish community. Baron Lionel de Rothschild, Sir Moses Montefiore, Isaac and Francis Goldsmid, David Salomons, and Louis Cohen all attended, as did a French visitor, the lawyer Adolphe Crémieux, who had come from Paris especially for the meeting. News of the events in Damascus had already generated sensational newspaper headlines in London. Another solemn resolution was no longer an option for the Board of Deputies.

The meeting opened with the reading of a letter from the aged chief rabbi of England, Solomon Herschel, which included a solemn oath that the charges against the Damascus Jews were "false and malicious"; letters sent to the Rothschilds from the Jews in Damascus, Constantinople, and Rhodes; and an address by Adolphe Crémieux on behalf of the French Consistory promising their cooperation in seeking to halt the cruel prosecution of "our Eastern brethren." The board then voted resolutions describing the ritual murder charges in Damascus and Rhodes as medieval phenomena that had "long disappeared from this part of the world, [along] with the fierce and furious prejudices that gave [it] birth." They called upon the governments of England, France, and Austria to intercede in Constantinople and Alexandria to put an end to the "atrocities"; set up a publicity committee to pay to have the resolutions of the board printed as advertisements in a list of London and provincial journals, including twice in the most important newspapers; and nominated a delegation to request an appointment with the foreign secretary, Lord Palmerston.[8]

The Board of Deputies had every reason to assume that the foreign minister would receive them. Palmerston had been interested in the Middle East since he took office in 1835. As a counterweight to Russian protection of the Orthodox Christians and the French and Austrian protection of the Roman Catholics of the Ottoman Empire, Palmerston had been exploring the idea of Britain asserting protection for the Jews of the Middle East.[9] Although he was not a supporter of the London Society for Promoting Christianity Amongst the Jews, in 1839 he had married Lady Emily Cowper, whose son, Lord Ashley, later the seventh Earl of Shaftesbury, was a vice president of the London Society and was active in promoting its mission. Ashley, at least, thought the family tie promising if not providential: "Things the most unpromising are oftentimes fruitful," he wrote in his diary after the marriage. "May it be so here."[10]

Palmerston had a strong personal reaction to the reports he had received from his consul in Damascus, Nathaniel Werry. After he read one of Werry's reports with its comments sympathetic to the prosecution of the Damascus Jews, Palmerston wrote, "I am sorry to find Mr. Werry entertains opinions so un-English about torture and justice. He has been too long in the Levant, and must come home and spend a year in England from Christmas next."[11] Werry seemed not to realize that his almost verbatim repetitions of the French consul's accusations of ritual murder ran against both Palmerston's personal beliefs and attitude and the grain of British (at least *official* British) thought on what was beginning to be called the Jewish Question. Ironically, by pointing out the complicity of Sherif Pasha in the French consul's accusations and legal process against the Jews, the British consul's reports had provided additional ammunition that the British could use in their campaign to force Muhammad Ali and the Egyptian administration out of Syria.

When Werry stuck to his position, Palmerston wrote back: "The manner in which you make mention of those transactions [the torture and other atrocities committed against the Jews in Damascus] either proves you to be wholly uninformed of what takes place in the City in which you are stationed, or evinces on your part an entire want of those principles and sentiments which ought to distinguish a British agent." Palmerston was so outraged by Werry's reports, which he found wholly unbefitting a British statesman and gentleman, that he ordered Werry to justify himself and his actions by providing a "full and detailed report" of everything that had taken place and told him instructions had been addressed to Alexandria that the consul-general there was to protest to Muhammad Ali the "extreme disgrace which the barbarous atrocities perpetrated at Damascus reflect upon his administration."[12] Werry, recognizing that his career hung in the balance, immediately set about collecting reports on the background and course of the investigation and prosecution, which he would eventually forward to London.

At the end of April the delegation from the Board of Deputies had their meeting with Lord Palmerston. Palmerston was cordial, assuring the delegation that he would send dispatches to Colonel Hodges in Alexandria and to Lord Ponsonby in the Sublime Porte expressing his "surprise that the calumny which had been invented [against the Jews] . . . should have received the highest credence," and he promised that the influence of the government would be exerted to put a stop to the atrocities against the Jews.

Unlike Metternich's quiet negotiations with Solomon Rothschild, which were kept completely private, Palmerston's meeting with the delegation from the Board of Deputies was promptly publicized.[13] And Palmerston did as he promised, ordering Hodges to communicate to Muhammad Ali that in the view of the British government and Europe the atrocities in Damascus reflected on his administration, that the atrocities appeared to be not the acts of an "ignorant rabble" but the "deliberate exercise of power by the pasha to whom . . . the city of Damascus has been entrusted," and that "Her Majesty's Government can entertain no doubt that Muhammad Ali will . . . make immediately the most ample reparation in his power to the unfortunate Jews . . . [and] dismiss and punish those officers who have so greatly abused powers."[14]

It was a strong statement, exactly what the Board of Deputies sought. Yet despite the publicity of the newspaper advertisements of the board's resolutions and the ringing endorsement of its views by Lord Palmerston, the situation in Damascus had still not been raised in Parliament. And it was Parliament that set British policy.

In Paris the Central Consistory was the highest body of Jewish representation to the government, roughly corresponding to the Board of Deputies in London except that French law had made the religious consistories quasi-governmental bodies by making rabbis and priests effectively employees of the state. The members of the Central Consistory were elected by select groups of voters, but neither the members nor the body itself were widely known. Only six people attended their first meeting on the events in Damascus, held at the end of April. Adolphe Crémieux, a radical lawyer and member of the consistory, made a report based on information he had been able to gather from Damascus and from other European capitals. Crémieux had already written about the events in Damascus in the *Journal des Débats*, relying on irony as his weapon against the relentless repetition of alleged atrocities by the Jews in the rightist and ultramontane press. "Almost 1,250 years ago Islam raised its standard in the Orient, in the city of Damascus," Crémieux wrote. "Never during this period have the Jews had this stupid accusation leveled at them. Christians are starting to make their influence felt in these lands and all of a sudden Western prejudices come to life in the Orient! What a subject for contemplation!" His report to the consistory included strong criticism of the French consul in Damascus, Count Ratti-Menton, "who had shown himself to be unworthy of the nation which he represents." Like the Board of Deputies, the Central Consistory concluded that the most important step on its agenda was to meet with the head of the government, Adolphe Thiers, to ask him to intervene and send prompt and proper instructions to the French consul in Damascus.[15]

Crémieux was well-known in France as a lawyer and orator. Even as a lycee student in the south of France he had been called *l'avocat* in recognition of his rhetorical eloquence and the career for which he seemed predestined. But as a Jew, in order to practice law in France,

Crémieux had faced the dreaded *more judaico*. This archaic and humiliating ceremony forced Jewish candidates for the bar to stand before the court wearing a crown of thorns, and to call down the maledictions in Leviticus and Deuteronomy—the plagues of Egypt, the leprosy of Na'aman and Gehazi, and the fate of Dathan and Abiram—as an oath. The more judaico had been suppressed by the Revolution in 1791 only to reappear in the Restoration. French rabbis repeatedly declared that the simple words "I swear" were sufficient as a binding oath, but their collective decree was ignored as the Restoration monarchy used this token issue to humiliate and restrict Jewish lawyers.

At the Nîmes courthouse where Crémieux was to be admitted to the bar, when the president of the court demanded, "M. Crémieux, will you take the oath more judaico?" Crémieux answered, "Am I in a synagogue? No, I am in an audience chamber. Am I in Jerusalem, in Palestine? No, I am in Nîmes, in France. Am I only a Jew? No, I am also a French citizen. Therefore, I take the oath of a Jewish French citizen." Whether it was Crémieux's defiant eloquence or a readiness by the court after so many years of protest against the special oath, the president of the court ruled in Crémiux's favor, effectively ending the use of the humiliating oath in France. The incident catapulted Crémieux to notoriety in French legal circles. His reputation for controversial stands and tales of his eloquence quickly spread north to Paris.

At an early trial the public prosecutor, paraphrasing God's words to Cain, asked the defendant Polge, who was alleged to have murdered Donnadieu: "What have you done with him? Answer, Polge, answer the voice of God which speaks in the Heavens and asks you the terrible question: Polge, what hast thou done with Donnadieu?" Crémieux, for the defense, pointed out that when Cain slew Abel no one else was present, hence no one else could have slain Abel. Yet God, who had seen it all, waited until after Cain's own self-accusation—"Am I my brother's keeper?"—before demanding of Cain, "What hast thou done? The voice of thy brother's blood crieth unto Me from the ground."[16] If God, though infallible, exercises such caution before pronouncing guilt, Crémieux asked the court, should we be any less cautious?

On another occasion, when he was referred to as a Jew during a trial in Nîmes, Crémieux demanded to be told the religion of everyone else in the court and that the religion of each person in the courtroom be mentioned with every reference lest the trial weigh to the advantage of one or the other of the two lawyers defending the appellant (the other lawyer was Catholic). After that trial there were no more special identifications of Jewish lawyers in the Nîmes courts. In still another trial, when the prosecutor said the accused was "nothing but a Jewish peddler," Cremieux objected, proclaiming the sovereignty of equality in the court and asking whether in the eyes of God a Jew is less than a Christian, or a French Jew less than a French Christian. He demanded of the prosecutor that since Crémieux too was a Jew, did the prosecutor intend to insult him as well as the defendant?[17] After being delegated by the Marseilles Consistory to represent it to the central Jewish administration in Paris, Crémieux became a member of the Central Consistory in 1830.

Crémieux and the Central Consistory had every reason to expect a favorable response to their request for a meeting with Adophe Thiers, the premier of France. The Jews of France had been emancipated since the Revolution, and full Jewish equality had become a tantalizingly realizable goal after the revolution of 1830. Thiers was widely admired for his liberal views as a politician, lawyer, journalist, and historian of the French Revolution. Even Heinrich Heine suspended his usual skepticism: "Others are only orators or administrators or scholars or diplomats or honest men, Thiers is all of these things . . . one of those souls whose talent for rule is inborn."[18] Thiers was also on friendly terms with Baron James de Rothschild, who had been willing to discuss financing new railroads in France after Thiers took office. It would have been difficult to imagine anyone more likely to be sympathetic to the questions that had been raised about the prosecution in Damascus.

But when the Central Consistory requested a meeting with the premier to discuss matters in Damascus, Thiers sidestepped the request, saying he had not had time to examine the materials arriving from Syria. Repeated requests were postponed without explanation. The official government newspaper, controlled by the premier, also ignored the reports from Damascus, pretending that the matters in Damascus and the heavy involvement of the French consul there never happened. The meeting the Central Consistory requested never took place.[19]

Crémieux was not one to give up easily. In recognition of his renowned eloquence, the Central Consistory called on him to give the formal addresses presented each year to Louis-Philippe on New Years day and on the king's official birthday, May 1. When it became apparent that Thiers would postpone indefinitely any request from the consistory for a meeting, Crémieux went to the official reception at the Tuileries on the king's birthday, began with the usual praises of the tolerance of France and the king appropriate to formal addresses on such occasions, and then asked the king to direct his "glance toward the Near East, where fanaticism is aroused and whence our brothers appeal to us with tears."[20] The progovernment press, which by tradition printed the full text of all formal birthday greetings to the king, ignored Crémieux's speech.

The explanation of Thiers's resolute silence is perhaps to be found in his replies to the reports he received from Ratti-Menton. From the earliest report, Thiers urged caution and moderation on his consul in Damascus, warning Ratti-Menton against excessive enthusiasm for the prosecution and praising him for demanding a stay in the execution of the accused Jews. He observed that whether the crimes in Damascus were rooted in fanaticism or vengeance, they were "evidently an isolated incident" and suggested that Ratti-Menton, "without question, will feel as I do that now every effort must be made to prevent this unfortunate affair from becoming the cause or pretext for an assault on the Jews" and urged that he use the influence inherent in his position to "calm the passions and to frustrate the schemes that tended toward a deplorable outcome."[21] Whatever his personal beliefs, the cautious and statesmanlike Thiers seemed determined not to let the affair in Damascus poison the outcome of the delicate negotiations with Britain and Austria about the future of the Middle East. By avoiding any public position on the matter, he could protect his consul in Damascus and at the same time avoid committing himself on the thorny questions of whether the Damascus Jews were guilty, whether they held fanatical religious beliefs, and whether the investigation and prosecution had been judicially sound.

Yet if the French government stringently avoided taking a public position, the Quai d'Orsay and the Elysée Palace were busily formulating policy behind the scenes. Baron James de Rothschild wrote his brother Solomon in early May to complain that the "steps I have taken so far have not had the desired results," that it appeared that Ratti-Menton would not be recalled, that the affair was "too distant" to attract sufficient notice, and that the only recourse was to turn for help to the "omnipotent" press. A week later he was even more pessimistic, reporting that Thiers had privately told him that "the case is based on the truth; that we had better let the matter rest; [that] the Jews in the Middle Ages were fanatical enough to require Christian blood for their Passover; [and] that the Jews in the East still maintain such superstitions."[22] Here, as in his other public and private statements about the events in Damascus, it is hard to determine where Thiers's personal beliefs ended and what he perceived as a required public stance began.

The slow camel trains and packet steamers meant that Ratti-Menton was among the last to learn about the repercussions of his investigation in the European capitals. But even in remote Damascus, he slowly began to realize that the reaction to his initial reports, and to the procedures used in investigation, were not at all what he had anticipated.

By mid-April dispatches from his superior Cochelet in Alexandria convinced the French consul that serious questions were being raised in Europe about the methods used in the investigation, the motives attributed to the accused Jews, and the legitimacy of the legal proceedings that had resulted in the death sentences. Ratti-Menton tried to bolster his justifications of the prosecution. As Ayyub Shubli finished each portion of the trial transcripts, they were sent off to Paris accompanied by additional material, including excerpts from the Moldavian monk's book and explanatory notes dictated by the consul. Ratti-Menton also began to build a defense for his own actions, soliciting character testimony and vouchers of his conduct from local notables and clergy in Damascus. He asked the chancellor of the British consulate, Sa'id Ali, to sign a statement certifying that Ratti-Menton had not personally used violence against the Jews or urged the use of violence during the investigation, confirming Ratti-Menton's initial skepticism of the charges against the Jews, and describing the "prevailing attitudes of the Muslim and Christian populations toward the Jews" from the perspective of someone whose "social position," marriage to a Muslim, and knowledge of Arabic enabled him to follow local events. Sa'id Ali was circumspect in his response but did allow that "it would appear . . . that the Jews use human blood . . . at their Passover" and that the affair might not have been exposed "if anybody but you [Ratti-Menton] had been responsible for its prosecution."[23]

Ratti-Menton also sent defenses of his conduct to Thiers, explaining why he had entered the apartment of one Austrian citizen during the searches and why he had called Picciotto a "murderer," and claiming that he had not protested the use of torture in the investigation because it was "customary" in judicial proceedings in the region. He also took credit for securing the release of the incarcerated Jewish boys and for saving some of the prisoners from execution. In another dispatch he predicted that "the Jews, clumsily turning the event into an issue of religion, would pass up no means of corruption to prevent the truth from seeing the light of day." If Thiers would study the French translations of the judicial protocols and Ratti-Menton's own explanatory notes, the consul assured him, the "incontestable facts" would give the lie to those who had accused him of "fanaticism and barbarity." Finally, Ratti-Menton requested the appointment of "a commission of inquiry to examine my conduct."[24]

The French consul sent his request for a commission of inquiry on May 7. It was an irony of the geography of information in the late spring of 1840 that on that very day, in Paris, the French government finally announced its official policy toward the prosecution in Damascus. A tersely worded notice in the *Moniteur*, the official government newspaper, reported that the government would be sending a vice-consul to Damascus with the official assignment of collecting information about the "assassination of Father Thomas and everything relating to this unfortunate event."[25]

As diplomacy, it was a brilliant move. With a special investigator appointed, Thiers had bought time: he could delay any action or public statement on the matter until the investigation was complete. By giving the appearance of devoting serious attention to the problem, he could avoid both the embarrassment of a strong statement of support for Ratti-Menton and the prosecution of the Jews and the equally troubling position of publicly criticizing or overruling his consul. The appointment of a special investigator also seemed to address the quiet pressure of the Rothschilds, the public pressure of the press, the demands of the Central Consistory, and the public challenge of the British and Austrians to the traditional role of France as defender of the Rights of Man.

Of course it would be weeks before Ratti-Menton, the pasha, or the Jewish and Christian communities in Damascus would learn that the French vice-consul in Alexandria would be holding a formal inquiry into the Damascus affair.

16

Inquiries

MAXIME RENAUD D'AVÈNE DES MELOIZES, the French vice-consul at Alexandria, was twenty-six years old, fifteen years younger than the consul at Damascus whose prosecution of the accused murderers of Father Thomas and his servant des Meloizes was to investigate. The vice-consul's diplomatic experience was as limited as his rank. Von Laurin wrote that he was a "sufficiently limited young gentleman." Colonel Hodges, the British consul-general, called him an *élève consulaire*. Hodges predicted that with the French subjects all so "strongly impressed with a belief in the culpability of the Jews," it was unlikely that the accused Jews would receive "impartial consideration" before "a tribunal so completely biased."[1]

Though young and inexperienced, des Meloizes was self-composed, intelligent, and cool tempered. His preparation for his assignment was months of following the dispatches about Ratti-Menton's prosecution and the interminable coming and going at Muhammad Ali's divan, where French consul-general Cochelet had defended the Damascus investigation against British and Austrian criticism. The French had never been quick to abandon their diplomats, and this was no exception. If des Meloizes's ostensible charge from Paris was to investigate and present an objective evaluation of the facts of the Damascus case, the young vice-consul was close enough to the diplomatic maneuvering at the viceroy's court in Alexandria to realize that French aspirations in the region and the goal of not losing diplomatic face had created a second, unstated, but perhaps more important, objective for the investigation: French interests required that he use his supposedly objective inquiry to compile or at least supplement a defense brief for the conduct of the French consul in Damascus.

When he arrived in Damascus on June 19, des Meloizes stepped into a volatile situation. In the four and a half months since Father Thomas had disappeared, opinions on both sides of the issue had hardened. Picciotto's vigorous denial of the charges made against him and his accusations of slander, perjury, coercion, and subornation of testimony on the part of Ratti-Menton, Beaudin, and the pasha had all been recorded in the trial protocols. However scanty the procedural guarantees to the accused in the Ottoman trials, the clerks were scrupulous about recording even potentially exculpatory testimony in the signed pseudotranscripts that constituted the trial record. There had been much talk in the city about Picciotto's testimony, and for months there had been rumors afoot—which may have originated at the Austrian consulate—that many of the prisoners were ready to recant their previous testimony as soon as they were given the opportunity to testify without the threat of torture.

Sherif Pasha, after three separate messages from his father banning further use of torture in the investigation, had backed off his own commitment to the case. If he still favored the Greek Catholics and was wary of the consequences of the diplomatic maneuvering in Alexandria, he was no longer ready to risk his status and authority to defend the French consul and Beaudin in their prosecution of the Jews. British consul Nathaniel Werry, who had been a staunch ally of the French consul both locally and in reports to London, had also backed away from his defense of the French consul, Beaudin, and the pasha as he busied himself preparing a defense of his own conduct in the matter.

Indeed, by late June it may have seemed that it was not the Jews but the French who were under siege. Much of the Christian quarter did not waver in its conviction that the accused Jews were guilty and continued to clamor for the executions of the incarcerated prisoners. But between the different public and private goals of his assignment, the open hostility of the Jewish quarter and the Austrian consulate, the unambiguous restrictions on the further use of torture imposed by Muhammad Ali's orders, and the realization that his inquiry was being watched from Alexandria and from the capitals of Europe, des Meloizes faced a formidable task.

Before he took any testimony, des Meloizes (or perhaps his superiors in orders that have been lost) decided that his investigation would be confined to "the circle of the condemned men," which effectively precluded any verification of the alibis that had been offered and all testimony from witnesses other than the accused men. Des Meloizes further narrowed his inquiry by announcing that in his reexamination of the prisoners he would seek only to verify whether the protocols had been an accurate transcription of their previous testimony, whether they had been motivated by personal animosities in accusing one another, whether their testimony had resulted from "illicit maneuvers," and whether the staff of the French consulate had played any role in the use of torture during the original interrogations.[2] If his methodology sounded thorough, it conveniently narrowed the scope of his investigation so that the accused men were caught in a trap: if they revoked their prior testimony, they could be impugned as having perjured themselves in at least one of their interrogations; yet since no new testimony that might serve to verify their alibis or otherwise discredit Ratti-Menton's investigation would be admitted in the new inquiry, the accused men could not exonerate themselves.

Des Meloizes did not begin taking testimony until after he first visited the various venues mentioned in the testimony, including the homes where the murders were alleged to have taken place and the locations where the supposed evidence of the murders was found. The first witnesses des Meloizes interviewed, on June 24, were the barber Solomon al-Hallaq and Murad al-Fatal, David Harari's servant, whose sensational testimony had initiated the charges against the Damascus Jews. Beaudin and Ratti-Menton were present for the new session, and both witnesses stood by their original testimony, insisting that their descriptions of the murders were true. Des Meloizes found the witnesses cynical and identified a few details in which their testimony under cross-examination differed, but he concluded that the discrepancies were not substantial enough to warrant discarding or discounting their testimony, the core of the cases against the accused Jews. The re-examination of the two principal witnesses took only one day.

It then took des Meloizes seven weeks to interview the eight accused Jews who were in custody, as each witness, no longer under threat of torture, recanted his original confession.

Abulafia was the first of the accused men to testify. He identified himself by his original name, saying that Muhammad Effendi was only a name the pasha now called him. He admitted to his previous testimony but said that he had been forced to interpret Jewish texts and to sign the incriminating trial protocols.

Des Meloizes asked, "Was what is written [in the trial protocols] the truth?"

"No," said Abulafia. "It is a lie."

"Do you mean that your whole written statement is false, or only a part?"

"It is all a lie," said Abulafia. "My whole statement is false. We are merchants. We are not people who would kill anyone. It is impossible."

"What is impossible?"

"That Jews kill for blood."[3]

150

Asked how he knew the details of the murders in his statement, Abulafia said he had heard them described by the barber and David Harari's servant in the courtroom.

"What about the use of the blood?" des Meloizes asked him.

"I made that up."

Abulafia admitted that he had falsely accused five of the other men of killing the monk's servant, explaining that he had been frightened: "If I had written anything else, he [Sherif Pasha] would have had me flogged and killed." He also admitted that he had refused to confirm Meir Farhi's alibi that he had been in synagogue because he was "afraid" and that he had begged the pasha for a pardon.[4]

Des Meloizes reminded Abulafia that he was still under a death sentence, that his pardon had been granted on condition of his giving truthful testimony, and that if his present testimony were found to be false the pardon would be annulled.

Abulafia, finally finding courage when the threat of torture was taken away, stood by his retraction. "It is all a lie," he said.

The retractions by the other convicted men were equally dramatic. Isaac Harari, when asked how it was possible that his testimony agreed so exactly with the testimony of the barber and David Harari's servant Murad al-Fatal, said that Sherif Pasha's scribe, Mansour Tayan, had read him their statements before he confessed.

"Your statements were dictated to you, you did not devise them yourself?" des Meloizes asked.

"No," said Harari. "I did not devise them. The pasha ordered Mansour to read the minutes to me before he had me put into the pool [of freezing water]."[5]

This testimony was dutifully recorded. But when Harari and other defendants tried to articulate the alibis they had not been able to present in their initial testimony, or when they named witnesses who could confirm their alibis, des Meloizes quickly redirected the interview. He refused to summon any of the witnesses they named, announcing that it was not within the scope of his inquiry to take testimony from new witnesses. He also reminded each of the accused men that they were still under a death sentence and threatened that if either their initial or their present testimony was determined to be false, it would aggravate the charges against them.

Aslan Farhi, the son of Raphael Farhi, as in his earlier testimony, was an exception in this phase of the investigation. During his imprisonment Aslan had written a retraction of his confession in a letter addressed to Muhammad Ali in Alexandria, which he managed to smuggle out to Caspar Merlato, the Austrian consul in Damascus.

When this information came out during his new interrogation, des Meloizes threatened Aslan with grave consequences if any of his testimony proved to be false. Aslan, who had taken the cowardly route in every other stage of the investigation, was consistent this time too. Still afraid of the wrath of Sherif Pasha, he—alone among the accused men—retracted his retraction.[6]

Predictably, the initial enthusiasm of the Jewish community for the inquiry quickly faded. The prisoners, who had waited months for the chance to present their case, no doubt welcomed des Meloizes's moderate temperament, which was so much less volatile and caustic than Ratti-Menton. The vice-consul at least controlled his temper during the interviews, lending the semblance of a proper judicial hearing. But their hopes were soon dashed as the severely limited scope of his inquiry and his strict control of what could be discussed in the interviews made it clear that his objective was nothing more or less than the exoneration of Ratti-Menton and the French consular staff. For the members of the Jewish community who had avoided prosecution, and who had hoped that the new inquiry would aid their efforts on behalf of their family members or friends in prison, the new inquiry was equally frustrating. Instead of the judicial rehearing that had been rumored for so long and the chance to clear the opprobrium that hung over the entire community, the inquiry served only to raise the old accusations and rehash the alleged confessions and evidence. Instead of providing relief to the prolonged siege of the Jewish quarter, des Meloizes's inquiry encouraged the Christian quarter to more street taunts, petty mob violence, and renewed calls for execution of the prisoners.

Des Meloizes ultimately agreed to interview a few witnesses other than the prisoners, possibly in response to pressure from the Austrian and British diplomats who had received formal complaints from the Jewish women Ratti-Menton had offended with his bumbling attempts at seduction. Esther Leniado, an Austrian citizen; Lulu Harari, the wife of David Harari; and Sarah Salonicli and Ora Abulafia, the wives of two of the rabbis, had appealed to Caspar Merlato, and their complaints against Ratti-Menton had been relayed up the diplomatic hierarchy to Vienna and London. A report from Damascus in the European press suggested that the complaints filed by the "beautiful Jewesses" could make it "difficult for the consul [Ratti-Menton] to continue to fulfill his duties."[7]

Des Meloizes agreed to a meeting with the women, but the women refused to allow Beaudin, who was especially detested in the Jewish community, to serve as the translator for the session. After long and acrimonious negotiations, another translator was ultimately found, but the women refused to sign the transcript of the session—which they may not have been able to read—effectively precluding the use of their testimony.[8]

Five weeks later, des Meloizes again tried to interview Esther Leniado and Ora Abulafia. When they discovered that Ratti-Menton would be present during the interview, the women remained resolutely uncooperative. After admitting that she had filed a complaint against Count Ratti-Menton with the Austrian consul, Ora Abulafia was asked who wrote the complaint.

She answered, "I've forgotten."

Des Meloizes asked her about the details of her complaint, whether she had in fact seen the consul put a rope around her husband's neck and the other humiliations listed in her written statement.

"I know nothing," she said. "I refuse to say anything. The petition speaks for itself."

"Are you going to keep refusing to answer?" he asked.

"If any good would come of answering, I would. Otherwise, I refuse."

The understandably furious and distrustful women kept up their invective against Ratti-Menton throughout the meeting. Esther Leniado, whose husband had been beaten to death in the pasha's dungeons during the early investigation and who had herself been the target of the French consul's most persistent and clumsiest seduction effort, was particularly vehement. Ratti-Menton labeled the charges of the women total fabrications. He claimed that he could not have sung a love song because he never knew Arabic before coming to Syria, did not know any songs or poetry in Arabic or how to sing the Arabic melodies, and that the complaints of the women were "probably a last desperate effort" at a defense of their husbands, their entire testimony nothing but "subterfuges and plots by the Jews."[9]

The two women were still shouting accusations and invective against the French consul when they left the consulate. Des Meloizes and Ratti-Menton decided that their behavior warranted punishment because some of the women's accusations had been made in public. They asked the pasha to imprison the women for eight days.

Before his interviews were finished, des Meloizes had already formed strong opinions about the situation in Damascus and the thrust of his planned report. In a dispatch to Thiers he announced that the prisoners had all given contradictory testimony and hence had perjured themselves in either their original confessions or their recent retractions. He allowed that torture had been applied in the original investigation, but it had been the responsibility of the Egyptian government and not the French consul or his staff, that Ratti-Menton had protested at least twice against the use of torture and that although two prisoners,

Isaac Yavo and the watchman, had in fact been beaten to death, since the pasha had been seeking confessions and not the death of witnesses, he was not to blame for the unfortunate deaths. The only parties with an interest in silencing witnesses during the original investigation, des Meloizes wrote, were the accused Jews.

He rejected the "alleged alibis" of the accused men, declaring that the efforts of the accused men and their families "to provide evidence of their innocence" could not be proved. Des Meloizes noted that Hanna Bahri Bey—who of course had every reason to see a successful prosecution of the Jews—had assisted his investigation and claimed that public opinion in Damascus also appeared to be on the side of Ratti-Menton and his staff: "Disinterested people have rallied spontaneously in praise of the character of the French consul . . . and the chancellor-dragoman [Beaudin]" while their detractors show "lack of resolution and timidity."[10] Whatever his charter or his original intentions, des Meloizes's inquiry had turned into a whitewash of the original investigation.

His was not the only inquiry into what in the early summer of 1840 was beginning to be called the Damascus affair.

Nathaniel Werry, whose early dispatches on the disappearance of Father Thomas had earned him a sharp rebuke from Lord Palmerston, was busily gathering information to bolster the positions he had taken supporting the French consul's prosecution of the Damascus Jews. Werry was angry and defensive about Palmerston's charges of ungentlemanly conduct. To John Bidwell, who was in charge of the consular corps, he wrote, "I am excessively chagrined at Lord Palmerston's despatch to me. If we are not supported by our superiors to whom are we to look and what is to become of us? . . . If I was a little easier in my circumstances I would not serve under him [Palmerston]."[11]

Werry did not share des Meloizes's burden of trying to appear to be objective, and since he was not a party to the original investigation, he did not have the authority to interview the accused prisoners. He confined his research to the preparation of a series of memoranda on specific topics: "On the character and occupation of the Father Tomasso . . . ," "On the general state of the Jew population at Damascus during the accusation and investigation . . . ," "On the Egyptian jurisdiction, in the case of the accused Jews . . . ," "On the punishments and tortures practiced at the Palace and at Sherif pasha's private dwelling . . . ," etc. These were sent to the Foreign Office as numbered enclosures, totaling over one hundred pages of documentation, and were accompanied by copies of the trial protocols of the monk and his servant and copies of other investigation documents that had been translated from the original Arabic to French or Italian. Werry's goal was to defend his own actions. If the documents he sent to London influenced opinions in the Foreign Office and perhaps shaped British diplomatic positions, they did nothing for the men incarcerated in the Pasha's serail or for the residents of the Jewish quarter who were still afraid to leave their houses lest they be accosted by the jeers or blows of Christian mobs.

There was still another investigation in Damascus that summer. Two delegates from the Jewish community in Alexandria, Isaac Loria and a Mr. Ventura, arrived in Damascus in July. Des Meloizes reported to Paris that the Jewish investigators had been sent "under the patronage of the Austrian consulate."[12]

Loria and Ventura followed the trails that Ratti-Menton and des Meloizes had diligently avoided: they tracked down witnesses who had been named in the alibis of the accused men and gathered testimony that could be introduced in a retrial or appeal of the sentences against the condemned men. When Loria and des Meloizes met in mid-July, Loria told des Meloizes that he had a list of Jews who were ready to testify on the case but were not yet willing "for want of an impartial interpreter." Because Beaudin, the official interpreter for both the initial investigation and for des Meloizes's inquiry, was still mistrusted and feared in the Jewish community and seen as a primary instigator of the actions against the Jews, Loria offered his own services as interpreter or to be present with Beaudin during any testimony. Des Meloizes rejected the offers on the grounds that either option would have made Loria the guarantor of any complaints made by the Jews.[13] In fact, of course, des Meloizes had no intention of allowing anyone except the prisoners to testify. Loria probably knew that and may have raised the whole issue to embarrass des Meloizes.

Four days after their meeting des Meloizes returned the favor. At a special hearing at the Pasha's palace on July 22 a document was revealed in which a high government official agreed to testify that Joseph Farhi, who had been convicted of the murder of Ibrahim Amara in absentia and was now a fugitive, had been at the official's home on the evening of February 5 The official claimed that in return for providing an alibi for Farhi, he was to receive a payment of 6,000 piastres, most of it provided by Farhi's wife. Two Muslim go-betweens for the transaction had been arrested leaving the Austrian consulate, and Ratti-Menton, des Meloizes, and Beaudin were summoned to the serail to take part in the examination of the arrested men. One Muslim identified Isaac Loria as the author of the bribery agreement; he said he had been told that "there's a consul [Loria] in charge of this case who is pursuing it with the justice of God."[14]

Des Meloizes and Ratti-Menton tried to bring charges against Loria and Ventura for the bribery episode, but Sherif Pasha, who had been distancing himself from the Father Thomas matter, refused even to send a complaint to the Austrian consulate. Diplomatic pressure from Alexandria also intervened. After Cochelet, the French consul-general in Alexandria, warned Ratti-Menton that it was better to allow Loria and Ventura to proceed with their inquiry in Damascus than to face the possibility of having "Jews sent to Alexandria" for a new investigation of the entire matter, des Meloizes and Ratti-Menton quietly backed off from pursuing the bribery charges.[15]

The inquiries went on for weeks, a propaganda match on which the local audience had already chosen sides. It had become clear to both the Christian and Jewish communities from the first days of des Meloizes's inquiry that despite the weighty language of the announcements from Paris, his investigation was another layer of cover-up, a defense of Ratti-Menton, his staff, and the French diplomats who had participated in the prosecution of the accused Jews. Nathaniel Werry did not so much investigate as collect evidence to build a defense of his own actions. And while the two investigators sent from the Alexandria Jewish community seemed eager to investigate beyond the limits of the original prosecution, their involvement in what appeared to be a clumsy bribery scheme to clear the name of one of the accused men backfired enough to embarrass their efforts.

In the end the inquiries would hardly matter. Even in Damascus it was becoming clear that the case would be resolved not in the pasha's court but in Alexandria. The viceroy, Muhammad Ali, would make the final decision, and enough rumors and fragments of news floated through the Jewish and Christian quarters for everyone to realize that the case would be decided not on the basis of the contradictions in the testimony of the accused men, their alibis, or the alleged evidence discovered in the sewers of Damascus but through the realities of great power diplomacy. The British, French, Austrians, and most of the other great powers had sent their best negotiators to Alexandria. The stakes in the Middle East were high enough that troops and fleets were being marshaled to influence the wavering stand of the viceroy of Egypt.

One very interested group had no delegate to represent their interests in those fierce diplomatic negotiations—the Jews. That would soon change.

17

Politics

E VEN DURING the long stalemate when there was little to report
beyond rumors about when Muhammad Ali would finally allow
the execution of the condemned Jews, the European press kept
the Damascus affair alive. The reactions of the different national presses
reflected the European political spectrum.

In Austria, Metternich, ever wary of the press, trusted the newspapers least when delicate diplomatic consequences or challenges to
Habsburg policy on minorities were at stake. Once he voiced his skepticism about the ritual murder charges, Austrian press coverage seemed
to shift overnight. Newspapers that had previously featured fulsome
portraits of the "murderous" Jews of Damascus suddenly claimed in
mid-April that there was no evidence that Father Thomas had even
been murdered, reporting that the bones found in the sewers were old,
had been there for a long time, and were definitely of animal origin.[1]

In Germany respected newspapers like the *Allgemeine Zeitung* of
Augsburg or the *Leipziger Allgemeine Zeitung* were in theory independent, but they had to cope with the censors; most pretended to be neutral
on the ritual murder charges while publishing frequent, harsh stories
about the accused Jews. In the Netherlands there was general apathy in
the press after the first sensational reports; only the French-language
Journal de la Haye provided regular coverage of events in Damascus.[2]

French newspapers were—again, in theory—free from censorship,
but were so dependent on subventions from the government and the
political parties that, as Heine put it, French editors and journalists had
to toe the line as good "lieutenants and soldiers." Predictably, the
government-sponsored press maintained the same resolute public
silence on the case as the Thiers government. The leftist press generally
refused to print reports on the events in Damascus, lest a perceived

alliance with either side of the issue dilute their political positions on more confrontational issues, while the ultramontane newspapers, taking their cues from directives and materials distributed by the Vatican, aggressively pursued the case. That left only the conservative *Journal des Débats* to defend the Jews, its occasional columns on the Damascus affair no match for the raucous sarcasm and cudgels the rightist papers wielded against their favorite target: "the man who owns the splendid mansion on the rue Laffitte." The Catholic press mercilessly accused Rothschild of seeking "a *coup d'état* against M. de Ratti-Menton, our consul at Damascus, who appears to have been well-behaved throughout the entire Damascus affair" and noted "this immense expenditure of money which is not usual among the Jews [but which] raises an enormous presumption against the accused." In editorials the rightist press pretended shock that even as the events in Damascus unfolded, "the philanthropists are demanding that this people [the Jews] be granted naturalization and political rights in all European societies."[3]

While the rightist press in France used the affair as a pretext to wage a campaign against the Jews of both France and Syria, much of the English press was consistently skeptical, dismissing the stories of ritual murder as humbug—ridiculous, medieval myths. Some of the British papers took Lord Palmerston's stance, treating the charges as unworthy even of repetition. A few papers documented their skepticism by publishing correspondence from Isaac Picciotto, Haim Nissim Abulafia, and other advocates for the Jews.

The glaring exception among the British press was the *Times*, then the most prestigious, and with its extensive front-page advertising perhaps the most profitable newspaper in the world. Whether out of opposition to Palmerston and sympathy for the French position in diplomatic matters or because of the commercial value of the sensational issue or because, as the self-appointed newspaper of record, they felt compelled to provide a forum for disparate viewpoints, the *Times* took what they declared to be a "neutral" position on the question of the guilt of the accused Jews in Damascus and the charges of ritual murder, opening their columns to descriptions of seventeenth-century blood accusations, extracts from the Passover Haggadah, reports from Sherif Pasha, allegations of ritual murders in Poland, and speeches of Thiers. In June the *Times* published a long extract from the infamous Moldavian monk's book under the heading "A Mystery, Hitherto Concealed and Now Published for the First Time, Concerning the Hebrews, the Blood that They Take from Christians, and the Use that They Make of it, with Proofs from the Holy Scriptures."[4]

The Jews of England were appalled. While the *Times* pretended to be neutral by granting equal (actually more) space to documents like the

Moldavian monk's book and pseudonymous letters that went so far as to enclose sample matzos for testing, the respected newspaper was effectively offering a mantle of credibility to the most outrageous charges against the Jews. An anonymous letter from "a member of the Jewish community" took the editors to task with a properly British tone: "While you expressed the warmest desire that they [the Damascus Jews] should have a fair trial . . . you scarcely appear thoroughly convinced of the absurdity of the charge." The newspaper defended itself by declaring that they had to publish arguments and documents from both sides of the issue in the interest of "our own impartiality," noting that if the accusations against the Jews proved to be true, "then the Jewish religion must at once disappear from the face of the earth. No honorable or honest man could remain a member of such a community. We shall await the issue, as the whole of Europe and the civilized world will do, with intense interest."[5]

While the *Times* opened its columns to a debate that many in Britain, including Lord Palmerston, must have thought unseemly if not ridiculous, it was Sir Robert Peel, the head of the Tory party and a former prime minister waiting to return to power, who finally spoke out on the Damascus affair in Parliament. On June 19 Peel rose to say that he "had been requested to say a few words by persons of the highest character belonging to the Jewish persuasion." Although the Tories had consistently voted against Jewish emancipation, Peel may have thought a public stance on the issue would attract Jewish support.

"The greatest prejudice against the Jews," Peel said on the floor of the Commons, "had been excited among the whole population of Damascus and the neighboring country," a prejudice that would "affect the entire body of the Jews throughout the world unless some effectual step were taken to appease it." To cheers ("Hear, hear!") from the benches, he called on Palmerston to assure the Commons that he was doing whatever could be done "to inculcate on British functionaries the exercise of their influence for insuring" a fair trial for the Damascus Jews, since "they could not have a trial according to British forms." By so doing, Peel concluded to more cheers, "the noble Lord [Palmerston] would be enabled to rescue that great portion of European society, the Jews . . . from a charge which was founded on prejudice and would subject them to the most grievous injustice."[6]

Palmerston was not there to answer Peel. It was not until the session resumed after a weekend that Palmerston rose to say that if the reports coming from the Middle East were true, this was indeed "an instance of barbarity and atrocity" that one would not expect to hear from any country having communication with "the civilized world." He assured the members that the British consul-general in Alexandria, Colonel

Hodges, had been instructed to present the British position to the Egyptian viceroy, that the British consul in Damascus was under instructions to make a "detailed report" on the case and on "the part which he and the other consuls might have taken in it," and that Werry's report would be shared with the Commons.[7]

Other members of the Commons, including representatives close to the London Society that had sent George Pieritz to Damascus, rose to praise "the great zeal and activity" Palmerston had directed toward the plight of the Damascus Jews and "in the affairs of the Jews generally." With debate focused on the plight of the Jews in Damascus, and no one from the major parties raising the touchy question of the existing limitations on the rights of Jews in Britain, the speeches took on the flavor of a celebration. The only dissenting speeches, from the Irish leader Daniel O'Connell and the radical Joseph Hume, pointed out that Peel's statement would have been "much more forcible if it had proceeded from a Hebrew gentlemen in that House" and asked whether the government was going to introduce a bill "conferring equal rights upon the [English] Jews." The reply from Lord John Russell was inaudible. Afterward Russell told reporters that while he personally favored such a bill, the Whig government did not consider it of pressing importance because there were so few British Jews. As long as the Jewish issue stayed in Damascus, the Commons seemed to be saying, they were of one mind.

There was no such friendliness between the government and the opposition when the Damascus affair was brought up on the floor of the Chambre des Députés in Paris.

Benoît Fould, a banker and the only Jewish member of the Chambre, used the consideration of the budget of the consular service as the opportunity to deliver a scathing attack on the handling of the case in Damascus. In the soaring rhetoric typical of debates in the Chambre, he called the affair "a question which not only impinges on the national honor, but concerns mankind as a whole," and then took to task Ratti-Menton, who "faced by the murder [of Father Thomas] chose to accuse not an individual, not a family, but nothing less than an entire nation."

To back up his attack Fould declared that all of the foreign consuls in Damascus had united in opposition to Ratti-Menton (actually, all but Caspar Merlato had sided *with* the French consul); that appointing a junior consular officer in charge of the inquiry into the matter meant that either "he will have to bend, or else he will create an intolerable case of insubordination"; and that "with the fate of two million people at stake, it [the inquiry] merited the dispatch of a special agent." (The two million was presumably a reference to the number of Jews in the Ottoman Empire; the world Jewish population was usually estimated at six million in 1840.)

Fould also attacked the papacy, noting that censorship in Italy had made it impossible to publish the statements of those medieval popes who had publicly opposed the blood libel.[8] He concluded by quoting a sermon given at St. Stephen's in Vienna by Johann Veith, a converted Jew and the official preacher to the Habsburgs who swore "by Him who gave His blood to save us, by this Christ that I hold in my hands, that the accusations made against the Jews of Damascus are as false as they are absurd."[9]

Thiers's reply to Fould took the lofty yet thoroughly unforthcoming tone he had maintained all along. He declared that while he had read the pertinent documents and the trial protocols, "I would consider it reprehensible if I were to express an opinion about the innocence or guilt of the accused in Damascus from this tribunal." The sole goal of his policy, Thiers claimed, was to "vindicate the conduct of an agent [Ratti-Menton] who we have to declare—until we are more fully informed—behaved in the manner that an agent true to his duty would have followed." Sending a high-ranking official to conduct the inquiry would have been impossible, he said, because it would have required removing Ratti-Menton, which would have "sacrificed him to a foreign consul." The dispatch of an agent from France would also have meant a delay of two or three months.

Two liberal deputies answered Thiers. Alexander de Laborde, an archaeologist who had traveled through the Middle East with Lamartine in the 1820s and 1830s, said that from his experience of the region the task of the inquiry was far too complex for a vice-consul. Then François Isambert, the leader of the anti-slavery society—speaking through shouted interruptions from the galleries and the floor—argued that in spite of the resolute silence about torture in the consul's reports, there was ample evidence that Ratti-Menton knew the suspects were being tortured and that he had made the "grave mistake of taking part in infamous proceedings" in which "four people have already perished as victims of this horrendous treatment" instead of opposing the proceedings "with all his might."

Thiers had the last word, mocking the "confidence with which certain of our colleagues declare their knowledge of the facts" and pointing to the "vigor and . . . ardor which can hardly be imagined" with which the Jews "all over Europe" were "putting forward their claims in every foreign chancellory." If the Jews of Damascus "constitute cause for concern," he asked, "does not a French agent totally alone in Damascus . . . deserve our protection? He is a Frenchman." The appeal to patriotism brought shouts of approval from the chamber.

Chauvinism was an uncharacteristic position for Thiers. He had made his reputation as a critic of the excesses of the revolutionary regimes and was now in the position of staunchly defending the government and the diplomatic hierarchy, including Ratti-Menton's own conduct. Thiers's early position of postponing any official position pending the receipt of additional information could be construed as at least consistent with the caution of a scholar, and his early correspondence to the French consuls in Alexandria and Damascus had been skeptical toward at least some of the testimony. Even Heine, who had been an admirer of Thiers, had trouble explaining the contradictions between the premier's writings as a historian and his public statements on the events in Damascus. Heine suggested that Thiers's support for Ratti-Menton may have been an effort to assure the political support of the widely read *Univers*, even if the newspaper "published everything imaginable . . . to make the world believe that Jews gobble up old Capuchins and that the Count Ratti-Menton is an honest man." Thiers seemed reluctant to challenge the ultramontane factions. During the Restoration the Jesuits had promoted the identification of the revolutionary regicides with "Christ-killing Jews"; by extension, in 1840 anyone who defended Jewish ritual murderers in Damascus by attacking an agent of the king was an enemy of France.[10]

Thiers may also have been forced to his positions by quiet accommodations he had made with the papal nuncio. The papal police in Rome had recently seized the child of French Jewish parents, claiming the child had been baptized. A flurry of negotiations followed, and as one condition for the release of the child, Thiers may have agreed to a public stance against the Damascus Jews.[11] Whatever Thiers's reasons—and his position may have had less to do with either domestic politics or his own beliefs than with the needs of France's diplomatic stance against the advances of British influence in the Middle East—by all but agreeing that the Jews were guilty of the ritual murder, he had thrown down a challenge to the Jewish leaders in France.

Adolphe Crémieux, never one to shy away from a fight, took up the challenge. After the premier's pointed comments in the Chambre, Crémieux wrote to Lionel Rothschild that the debate had not been "marvelous" for the "poor Jews in Damascus." Crémieux was especially upset by Thiers's report that the British consul in Damascus had supported Ratti-Menton's findings—which, though true, was shockingly contrary to what Crémieux and Rothschild expected of a British consul. Nathaniel Rothschild, who was in Paris to race his horses, wrote to London about the alleged behavior of the British consul and urged Crémieux to write an official letter from the Central Consistory in Paris to the Board of Deputies in London, which would afford the London group an opportunity to raise the matter with Lord Palmerston. "It is an unpleasant business," Rothschild wrote, "but one must exert oneself to prevent such calumnies being spread against our religion and such horrid tortures being practiced against our unfortunate brethren in the East."[12]

Back in mid-May, when Jewish leaders in Europe were still hoping that the efforts of von Laurin in Alexandria would result in a truly independent inquiry into the events in Damascus, Crémieux had said that if it would help the cause he was ready to "drop everything" and go to Alexandria or Damascus. At the time his offer was little more than an expression of the earnestness of his convictions. He had no experience abroad and certainly could not pretend to be an official representative of any group other than the Central Consistory in Paris, which had rarely managed to attract more than a dozen people to any of its meetings.

Two days after the debate in the Chambre, Nathaniel Rothschild wrote from Paris to his office in London that the "affair of the Jews of Damascus still makes a great noise here" and urged the office to "get up a good subscription to pay the expenses of sending Crémieux there [Damascus] fast." He suggested putting the House of Rothschild down for £1,000 to make a "good beginning" and wrote that he was "curious to know what Isaac Goldsmid will do." Even in philanthropy there was a lively competition between the leading families.

Crémieux's offhand comment of a month before was suddenly the seed of a bold and unprecedented plan.

For all the talk in the rightist press of international Jewish conspiracies and the power of "international Jewry," the rumored worldwide organization of the Jews was a myth. Even in the middle of the nineteenth century, the lasting effects of the diaspora and subsequent migrations had left the Jews of the world scattered and without any institutional organization that spanned borders and oceans. The famed banking network of the Rothschilds, like earlier instances of financial arrangements across borders or continents, was based not on some mysterious international Jewish network but on close family relationships; to keep business matters within the family, the Rothschilds adopted a policy of requiring Rothschild men to marry within the family.[13]

The idea that the Jews of France would send their own representative on a quasi-diplomatic mission to the Middle East was a remarkably bold notion in 1840. Except for relatively new and inexperienced representative bodies like the Consistory in France and the Board of Deputies in London, or the chief rabbis in some states who served as a focal point for interaction with political authority or with the heads of other faiths, there was no official Jewish institution in whose name a delegation could offer credentials. That Nathaniel Rothschild promoted the idea testifies to the financial, social, and political status the Rothschilds had achieved in France, where he made the suggestion, and in England, his home. Sending an independent delegation to the Middle East that would represent a separate and distinct Jewish position was both an open challenge to the official French government position on the matter and strong ammunition to those who, since the Revolution, had charged the Jews with being a separate nation within France.

Crémieux, with his celebrated eloquence, his experience and successes in the courts, and his knowledge of Jewish affairs as the vice-president of the Central Consistory, had much to recommend him as a delegate. But if he was well known in France, indeed infamous in circles that opposed further Jewish emancipation, Crémieux had little experience abroad and little prestige among Jewish communities outside France. His reputation for confrontation and sharp rhetoric also suggested that an effective delegation to the Middle East might profit from a counterweight to dampen the excesses of Crémieux's style and to broaden the prestige of the delegation outside France.

On June 5, only three days after Thiers took his strong stand in the Chambre, the Central Consistory in Paris wrote a letter to the Board of Deputies in London announcing that Crémieux would "leave without delay for Alexandria" and asking if it would not be "most advantageous if Mr. Crémieux were accompanied to the East by an eminent and influential personage who would worthily represent our brothers in England."[14] The person they had in mind was Sir Moses Montefiore, the new president of the Board of Deputies and a distinguished leader of Sephardic Jewry in Britain. A former sheriff of London, one of the few Jews in England to have been knighted, and an experienced traveler to the Middle East who had been in Palestine on behalf of the pious Jews of Jerusalem and Safed only a year before, Montefiore was an imposing figure. He was fifty-five years old, stood six foot three inches tall, and often dressed in his full uniform as a Lieutenant of the Guard of the City of London. His house on Park Lane had been the site of the April meeting of the Board of Deputies that had taken up the issue of the Damascus affair, and because he had returned from Jerusalem via Alexandria on his previous trip to the Middle East, he was personally acquainted with Muhammad Ali. That Montefiore was wealthy enough to finance much of the mission, related to the Rothschilds by marriage, and renowned for his piety and observance made the pairing with the unobservant Crémieux even more inviting.

But if the mission seemed an ideal calling for Montefiore, he was a proud man, enamored of attention and authority, with an inordinate fondness for uniforms and ceremony, a reputation as a statesman and leader that he fiercely guarded, and was blissfully unaware that many who had dealt with him found him insufferably phlegmatic and pompous. Montefiore cautiously reserved his decision when two meetings of the Board of Deputies, each swelled by the attendance of a gallery of the best-known members of the Jewish community in Britain, formally asked him to join the mission to Damascus. A public subscription was organized to raise funds for the mission, with Lionel Rothschild as the receiver of funds, and a public meeting was scheduled for June 23 to mobilize public support. Montefiore, never one to shy away from publicity, was scheduled to attend the rally.

Crémieux spoke at one of the meetings of the Board of Deputies, personally inviting Montefiore to join the delegation as someone "particularly fitted to be the representative . . . of the British Jews at the court of the pasha of Egypt and [as] the defender of our persecuted brethren."[15] Like the invitations from the distinguished members of the Board of Deputies and the other notables among British Jewry, it was a gracious and highly complimentary invitation. But Moses Montefiore was not the man to go along as second fiddle on a mission led by a brash, young Frenchman.

18

The Mission I

THE ROTHSCHILDS liked to work behind the scenes. Using what they hoped were discreet private channels, the family sent 20,000 francs (over $5,000) directly to Damascus for the aid and support of the distressed families in the Jewish quarter of the city. Despite efforts to keep the transfer of funds quiet, word of the donation slipped out to the press, and in Paris the *Univers* promptly announced that the real purpose of the funds had been to buy the silence of prisoners who had so far refused to cooperate with the prosecution. As word of the contribution finally reached Damascus, there were accusations that the reports of tortures inflicted on the accused men had been deliberately exaggerated so the incarcerated Jews could share "the bounty transmitted to this place for that purpose [relief of the accused] by Baron Rothschild."[1]

There was little anyone could do about newspapers like *Univers*, but the battle in the press was almost as important as aid to the beleaguered Jews of Damascus. In the European capitals there was always a hope that favorable press coverage would find its way back to the Middle East, where the weight of editorials or the slant of coverage might influence Muhammad Ali's decision on the pending execution of the convicted Jews. If nothing else, favorable press coverage would lend support to the beleaguered Jewish community of Damascus, assuring them they had not been abandoned. Wealthy members of the Jewish community in Constantinople quietly contributed 3,000 piastres to have the *Journal de Smyrne* publish their side of the Damascus story. From Naples Karl Rothschild wrote to associates in Malta to urge moderation on the Damascus case in the Italian-language newspapers there. The Board of Deputies in London also made a modest payment of £20 to ensure friendly coverage in the English-language *Malta Times*.[2]

Another private effort arrived in the form of a letter delivered by the Austrian ambassador to the Holy See. The letter reported that "the most insistent appeals are currently being made to the Imperial Court of Austria from different quarters" and called on the Holy See to interest itself in the disappearance of Father Thomas, "on behalf of outraged humanity, in ensuring that this [cause] is served by the strictest and most impartial justice and is not left to purely arbitrary action." As supporting evidence, the letter offered a mélange of alternate explanations of the disappearance of Father Thomas, suggesting that he may have been pursued by an "Arab Muslim" enemy on a vendetta and that since the Father and his servant had been seen leaving the city, they probably fled toward "Palestine and Mount Lebanon" where they might still be hiding in one of the convents, if they had not been killed on the dangerous roads. "In order to clarify these suppositions," the letter asked if it would not be "desirable for His Holiness to address circular letters to the religious heads of Palestine, the Holy Land and Mount Lebanon" to undertake "a thorough search for Father Tomasso in those convents and in all other religious buildings and parishes" or at least to find out "if a priest or anyone else has seen or encountered him on his way after his disappearance with his servant."[3]

The letter carefully avoided admitting that the "insistent appeals" were from Solomon Rothschild, who had ready access to Metternich's ear. Cardinal Lambruschini, the secretary of state and the second most powerful figure in the Vatican, may have realized that Rothschild was behind the letter when he answered that "the news that has reached both me and the Congregations for the Propaganda [of the Faith] from highly trustworthy individuals living in the Levant, and especially in Syria and Egypt, leaves not the slightest shadow of a doubt of the truth of this accusation, notwithstanding its wicked and atrocious nature." His letter went on to suggest that if Father Thomas were alive, he surely would have heard that individuals were being tortured to discover his whereabouts and would have found a means to communicate that he was alive without revealing his whereabouts. Hence, Cardinal Lambruschini concluded, "Your excellency will recognize the reasonableness of the negative decision that I have taken with respect to the inquiries requested by the Austrian Government."[4] The cardinal seemed quite proud of his logic.

The frustrating lack of success of the private efforts to aide the accused Jews focused attention on Crémieux's planned mission to the Middle East. In London the Board of Deputies had organized a grand rally in support of the mission for the evening of June 23 at the Great Synagogue in Duke's Place. Representatives from across the spectrum of British Jewry attended, listening to an official report on the situation in Damascus and to speeches that rallied support by pointing out that it was not only the Jews of the Middle East but "the Jewish religion," which had to be rescued from the charges. David Solomons warned that if the "calumny" was not "nipped in the bud, its effects will be extended to the remotest parts of the earth." He carefully distinguished between Thiers's position on the issue and "the French people" and took the opportunity to advance his own agenda by pointing out that while no Jew was able to speak on the matter as a member of Parliament, in France Benôit Fould, a Jew, had been able to raise the issue in the Chambre des Députés. Other speakers took a more cautious slant, characterizing the mission as a bulwark to confine the threatening issue in the East "lest it should travel westward."[5]

The crowd cheered, especially when Moses Montefiore agreed to lend his prestige and leadership to the mission. In the exuberance of the hour, splits within British Jewry between conservatives like Montefiore and Rothschild and liberals like David Salomons and Isaac Goldsmid were temporarily put aside, lending an impressive display of unity and commitment for the occasion. The pairing of the distinguished Montefiore with his gravitas and experience and Adolphe Crémieux's firebrand rhetoric and quick mind suggested to all that the mission had not only brought together representation of England and France, the two great powers that had done the most to liberate the Jews in their own nations, but also an apparently ideal combination of talents for the mission.

A second public meeting to support the mission was called for the afternoon of July 3 in the Egyptian Hall at Mansion House. This time the elite of British Jewry—the Goldsmids, Rothschilds, and other prominent Jews—were again present, but the speakers were all non-Jews. John Bowring, an expert on international trade, pointed out that on the basis of statistics he had collected in a recent trip to the Middle East, the Jews under arrest in Damascus collectively controlled some 16 million piastres ($800,000) of capital, making them a significant force in the economy. Bankers and representatives of merchant firms in the audience were no doubt impressed by Bowring's numbers. From the podium portions of Peel's speech in the House of Commons and George Pieritz's reports from Damascus were read out loud, while other speakers, including the Lord Mayor, praised Jewish philanthropy and assured the Jews that they were esteemed and respected members of society. A formal resolution called "for an immediate and impartial investigation" to disprove the "atrocious calumnies invented . . . as a pretext for the infliction of cruelties almost unknown to the previous history of mankind." The final speech by Daniel O'Connell, the renowned radical orator, echoed the cadences of Shylock's plaint in

The Merchant of Venice: "Was there a human being so degraded as to believe that they [Jews] made human blood a part . . . [of] their ceremonies? Was not the Hebrew exemplary in every relation of life? Was he not a good father, a good son? Did they not make good mothers and daughters? Were they not firm friends?"[6]

The meeting ended on a chorus of cheers, a fitting send-off for Montefiore and Crémieux, who were scheduled to depart the next week for the Middle East. The Lord Mayor asked the foreign ambassadors in London to convey the resolutions of the Mansion House meeting to their governments, and the enthusiasm displayed at the two public rallies persuaded the Board of Deputies to openly publicize the mission in Britain and abroad.

As news of the mission and the London rallies wended its way to Jewish communities in Europe, the Caribbean, and the United States, rallies of support were held in Manchester, Liverpool, Dublin, Portsea, Falmouth, Altona, Hamburg, Bridgetown (Barbados), Kingston and Spanish Town (Jamaica), Curaçao, Richmond (Virginia), New York, Philadelphia, Charleston (South Carolina), and Cincinnati (Ohio). There were also solidarity meetings with non-Jewish speakers on the model of the Mansion House meeting in Manchester, Savannah (Georgia), and other cities.[7]

At the rallies speakers read from copies of the original letters written from the Damascus community and from Pieritz's report. It was an era of rousing rhetoric, and speakers like the Rabbi Isaac Leeser in Philadelphia perorated on those who had been forced to confess or adopt the Muslim religion under torture, those who had "died under the excruciating pain they had to endure," and those who "enduring the most intense suffering, still clung to the truth, and refused making any confession of guilt in themselves or others, of which they were guiltless."[8]

Liberal newspaper editors, Protestant ministers, and politicians joined the rabbis and Jewish community leaders in speaking out on tolerance, justice, the threat that the accusations in the East could ultimately mean to the Jewish communities of the West, and in celebration of the solidarity of world Jewry expressed for a single purpose in so many communities. Hirsch Lehren wrote Crémieux from Amsterdam to express "the unanimous gratitude of our entire, insulted nation for the fact that you have selected to undertake the defense for which your exceptional talents so uniquely qualify you." Many echoed Isaac Leeser's proclamation in Philadelphia that "the times . . . have produced spirits adequate to the emergency and a Crémieux . . . and a Montefiore will be long remembered as the generous, active friends of their people."[9]

The rallies drew substantial contributions, from the £1,200 raised in Kingston, Jamaica, and $850 from the Jewish community of Philadelphia to £186 from the community in Gibraltar and £115 from St. Thomas. Christians in some communities contributed to the funds, and communities that decided against public rallies sent funds directly to Lionel Rothschild, who served as treasurer for the subscriptions. From Amsterdam, 250 individuals contributed 5,600 florins. The total raised for the mission, including the original Rothschild pledges and Moses Montefiore's contribution of £2,400, was over £10,000.[10]

The reports that crisscrossed the Atlantic, quoting the soaring rhetoric of the speeches and documenting the enthusiasm of the crowds and the successful fundraising on the Continent, the British Isles, the Caribbean, and the United States created the sense of an international and intercontinental rally of the Jewish people, bringing communities on both sides of the Atlantic together in support of a single purpose. For many the feelings of distress, embarrassment, guilt, and anxiety that had previously tempered active interest in the events in the Middle East finally turned to enthusiasm for the defense of the Jews of Damascus, as the mission of Montefiore and Crémieux provided a focus for rallied support and, for the first time since the diaspora, brought the Jewish communities of the world together in a common cause.

Yet while many rabbis composed special prayers to be recited in support of the mission and the beleaguered Jews of Damascus, there were dissents: the Sephardic community in America, traditionally aloof from the rest of American Jewry, and perhaps afraid that they would be tainted by association with the Jews of Damascus, chose not to take part in any of the public meetings. Some Italian Jewish communities worried that public efforts on behalf of the Jews would generate a backlash. A rabbi from Jerusalem argued that by failing to observe the laws of sexual purity the pleasure-loving Damascus Jews had invited punishment from above: "They transgressed in blood and were penalized in blood." A rabbi from near Belgrade blamed the entire Jewish people: "We have sinned against God," he wrote, using a familiar phrase (*anahnu hata'nu*) from the Yom Kippur service. Even Hirsch Lehren, who had first publicized the persecution of the Damascus Jews from his office in Amsterdam, asked if the events in Damascus could be explained by anything "but punishment from God for the transgressions against the Divine Law which, alas, are increasing every day among our co-religionists."[11]

A more threatening exception to the widespread enthusiasm for the mission was the situation in France, where even Crémieux's sharp oratory had not been enough to rally a public challenge or appeal of the official government position. Heine observed that "with the exception of one beautiful woman and a few young scholars," the only voice in Paris active in the cause was Crémieux's "generous eloquence." The beautiful woman was Baroness Betty de Rothschild, Salomon Rothschild's daughter and the wife of Baron James, who at thirty-five was a famed beauty and fiercely active in Jewish causes. The scholars were probably Salomon Munk, a distinguished linguist and Orientalist, the curator of Semitic manuscripts at the Bibliothèque Nationale, and professor of Hebrew and Syrian literature at the Collège de France;[12] and Albert Cohn, the Vienna-educated Jewish tutor to the Rothschilds who had urged Crémieux's first response to the events in Damascus. At a private gathering in Paris, the Foulds, Baron James de Rothschild, Anselm Halphen, and Worms de Romilly each contributed 3,000 to 7,000 francs to the mission and agreed to double their contributions if additional funds were needed. They asked that their contributions, which totaled over 20,000 francs, be kept quiet.

Why were the French Jews, though generous in private, so reluctant to take a public stand? Heine thought it was because the French Jews had been emancipated so long they had submerged their Judaism into a French identity: "They are Frenchmen just like the others, and have outbursts of enthusiasm that last for twenty-four hours, or if the sun is hot, for three days!" If they still practiced Jewish ceremonies, he observed, they did so mechanically, from habit, without knowing why: "Among the French Jews, as among the rest of the French, money is the god of the day and industry the dominant religion."[13] There was a grain of truth in what he wrote, but it would have been just as fair to note that the French Jews, who had come so far since the reversals of the Restoration, were reluctant to risk the gains they had achieved by fighting for a cause so far from France or to see the heinous accusations that had been made in Damascus come back to taint their own hard-earned social, economic, and political achievements.

But France, with the special circumstance of the government protecting their consul at Damascus and their alliance with Muhammad Ali, was an exception. Elsewhere enthusiasm and optimism reigned. At the rally in London on July 3, a speaker had enthusiastically proclaimed to much cheering that "he had a letter in his possession [confirming] . . . that the sovereign of Egypt was ready . . . to assent to any species of tribunal which the English consul would wish to have."[14] Muhammad Ali had indeed agreed to a tribunal in his early negotiations with von Laurin and Colonel Hodges, but the geography of information was playing tricks again. It would be weeks before London learned that once the French had begun their own inquiry under des Meloizes, the viceroy had quietly withdrawn his offer to allow a further tribunal to investigate the Damascus matter.

The widespread optimism and anticipation of the mission left little room for caution, and those with reservations kept them private. After the first rally in London, Nathaniel Rothschild wrote privately, "I do not think Sir Moses will find it a very easy matter to establish the innocence of the poor Jews; the French interest at Alexandria is now the prevailing one and the French authorities will do all in their power to prevent the truth from being brought to light." Palmerston also warned Montefiore privately that his mission might be "to no great avail." Across the Channel Crémieux met privately with Thiers, hoping to persuade him to grant the mission some official accreditation. Thiers refused to accredit the mission and never delivered a promised letter of introduction to the French consul-general in Egypt. Privately he told Crémieux, "Those people are guilty. They wanted a priest's blood and you do not know how far the fanaticism of the Eastern Jews goes. This is not the first instance of such a crime." Given Thiers's reputation and circumspect public comments on the case, this uncharacteristic private comment is difficult to explain. His argument sounds strikingly like Voltaire's least-enlightened treatise, the pamphlet *Anthropophages*, in which he supported the idea that ancient Jews had offered up human sacrifices.[15]

If Crémieux would travel without official French accreditation, Montefiore made up for it with his voluminous formal credentials. Lord Palmerston wrote on his behalf to the British consuls at Alexandria, Beirut, and Damascus requesting courtesy and support for Montefiore and his mission. Palmerston would not accord British protection to the members of the mission who were not British, including Crémieux, and even Montefiore acknowledged that they would be up against the French influence in Egypt and that he would "have much greater difficulty to encounter with than I anticipated." But he remained a supremely confident man, assuring the Board of Deputies on the eve of his departure that "neither difficulty nor danger shall divert me from the prosecution of my mission, trusting on Him who can direct and overrule all things for good to His people, Israel."[16]

The statement was vintage Montefiore—pious, dignified, formal, and deliberate. As Nathaniel Rothschild had predicted, Montefiore was a polar complement to Crémieux's boldness, quick legal mind, and formidable eloquence. Between them they had recruited an impressive entourage. In addition to their wives, Crémieux and Montefiore would be accompanied by distinguished Orientalists and linguists Salomon Munk from France and Louis Loewe, a Prussian from England. Montefiore's entourage also included the British lawyer and alderman D. N. Wire and British physician John Madden. With strong and visible support from Jewish communities on both sides of the Atlantic, the personal backing of the Rothschilds, and the official recognition from the British government, the mission seemed destined to triumph.

The publicity attending the mission also attracted the attention of those who had long opposed Jewish emancipation. The plans for a joint diplomatic mission fit perfectly with the charges that had been heard in France since the Revolution—that the Jews were not like other citizens but constituted a separate nation within the nation and hence a threat to the fundamental values of France. Reports of Montefiore's journey to Palestine in 1839, during which he had met with Muhammad Ali and presented him with an ambitious plan for the settlement of Jewish farmers in Palestine, elevated rumors and fears about the mission to the Middle East, at least for those who were willing to believe conspiracy theories. The newspapers also carried stories about the widely discussed millenarian expectations for the year 1839–40 (5600 in the Hebrew calendar), suggesting that there were secret plans afoot to rebuild the Holy Land as a Jewish state. Rumors had already circulated that the Rothschilds would buy the Holy Land from the Egyptians or the sultan, and newspapers identified with Palmerston's positions wrote that although the Jews might not "return all at once to their native land . . . it seems highly probable . . . that numbers would repair to Judea, and help to make it what it was once, a region of traffic," and that there was a "blessing on record for those who show kindness to the children of Abraham. Now is the time for Britain to set about deserving it."[17] The Paris papers that had been the most explicitly supportive of Ratti-Menton's prosecution of the Damascus Jews found just the ammunition they needed by quoting the British articles, adding that "the English are continuing to demonstrate the liveliest interest on behalf of the Jews; what is being considered is the sale of Syria to them and the creation of a Jewish kingdom."[18]

There was in fact a theological dimension to the British interest in Palestine and Syria. Lord Ashley's interest in the restoration of the Jews to the Holy Land as a prerequisite to the Second Coming was popular in Protestant England. Ashley's prescription for the problem was simple: "It seems as though money were the only thing wanting to regenerate the world . . . [and to] restore the Jews to the Holy Land." Although Palmerston did not share Lord Ashley's views, his marriage to Lord Ashley's mother-in-law gave Ashley access to the foreign secretary. They had dinner together one evening, and Ashley presented his scheme; when Palmerston asked questions and agreed to "consider" the scheme, Ashley concluded that "Palmerston has already been chosen by God to be an instrument of good to His ancient people; to do homage, as it were, to their inheritance, and to recognize their rights without believing their destiny. And it seems he will yet do more."[19]

Palmerston was only being polite to his nephew. Diplomatic questions and policy considerations for the future of the Middle East loomed far bigger in Palmerston's mind than Ashley's millenarian ideas.

While the final arrangements were being made for the departure of the Crémieux-Montefiore mission to the Middle East, Palmerston was huddled with representatives of Russia, Austria, and Prussia, determined to forge a treaty that would end the diplomatic stalemate in their negotiations with Muhammad Ali. Mutual though conflicting interests brought them together: Britain needed to protect the overland routes from the Mediterranean to the Red Sea and the channels through the Red Sea to India that Muhammad Ali controlled. Austria wanted to uphold the Ottoman Empire as a bulwark against revolution and Russian encroachment. The Russians wanted friendly powers controlling the straits that potentially throttled their access to the Black Sea. The Prussians, while not directly affected by the events in the Middle East, were a willing partner in the revival of the Holy Alliance that had faced France in the Napoleonic era.

Palmerston had begun to lose patience in the protracted negotiations. Muhammad Ali, who bristled that he was treated only as a renegade viceroy, had been by turns intractable and seductive, a master of procrastination, tergiversation, and brinkmanship. Since the fall of 1839 Muhammad Ali had built up his army to a formidable force of two hundred thousand men.[20] French advisers trained his forces for European technology and tactics, the Ottoman fleet was at his disposal in Alexandria harbor, and he had the potential backing of a substantial French Mediterranean fleet. He had repeatedly threatened that if pressed he would order his son Ibrahim Pasha to unleash the Egyptian armies across the plains of Anatolia to Constantinople itself and call for a jihad against the Christian powers that would invite revolts from every subject people in the Ottoman Empire. The Ottomans had initiated reforms in their own army, with uniforms, conscription, Polish and German officers, and new regulations limiting the length of beards to the width of two fingers and moustaches to the width of eyebrows. But the inexperienced nineteen-year-old sultan, his court and harem engulfed in his mother's intrigues, was no match for the Egyptians.

Britain was already heavily involved in wars in Afghanistan and China in 1840, but by summer Palmerston, weary of the months of fruitless negotiations with Muhammad Ali, whom he had privately labeled "an ignorant barbarian," had concluded that a few thousand Turkish soldiers reinforced by British marines could engineer a successful Druse and Maronite uprising in Lebanon that would distract the

Egyptian troops, and that if the Royal Navy could control the sea routes between Egypt and Syria, Ibrahim Pasha's army would be nullified.[21] Palmerston was willing to gamble on the strategy, and on July 15 Britain, Russia, Austria, and Prussia signed the Treaty of London, an ultimatum that offered Muhammad Ali hereditary possession of Egypt and southern Syria (Palestine and Gaza) for his lifetime if he returned to the sultan Crete, northern Syria, the holy cities of Mecca and Medina, and the Turkish fleet. Muhammad Ali was given ten days to accept the terms of the treaty, or he would lose southern Syria. After ten more days the treaty would grant the sultan the right to make other arrangements for all of the lands occupied by the Egyptians, including Egypt itself.

The French expansion in the Middle East was as much a target of the treaty as Muhammad Ali. Ever since he came to office, Thiers had been making strong public statements of French support for the Egyptian viceroy, calling Muhammad Ali "a man of genius." Diplomatic posturing and feints, an art Thiers had mastered, was a skill that eluded the Egyptian viceroy, who refused to understand that despite the bold public statements, France was not willing to be dragged into war to support Egyptian ambitions. Cochelet wrote from Alexandria that "it would be difficult for you to conceive how opinionated Muhammad Ali is—and how foolish—in everything that touches his glory and vanity. He is old and surrounded by flatterers . . . everything he had done has succeeded, and he believes that fortune will not desert him." When Cochelet warned the viceroy that Napoleon had lost everything because he had abused his power, Muhammad Ali—who liked to brag that he was born in the same year as Napoleon—was pleased by the comparison. He said that if his name survived he was oblivious to his own downfall.[22]

Given his titanic ego, Muhammad Ali's response to the ultimatum in the Treaty of London was unpredictable. What was predictable was that as soon as the text of the treaty arrived in Alexandria, the viceroy, Palmerston, and Thiers would be pitched into a three-handed game of poker, with the future of Syria and Muhammad Ali's other possessions as the stakes. All three were masters of the bluff and the aggressive bid. Little else would matter in Alexandria, including the fate of the accused Jews in Damascus, until their game played out.

19

The Mission II

THE MISSION did not begin well.

More than a hundred well-wishers from the Ecclesiastical Courts and the German and Portuguese congregations were at London Bridge Wharf on July 7 to give Montefiore and his entourage a proper send-off. But the wind was blowing hard when they reached Gravesend, and Sir Moses and Lady Montefiore, self-admitted "bad sailors," found boarding the *Arrow* and the Channel crossing in squally weather and rough seas unpleasant. On the French side of the Channel they had to anchor offshore for hours until it was safe for the *Arrow* to enter port, and they then faced an overnight journey by carriage to Paris via Boulogne and Abbyville. Sir Moses's carpet bag and his favorite traveling cap were somehow misplaced on the journey, leaving him in a foul mood.[1]

In Paris Montefiore and Crémieux met with a subcommittee of the Central Consistory. Everyone expressed a "keen desire to obtain justice at Damascus," but the committee made it clear that Crémieux was to do nothing that would compromise the position of the Jews in France. Even a letter against the official government position was ruled too dangerous, and Crémieux was admonished that if French consul-general Cochelet in Alexandria showed any hostility to his efforts, "open or veiled," Crémieux was to back off pending further instructions from the committee. Appalled by the pusillanimous attitude, Crémieux told the committee that he insisted on being in charge, that as a lawyer he seemed to know their own best interests better than they did, that as a Frenchman he was not so crazy as to "gamble with our future," and that as he had been "delegated to a mission which placed me in a special, eminent position, [he] would not hear of being kept in swaddling clothes." It was a brave statement, but he was arguing with the wind. Unlike the wealthy Montefiore, Crémieux had to negotiate for

176

the 40,000 franc honorarium that enabled him to undertake the mission. This was clearly an instance of "he who pays the piper calls the tune."

That evening, on the eve of their departure for Marseilles where they would board the steamer to Alexandria, Crémieux and Montefiore dined with Baron Anselm de Rothschild, the son of Solomon Rothschild who was married to Charlotte, the daughter of Nathan Rothschild. Anselm Rothschild explained that because Montefiore had been officially "delegated" by his government, he would be recognized as the formal head of the mission and would have the final word if there were a dispute. For Crémieux—who had first proposed the mission, volunteered without hesitation, suggested recruiting Montefiore to join him, and had repeatedly traveled to England to advocate the cause—Rothschild's ruling was a harsh blow. It was too late to back out, so Crémieux reluctantly acceded to the proposed arrangement with the qualification that if the judicial case of the Damascus Jews could be reopened, he, as an experienced lawyer, would be in charge of legal matters. Montefiore, speaking with the authority of his newly announced position as head of the mission, and with the status and familiarity of an uncle-by-marriage to Anselm Rothschild, said, "As for the law case, I will take advice from Mr. Wire and from Mr. Crémieux as well." Crémieux, protesting that he would make no more concessions, began keeping a journal of the mission.[2]

It is not clear whether Montefiore had privately made an arrangement with the Rothschilds even before the Paris dinner. Given Montefiore's initial public reluctance to join the mission, and his secure knowledge that Rothschild blood was thicker than French wine, the undisputed leadership of the mission may have been his price for joining, and one the Rothschilds gladly paid. Montefiore's own description of the predeparture arrangements did not acknowledge that he had effectively staged a coup. "Mons. Crémieux was present," Montefiore wrote to the Board of Deputies in London, "and it was then agreed that as he did not represent his government he should act as my counsel in conjunction with Mr. Wire. The committee [of the Central Consistory] was very cordial and anxious to meet my wishes."[3]

As if to demonstrate the new order of authority in the mission, before they set off for Marseilles the composition of the traveling party was rearranged. Lady Montefiore's maid would not be going with them, but Lord Montefiore took two servants, one a ritual food inspector to ensure that his food was kosher, along with his entourage of Wire, Madden, and Dr. Loewe. The Crémieux party, consisting only of Crémieux, his wife, and Munk, traveled to Marseilles separately. When the Montefiore party reached Lyon, where their dinner at the home of a Jew had been arranged by Crémieux, Montefiore announced that the food was not properly kosher. He wrote in his diary that he distrusted and disliked Crémieux.

The two parties met up in Avignon, and reached Marseilles on July 20. There, while Montefiore went to synagogue to pray for the success of the mission, Crémieux boarded the *Minos*, the steamer that would take them across the Mediterranean. When the Montefiores boarded, they discovered that Amélie Crémieux had already taken the best cabin. Judith Montefiore was at first gracious about the arrangement, but the next day a delegation of Wire, Madden, and Dr. Loewe called on Crémieux to complain that unless the better cabin were given to Montefiore, "his health would not permit him to make the voyage." At the moment they appeared, Amélie Crémieux had a fever and a stomach upset severe enough to warrant the attention of the ship's physician, but as Crémieux wrote in his journal, "the condition of my wife during her illness was of no interest to those people." Crémieux yielded the cabin, but from that point on Amélie Crémieux and Lady Montefiore snubbed one another at every opportunity, bickering over cabin assignments whenever they changed ships and blaming one another for each minor mishap.[4]

The two husbands mirrored the attitudes of their wives. Lord Montefiore found Crémieux intolerably French—intelligent, voluble, and quick but facile and determinedly nonobservant. Crémieux, who had conspicuously avoided accompanying Montefiore to synagogue services, at one point said that he intended to "turn Jew" when they were on their way to Beirut and to continue so until they visited Jerusalem. When Montefiore said that he hoped Crémieux would remain so, the Frenchman answered that "it would not be convenient to submit to such an arrangement." For his part Crémieux found Montefiore unbearably pompous, arrogant, and vain. "By character, Sir Moses and his wife are good people," he wrote in his journal, "but the arrogance born of money, and the English vanity of these two individuals surpasses anything that can be imagined." Crémieux was especially appalled at what he saw as Montefiore's unjustified optimism about the mission and apparent ignorance of the situation they faced. It was impossible to persuade Sir Moses and Lady Montefiore that as long as Muhammad Ali was under the thrall of the French, it was Cochelet, the French consul-general in Alexandria, and not Palmerston, in faraway London, who would hold sway over the viceroy. "I could not even begin to describe how little such ideas impinged on Sir Moses and his wife," Crémieux wrote.[5]

When they steamed into Alexandria on August 4, they could see the warships of the former Turkish fleet lying at anchor in the harbor. Montefiore and his entourage were received with great pomp by representatives of the Jewish community and the British and Austrian consuls-general. The Montefiore and Crémieux parties then sought out their separate hotels. That afternoon and evening the festivities and a round of calls on the various consuls lasted until two in the morning, but Montefiore was up at five to dress in his full uniform as a Lieutenant of the Guard so Colonel Hodges could present him to the viceroy at eight. Montefiore's entourage, he noted in his diary, wore "court or official costume." Crémieux and Munk did not join him, "for reasons best known to him [Crémieux]."[6]

Montefiore found the viceroy exactly where he had last seen him over a year before, reclining in his cool and airy divan, the harbor and his considerable fleet visible through the open archways that looked out over the sea. Montefiore read his long petition to the end: "The eyes of all Europe are fixed on Your Highness . . . the whole world will be much gratified . . . The great man, who has already such a glorious name, must love justice dearly. There cannot be a greater homage rendered to Your Highness's genius." The petition requested permission to cross-examine witnesses and collect evidence in Damascus on behalf of the accused prisoners. Before the Turkish version was read, the viceroy waived the translation as "too long." Hodges reported that all summer Muhammad Ali had sought "by every means in his power to avoid the subject [of the Damascus affair] when it is mentioned to him" and seemed determined to "only do what France wishes" and that once again he successfully avoided the subject. The viceroy promised a reply to the petition within two days.[7]

Crémieux made his own call on the viceroy two days later, appearing without a formal introduction from the French consul-general and presenting a petition with the same request Montefiore had made. He too was sent off without an answer. Muhammad Ali was probably more confused than impressed by the separate petitions. Whatever impact the mission was supposed to achieve as a joint delegation was already squandered, a victim of the unbridgeable differences in character and approach of Montefiore and Crémieux.

Shortly after Crémieux presented his petition, the viceroy left for a journey up the Nile to Cairo. On the basis of the viceroy's lack of response to his petition, Montefiore concluded that they should be prepared for a negative reply. He wrote the Board of Deputies asking that they petition Palmerston to intervene directly with Thiers. Since England and France were on the verge of war, the gesture seemed to ratify Crémieux's appraisal of Montefiore's understanding of the diplomatic situation. In fact, just before the viceroy left Alexandria he hinted to Austrian consul-general von Laurin that there was a possibility of a new trial in Damascus, with the Jewish delegations permitted to attend, although Muhammad Ali added that if the witnesses could not prove the innocence of the Jews, "they must be considered guilty."[8]

Interpreting the tea leaves of the viceroy's remarks soon would not matter. While Muhammad Ali was in Cairo, the Ottoman representative, Rifāt Bey, arrived with the official text of the Treaty of London signed by the four great powers and Turkey. He personally delivered the ultimatum to Muhammad Ali on August 16. The terms of the treaty were clear: if Muhammad Ali did not agree to accept the limited Egypt the great powers had offered him within ten days, they would withdraw the offer of lifetime rule of southern Syria and Palestine. After twenty days they would withdraw the rule of Egypt itself. The viceroy's only alternative was war.

As if to further heighten tensions, the day Rifāt Bey appeared saw an even more dramatic arrival in Alexandria: Count Walewski, the son of Napoleon, a special envoy from Paris. With Paris still celebrating the glorious entombment of Napoleon's remains in the Invalides, the appearance of the natural son of the emperor was guaranteed to invoke the memories of Napoleon's conquest of Egypt and Palestine and underline the earnestness of the French interest in the Middle East and especially Egypt. Muhammad Ali promptly received Walewski to request "the protection and mediation" of France in the current situation and was given a secret message, presumably from Thiers, instructing him to pursue negotiations with the Ottoman Empire and the four great powers as long as possible and ordering that if the negotiations failed, the Egyptian armies should launch an immediate attack on Anatolia, the underbelly of Turkey. Walewski did not have to point out that the previous attack in the same region by Ibrahim Pasha had easily driven back the Turkish armies. Concluding that the presence of an envoy as distinguished as Walewski constituted a promise of French support, Muhammad Ali promptly dismissed the ultimatum from the sultan and the four powers, saying, "France is ready to come to my aid and more than once has offered its intervention."[9] To those who had followed the diplomatic situation, it sounded like a declaration of war.

Crémieux and Montefiore, living in different hotels and consulting with separate advisers, had very different understandings of the politics of the situation and the strategy to pursue.

From the moment he agreed to go to the Middle East, Crémieux believed that the key to the success of the mission was the French consul-general in Alexandria, Adrien-Louis Cochelet. The French were the only ally of the Egyptians. With the other great powers and the sultan all but declared enemies of Egypt, Crémieux reasoned that the viceroy would rely on the advice and counsel of the French consul-general on any matter with diplomatic consequences. And whatever the issues separating them, Crémieux and Cochelet were Frenchmen, sharing that mysterious bond of language, values, and hauteur that infuriates outsiders. Crémieux's reputation was as a brilliant and relentless courtroom orator, but he was also an experienced negotiator, convinced that he could hammer out an agreement with his fellow countryman and that French support would persuade the viceroy to agree on a remedy that would realize the essential goals of the mission. Crémieux realized that the French government, like the viceroy, was proud to the point of arrogance. If they were to yield on the fundamental issues of the accusations in Damascus, they would need to be offered a solution to the situation that would not embarrass them before the world.

The day the mission arrived in Alexandria, while Montefiore had hastened to present his petition to the viceroy, Crémieux had been huddled with the French consul-general. Cochelet was reluctant to deviate from the official position he was supposed to represent. He told Crémieux that while he was personally skeptical of the ritual murder aspects of the case, it was clear to him that the murders must have been committed by the Jews, perhaps to satisfy some "personal hatred."

Crémieux instinctively cross-examined. "Where are the proofs?" he asked. "Where is the evidence? And why fifteen criminals?"

Cochelet answered that "the fanaticism of that country is enormous" and that even if there had been only "one or two fanatics," they could have inspired the others to join them in killing the priest. In any case, Cochelet insisted, the viceroy would never allow a review of the matter because it would embarrass his own judicial agents and process. Cochelet also objected that the Meloizes investigation was not yet complete, and he was particularly troubled that a new trial might raise charges against a fellow diplomat, Ratti-Menton.

Crémieux wrote in his journal that he felt the blood rise in his face at the idea that concerns about soiling the name of a French official could be put ahead of justice for the poor accused men in Damascus. He controlled himself, assuring Cochelet that if there were "well-founded accusations" against Ratti-Menton, he would know how to cover them over. He finally persuaded Cochelet to hear his proposal. His two demands, as he explained them to Cochelet, were that the Egyptian government declare the ritual murder accusations false and slanderous and that the prisoners in Damascus be released and declared innocent. In return, he agreed that he would make no demands for the case to be reopened. "As for the four dead men [who had been flogged to death during the interrogations]," Crémieux told Cochelet, "we can leave it to time to reveal the truth, and [allow] the murder accusations to rest on those poor victims."[10]

Cochelet was willing to endorse the first demand, that the ritual murder accusation be rescinded, but he would not agree to endorse the request for a declaration that the accused men were innocent, even with Crémieux's formula that allowed the inference that the men who had died in interrogation had been guilty of the murders.

When the two men met again, more than a week later, Crémieux used his celebrated rhetorical skills to present a history of the entire blood-libel accusation, a chronicle of "massacres, hecatombs in which blood flowed without pity." Madame Crémieux had joined him for the meeting, and she and Cochelet were moved to tears by Crémieux's presentation. But, Crémieux wrote in his journal, "the moment passed." It was painfully clear that Cochelet was under instructions, no doubt from Thiers himself, that the guilt of the accused Jews was not subject to negotiation.[11]

For his assessment of the situation Montefiore relied on the British businessman Samuel Briggs, who had made a fortune as an independent banker and as an agent for the Rothschilds in Alexandria. Briggs had visited Syria in June and July and had personally appealed to Sherif Pasha to reopen the investigation of the disappearance of Father Thomas. Sherif Pasha denied the request, but by the time Briggs returned to Alexandria, a few days after the arrival of Montefiore and Crémieux, Montefiore was reading positive signs from Briggs's appraisal of the situation. "Mr. Briggs, who returned last evening from Damascus and Syria," Montefiore wrote to the Board of Deputies in London, "assures me that the pasha will do justice." Montefiore also received a report from British consul Nathaniel Werry, who had written from Damascus that he hoped Muhammad Ali would approve a new trial in Alexandria.[12]

Briggs, who had attended the last meeting with Muhammad Ali, had said something that pleased the viceroy and came away with the optimistic conviction that Muhammad Ali had given "more than half a promise" that he would liberate the prisoners and declare "his entire belief in their innocence of the murder, and of the other charges made against them."[13] Montefiore used Briggs's optimism to justify his own stubborn positions.

There was one issue on which Crémieux and Montefiore silently agreed. Although the original impetus for the mission to the East had been the fate of the Jews who had been accused, convicted, and were now awaiting execution in Damascus, by the time the mission left England, the focus of rallies, the fund raising, and ultimately the mission itself had been transformed into abstract causes: a battle of Western reason against injustice, Oriental barbarism, fanaticism, and the threat that the ritual murder charges could taint the Jews of the West. The incarcerated men who had spent the long winter and simmering summer in the pasha's dungeons in Damascus had become tokens. From the time they left on their mission, Crémieux and Montefiore made no effort to contact the Damascus prisoners, and their diary and journal entries, the only record we have of their thoughts during the mission, do not mention the incarcerated men by name.

At the London rallies and meetings where the mission was conceived and given its send-off, Montefiore had promised to visit Damascus to see to the condition of the incarcerated men and personally intervene in the judicial proceedings. Once he reached Alexandria, Montefiore repeatedly said he was eager to go to Damascus, but each time the issue arose he found new evidence of the danger of a visit to Syria. He cited the letter Colonel Hodges had given him from Nathaniel Werry reporting that the uprising in Mount Lebanon had not been quelled, which left travel to Syria perilous. He also reported that the Prussian consul-general had advised him not to go to Syria.

On his previous trip to the Middle East, Montefiore had also declined to visit Syria, that time because of the onerous quarantine restrictions, the ban on European dress at the divan of the pasha, and the rumors of epidemics. This time the rumors were about war preparations. According to the cafe talk in Alexandria, three Egyptian transport ships had been sent to Syria, and the HMS *Gorgon* had been dispatched to intercept the ships and force them to Malta. Citing the war dangers, Montefiore decided that it would not be opportune to visit the condemned prisoners or to press his case in Damascus. He huddled with Briggs on a Saturday—making a note in his diary that, "in a case like this, where life and death are at stake, exertion and work [on the sabbath] are considered permissible"—to draw up a new plan. They decided to put aside the earlier request for a new investigation and instead appeal to Muhammad Ali to sign a firman that would announce the innocence and release of the prisoners and state his "disbelief that the Israelites committed murder for the sake of blood in their ceremonies."[14]

Crémieux, who had labored long and hard to obtain a limited version of the same outcome through Cochelet, dismissed Montefiore's new effort as quixotic: "A firman conceived on such lines . . . would condemn Sherif Pasha and Bahri Bey, [and] would be the most terrible accusation against Ratti-Menton. For his own sake and for that of Cochelet, the viceroy will never sign such a firman!" Montefiore, ignoring Crémieux's advice, sent a draft of the request to Muhammad Ali, only to have it summarily rejected.[15]

Publicly Muhammad Ali had dismissed the ultimatum of the great powers, but with Count Walewski still in Alexandria, and the consuls-general rushing daily to and from the pasha's divan, it was a field day for the war rumor mongers, especially when two large Austrian frigates anchored next to HMS *Bellerophon*, and HMS *Cyclops* began taking soundings outside the harbor.

The day after Muhammad Ali rejected the ultimatum of the great powers, Crémieux and Montefiore were received together at the viceroy's divan. It had been almost two weeks since they had presented their separate petitions and been promised a prompt reply. Samuel Briggs accompanied the delegation and reminded Muhammad Ali that the mission had been sent not just by England and France "but by the entire Jewish population of the world." The viceroy was not impressed. He assured the delegation that the prisoners in Damascus were being treated "humanely"—which contradicted the reports they had gotten from private sources—but admitted he had no answer to their petitions. "I have not thought much about it [the situation in Damascus]," he told them. "I have too many other matters at hand."[16]

Crémieux wrote in his journal that the whole mission was on the verge of going "up in smoke." In the desperate hope of salvaging at least something from the mission, he proposed a further concession to Cochelet, suggesting that the viceroy be invited to issue a firman renouncing the blood accusation and pronouncing the prisoners innocent, but with a clause that could obliquely suggest that "suspicion" had fallen on the two Jews who had died during interrogation in Damascus—Rabbi Leniado and Joseph Harari.

Montefiore had already expressed his disapproval of Crémieux's private negotiations with Cochelet, but Crémieux insisted on bringing up his proposal at a meeting of the entire mission. Everyone there opposed Crémieux's new proposal, not only Montefiore and his entourage but even Amélie Crémieux and Solomon Munk, Crémieux's own adviser. The meeting turned into a "violent dispute." Montefiore, assuming the idea of letting the two dead men bear the accusations came from Cochelet, declared adamantly that he would "never allow that any Jew committed the murder of Father Tomasso and his servant . . . from vengeance or any other motive." Such an admission, he argued, would invite talk everywhere that the Jews were in fact guilty and a repetition of "the same awful charges" against the Jews "over and over again."[17] We can only imagine Montefiore's reaction if he had been aware that the idea for the latest proposal was actually Crémieux's.

In fact, even Cochelet had no enthusiasm for the new proposal. "You'll never obtain it," he told Crémieux. "Perhaps a pardon for the prisoners, which might be possible if it could dampen the affair. Nothing more!" Crémieux told Cochelet that a pardon, with its implication of the guilt of the accused men, was unacceptable. With their stop-start negotiations at a standstill, Crémieux warned Cochelet that he was left with no options but extreme measures: he threatened to summon Ratti-Menton before the Council of State and to join von Laurin in defending the case against Picciotto, where the full testimony of the witnesses and the accused men, which had never been permitted in the cases of the men in prison in Damascus, could all be heard.[18]

Despite Muhammad Ali's public statements that he rejected the ultimatum from the great powers and the sultan, the city counted down the ten-day deadline he was allowed for an official response. Rumors circulated that British commodore Charles Napier, commanding a fleet off the coast of Lebanon with an invasion force of Albanian troops, had already intercepted transports carrying supplies to the Egyptian army in Syria. The consuls-general selectively shared the dispatches they received, adding to the war rumors. Samuel Briggs, whose banking business depended on stability, read the diplomatic signs and decided to leave for England.[19]

Montefiore and Crémieux decided to make a final attempt to salvage the mission. They drew up a new appeal, asking for nothing more than the liberation of the prisoners. Montefiore explained the move in a letter to London: "It was prompted solely by an anxious feeling to get the prisoners released ere hostilities commenced, being assured that after that event nothing could be done for them and that they might be left in prison exposed to sufferings . . . and as likely to end in their death when the protecting power of the consuls of England, Austria, Russia and Prussia was withdrawn." To lend the new petition authority, Crémieux and Montefiore circulated it among the diplomats in Alexandria for their signatures. Most signed, although some argued that the whole exercise was futile. The Neapolitan consul pointed out that Sherif Pasha was the viceroy's adopted son and that Muhammad Ali had raised him from the age of four and places "the greatest confidence in him." Why would the viceroy do anything against him? Besides, he added, "tortures are allowed by Turkish law."[20] Others, including the Prussian consul-general, also urged them not to submit the petition, arguing that it would only infuriate the viceroy. In the end they decided not to submit the petition. Dr. Loewe wrote that "the distress of Sir Moses was impossible to describe."[21]

Crémieux privately called on the viceroy on August 26 and 27. Muhammad Ali in earlier comments had been particularly impressed with the report that the alleged bones of Father Thomas had been found at the exact spot pointed out in the confessions of several of the accused men. Crémieux pointed out how easy it would be to stage such a discovery. The viceroy listened attentively but would concede nothing.

Crémieux, "without hope," decided to leave for Cairo with his wife the next day. He was a tourist on his first trip to the Middle East, and there was much that intrigued him, such as the sorry state of the schools in the Jewish communities.

Montefiore doggedly decided to stay "at his post."[22] Like the men held under death sentences in the pasha's dungeons in Damascus, ten days away by camel-train, there was nothing he could do but wait.

20

Muhammad Ali's Behind

B EFORE THE ADVENT of hygiene measures, sterile procedures, and effective antibiotics, a boil on the buttocks (or, as the physicians would describe it, an ischiorectal or perianal abscess) was a serious affliction. Rich and poor alike were susceptible to the embarrassing, painful, and dangerous abscesses. Even in the developed nations, as late as the first quarter of the twentieth century over 13 percent of the health claims for days off work were for ischiorectal abscesses. Lacking effective anesthetics or analgesics, the efforts of physicians to minister to boils were painful, often dangerous, and rarely effective. In 1836, when the Rothschild family gathered in Frankfurt for the gala wedding of Karl's daughter Charlotte and Nathan's son Lionel, Nathan Rothschild, the head of the British branch of the family, was suffering from what his wife described as "a disagreeable boil in a most inconvenient place." Six weeks later, after suffering terrible pain and despite treatment by the best German doctors, Nathan Rothschild was dead.[1]

At the end of August 1840, just when the deadline of the ultimatum demanding that the Egyptians give up Syria was due to expire, and when Moses Montefiore and Adolphe Crémieux were reaching a crescendo in their campaigns to persuade the viceroy to intervene in the case of the accused Jews in Damascus, Muhammad Ali was suffering the pain and indignity of a boil on his bottom. The weather was oppressively close that August, even in the shade of the viceroy's divan overlooking the Alexandria harbor, and the viceroy had to sit for long hours listening to the pleas and arguments of the endless stream of diplomats and petitioners. The pain of a posterior boil is persistent and sensitive to the slightest pressure; no amount of soft pillows could make the viceroy comfortable. Cochelet found him "very low, his voice feeble and broken." The boil was the talk of the cafes and the streets. A British diplomat wrote down the coarse jokes that were told about the viceroy's affliction and reported that a "common Bedouin" asked, "Are the Pasha's boils to trouble the peace of the world?" The complaint was an old one in the Ottoman world: in the sixteenth century the death of Sultan Selim I on the eve of an attack on Europe that had been two years in the planning had given rise to a Turkish proverb, "Yavuz Selim died of an infected boil and Hungary was spared."[2]

Muhammad Ali was under the care of two European physicians, Dr. Antoine Clot-Bey, a Frenchman, and Dr. Gaetani, an Italian. There was little they could do for the viceroy's boil besides applying compresses and ointments. The physicians were not political advisers, but they knew the viceroy's moods, whims, and his current thinking on the pressing issues of the day, and whenever he was being treated they had Muhammad Ali's ear. When they were not attending the viceroy, Clot-Bey and Gaetani, both European trained, gravitated to Crémieux's company, no doubt entertained by his eloquent conversation and his familiarity with politics and other current news from Paris.

By the end of August, whether because of the persistent discomfort of his affliction, fatigue at the relentless pressure of the diplomatic situation, a gradual awareness of the seriousness of the looming war against a coalition of the Ottoman Empire and the great powers, or the reality of seeing British and Austrian warships outside his harbor, Muhammad Ali was weary. On August 27, the day the ultimatum of the sultan and great powers expired, he announced to a large group of his counselors that he had changed his mind and was willing to forgo his claim to the hereditary rule of Syria. The next day he received Rifāt Bey and the consuls-general of the four great powers at his divan and told them that he accepted the terms of the second ultimatum: in return for the hereditary rule of Egypt, he was willing to give up his claims to the other territories he ruled, although he reserved the right to present a "humble plea" to the sultan asking for rule of Syria and Crete during his lifetime. He asked Rifāt Bey to convey his agreement to Constantinople, but the consuls-general of the four great powers insisted that a verbal surrender was not sufficient and that Muhammad Ali would have to demonstrate his acceptance of the treaty by withdrawing his army from Syria and by returning the Turkish fleet to Ottoman command. The consuls-general, wary lest their victory vanish in a change of mind as quick as the one that had led the viceroy to agree to the terms of the treaty, stayed at Rifāt Bey's side to make sure he did not depart for Constantinople before Muhammad Ali had agreed to their terms. The endgame negotiations went on for an entire day. The boil on the viceroy's behind had also reached a critical point, and he was especially uncomfortable.[3]

Cochelet, indignant because he was left out of the important negotiations, called it a "day of concessions." He explained the viceroy's shocking change of position as much by his low mood, brought on by the painful boil, as by his awareness of the looming threat of war.[4] In the end the French special envoy Count Walewski was designated to carry to Constantinople the message that Muhammad Ali had agreed to the sultan's terms. By having him also convey the threat that the Egyptian armies were poised to invade Anatolia if the viceroy's offer was not accepted, the French saved a measure of face in what had proved a disastrous diplomatic effort.

Early the next morning, on August 28, the physicians decided to lance the viceroy's boil. During the operation the conversation turned to the subject of the Damascus Jews, and Drs. Gaetani and Clot-Bey pointed out that with the international crisis in the Middle East at such a critical juncture, "the voice of six million Jews in your favor would be of great importance." Muhammad Ali suddenly announced, "I am going to grant the prisoners their liberty and permit the return of the fugitives. I shall be giving the necessary orders."[5]

As soon as they finished the operation, the two physicians rushed by horse-drawn cab for the Maḥmud canal, where Crémieux and his wife had already boarded the barge that would take them to Cairo. After the doctors boarded the barge and told Crémieux about their extraordinary conversation with the viceroy that morning, Crémieux changed his plans and decided to return to Alexandria. Aware that the viceroy was still in a delicate condition, and that after the intense diplomatic pressures of the recent weeks he might at any moment lose his resolve or reverse his position, Crémieux chose not to go to the serail and instead entrusted the two physicians with the responsibility of making sure that Muhammad Ali followed through on his promise to release the prisoners. Crémieux told the doctors to inform him as soon as the order had been drawn up. As a further insurance, Crémieux sent a note to Montefiore, passing along the good news and warning him to keep everything strictly confidential and that a visit to the palace "could ruin everything."

When he read Crémieux's note, Montefiore promptly assembled his advisers, Dr. Loewe, Wire, Madden, and Lady Montefiore. From Crémieux's note Montefiore assumed that the Frenchman and his wife had gone ahead to Cairo. He apparently felt safe in ignoring Crémieux's advice and rushing to the viceroy's palace.[6]

He arrived at the palace at two in the afternoon, was handed a beautiful pipe, and told to wait. Twenty minutes later he was told that the viceroy was leaving his room for the audience hall. From the doorway of the hall Montefiore saw Muhammad Ali smile and motion for him to enter and be seated.

Montefiore told the viceroy that he still wanted an answer to the petition he had presented in his first interview. Muhammad Ali then confirmed what Montefiore already knew from Crémieux's note, that he was planning to issue an order releasing all the prisoners in Damascus. Montefiore told the viceroy that he still wanted "to have the guilty punished" and that to that end he wanted a firman issued that would allow him to go to Damascus. The viceroy warned that the city was far too excited and the countryside too disturbed for safe travel, but Montefiore persisted, saying he wanted a firman that would permit him to travel there when conditions permitted. He did not raise the question of reopening the investigation, only his right to visit Syria. After the meeting, Montefiore wrote a note to Crémieux, assuming he was still in Cairo. He also reported the news of his meeting with Muhammad Ali to two leaders of the Alexandria Jewish community, Moses Valensino and Isaac Morpurgo, warning them to keep the news quiet until the proclamation the viceroy had promised was delivered.

Valensino and Morpurgo stopped by Crémieux's hotel to congratulate him. Crémieux, realizing that Montefiore had ignored his advice and would now claim all credit for the viceroy's decision, was furious. He ran to the palace, got an interview with the viceroy, and managed a flourish of uncharacteristic pleasantries and flattery of the sort that he normally would withhold even from the king of France at his birthday galas. Echoing the language the physicians had used that morning, he thanked Muhammad Ali in the name of "six million Jews scattered across the globe" and quoted Kléber's famous speech to Bonaparte. "You are as great as the world," he told Muhammad Ali. "You are as great as Napoleon."[7]

That evening—it was Friday night, and the Jewish sabbath had already begun—Crémieux went to Montefiore's hotel. Only Lady Montefiore was there, and she explained Sir Moses's conduct by the "political exigencies" that had so suddenly changed Muhammad Ali's mind, "and nothing else." Crémieux was reluctant to pursue the matter with her.

It was when Montefiore returned that the jealousy, distrust, and competition that had been brewing since mid-July found full vent. Pointing out that he had taken an active role in the Damascus case since early April, Crémieux credited the viceroy's doctors for their role in the recent events and accused Montefiore of being a passive bystander until there had been an opportunity to claim credit and glory. "You want to be an absolute master," he said. "Your vanity knows no bounds." He cursed the day he had sought Montefiore as a partner on the mission.

Montefiore answered that the real credit belonged to his friend Samuel Briggs. "You counted for nothing here," he told Crémieux. "Neither you nor your friends."

"Write to Europe if you dare," answered Crémieux. "Say that you and the English did everything. For my part, I shall write as well, describing all that has happened. Europe can decide between you and me."[8]

Later that evening Dr. Madden sought out Crémieux with consoling words, and enough peace was restored for Montefiore, Crémieux, and their wives to sit down to a polite dinner together. Montefiore's diary recorded of the evening only that it had been the sabbath with much coming and going. A month later he wrote in a letter that Crémieux had been "extremely angry" but that he gave "no reason for being so much displeased."[9]

On Saturday Drs. Loewe and Munk went to the palace to pick up copies of the viceroy's proclamation ordering the release of the Damascus prisoners and suspending the charges against the fugitives who had avoided arrest. Munk studied an Arabic version of the proclamation, Loewe had a Turkish version, and Crémieux read a French translation. One of the three men—all later claimed credit—discovered that the proclamation contained the term "pardon" (*afu* in Arabic or Turkish, *grâce* in French) which all agreed was totally unacceptable, since it implied that the imprisoned men and the fugitives were guilty. Crémieux ran to the palace to explain that the delegation would have to make a public protest unless the offending word were changed. The argument went on for a full hour until the viceroy agreed to substitute a Turkish term (*itlaq ve tervîhh*) that could be translated in English as "release."[10]

Montefiore, slower to get moving on the sabbath, had been about to set off to the palace with the same mission in mind when Crémieux showed up at his hotel, "praising and congratulating himself." Montefiore announced that "had I known it I should have been most indignant with the Pasha [Muhammad Ali] for inserting the word, it being in complete opposition to my request, as I would never, for an instant, admit any guilt, either of the living or the dead." The reference to "the dead" was a dig at the plan Crémieux had offered earlier. For good measure Montefiore then went to the palace, where he was told that the viceroy had already given the order to remove the objectionable word.[11]

The final step was a letter from the delegation to the Jewish community in Damascus reporting the good news. Montefiore agreed that they should write a joint letter when the sabbath was over to avoid the sabbath ban on writing. Crémieux discovered that despite the agreement Montefiore had already drawn up a letter, making certain that Crémieux's name would not be "joined to his in announcing the important news." Crémieux promptly wrote a letter of his own to the

Damascus community and dispatched it that night by government courier. "Mine," he gloated in his journal, "got a twenty-four hour head start—my reward and his just deserts."[12]

The story was not over. Muhammad Ali's order would have the condemned Jews released from their imprisonment at Sherif Pasha's palace in Damascus and the arrest orders for the fugitives vacated, but there was no official pronouncement against the charges of ritual murder. Although they were not tainted with the opprobrium of a pardon, the order had only liberated the prisoners. Until the prisoners and fugitives were officially declared innocent of the ritual murder charges, the Damascus Jewish community would have to live under the heinous blood libel.

On September 7, a week after the flurry of events that had led to the viceroy's proclamation releasing the imprisoned men, and long enough for the severest symptoms of the viceroy's boil to abate and leave him in a more receptive mood, Crémieux called at the palace. The aggravated split between Montefiore and Crémieux was no secret to Muhammad Ali, and Crémieux took advantage of the still-tense diplomatic situation and of the rumors of British and Egyptian fleet and troop movements to present himself as a Frenchman, an ally of Egypt and Muhammad Ali. He did not have to state the obvious, that Montefiore, as an Englishman, was on the other side of the dispute that was foremost in the viceroy's attention.[13]

Crémieux gave Muhammad Ali his own assessment of the military situation, that the combined Turkish and British forces were insufficient to invade Syria and that the most the British and Austrian fleets could muster would be a blockade of the Lebanese coast. The real outcome, the two men agreed, depended on the degree to which the French backed Egypt.

When the conversation turned to the Damascus affair, Muhammad Ali said he personally did not believe in the ritual murder accusations. But when Crémieux asked for a proclamation against the blood libel, the viceroy refused to commit himself. "Why should I put it in writing?" he said. "Do not involve me in this affair; I don't want to be involved in religious issues."

The next day, Montefiore and Crémieux visited the palace together to present a new petition to the viceroy. In addition to the usual encomiums of praise and gratitude, Montefiore had also insisted that the petition include a request for the abolition of the use of torture in Muhammad Ali's territories. Before they could present it, Montefiore learned that he would receive a gift of a granite column from the ancient temple of Serapis in Alexandria. He then handed the Turkish translation of the petition to the viceroy, who read a few lines and handed it to his secretary to read aloud. When the secretary came to the lines about torture, he "lowered his voice till he could hardly be heard." The viceroy then looked twice at his watch, and the delegation left without the viceroy uttering a single word on the subject of their visit.[14]

Crémieux was not willing to give up. The real goal of the mission had been a new trial for the accused men so that the absurd charges of ritual murder could be definitively proved false. The experienced advocate could no doubt picture himself arguing the case. When he had spoken about the issue, his eloquence had brought Madame Crémieux, who was generally insensitive to Jewish issues, and even Cochelet to tears. Crémieux could probably imagine himself arguing with the same persuasive eloquence to a judge, a courtroom audience, and the public who followed or read about the trial.

In Alexandria Crémieux had spoken frequently to Anton von Laurin, the Austrian consul-general who had himself pressed for a reopening of the trial. Once the viceroy's proclamation was secured, Crémieux wrote to Caspar Merlato, the Austrian consul in Damascus, to urge that when Muhammad Ali's proclamation released Isaac Picciotto from his protective custody in the Austrian consulate, Picciotto should draw up a formal complaint against the false charges that been brought and threaten to file a lawsuit for damages—which could be used to expose the paucity of evidence for the ritual murder charge. Crémieux also pondered the scheme of having von Lauren initiate a rearrest of Picciotto and Aaron Stambouli, the first an Austrian subject and the second a Tuscan, so they could be tried for murder and judicially exonerated.[15]

While Crémieux schemed for the public trial he had hoped for from the beginning of the mission, Montefiore contemplated the reception the reports about the mission would receive in Britain and in Europe. He continued to ask about conditions in Damascus and whether it was safe to travel there, pretending disdain for those, like Colonel Hodges, who cautioned him about the dangers of impending war. Publicly, he left the impression that despite any dangers, he was eager to leave for Damascus as soon as possible so he could personally see to the release of the imprisoned men. Privately, he told Crémieux that a visit to Damascus would be "not only a most rash and unwarrantable act, but almost an impossibility" but cautioned that they should "publicize widely that we are eager to go to Damascus and put up resistance to anyone who encourages us not to endanger ourselves. Then we'll be able to say that people were unwilling to let us go." In a letter to the Board of Deputies in London, Montefiore was equally candid on "the propriety of feeding the public mind . . . after all, it is London that must act upon the world, and through its press leave the imprint of its civilization, its liberal feeling and humanity upon the East."

Crémieux was appalled by Montefiore's obsession with his public image. "What is there to say about this hypocrisy?" he wrote in his journal. "What kind of wretch am I chained to?"[16]

21

Damascus, September 1840

THE SPECIAL government courier from Alexandria, the local equivalent of the pony express, arrived in Damascus on September 5.

The plague epidemic had temporarily abated, but the city was
still beset with "the usual maladies . . . fevers, ophthalmia and dysen-
teries" and buzzing with war rumors. Royal Navy commodore Napier
had appeared off the coast of Beirut on August 13 with four ships of
the line, later reinforced by the steam frigates *Castor* and *Gorgon*. On
August 14 he issued proclamations from his flagship the HMS
Powerful—a message to the diplomatic community and the British
merchants at Beirut "that Great Britain, Austria, Russia and Prussia
have decided that Syria is to be restored to the Porte" and an offer of
arms and ammunition to the Syrians so they could throw off their
Egyptian yoke. There had been reports of British marines and Turkish
soldiers landing on the Lebanon coast, of supply ships from Egypt
interdicted by Royal Navy ships, and a rumor that the British and
Austrian fleets were prepared to blockade Syria. For the first time
since early February the accused Jews were not the only subject of
Damascus cafe gossip.[1]

Sherif Pasha had sensed which way the desert breezes were blowing months before. The pasha's first loyalty was to his father, and he
unhesitatingly followed the orders in the proclamation the courier
brought from Alexandria. At eight in the morning on September 6, the
incarcerated Jews were released "in a most gracious manner," and the
search warrants for the fugitive Jews were vacated.

After six months in the pasha's dungeons, through the bitter cold of
a Damascus winter and the oppressive heat of summer, the prisoners
were filthy, their clothes rags. Their singed beards had grown back, but
other scars of their torture remained. Some of the men could hardly

195

walk; the untreated lacerations of their feet from the bastinado would never heal properly. David Harari had lost an ear, and many of the men had suffered crushed genitals with permanent consequences. Rabbi Salonicli's fingers were twisted and deformed.

Accompanied by crowds of Jews and Muslims, the liberated Jews went first to their synagogues, where "in unison with an immense multitude they prostrated themselves on the earth and prayed for peace and every blessing upon Muhammad Ali and all their other powerful benefactors." Before the same Holy Ark that Rabbi Antabi had dramatically thrown open in early February to first warn the community of the terrible crisis they faced, the released men blessed the God of Israel for their deliverance from the hands of their persecutors and prayed for the happiness of the pasha, "whose justice and humanity" had restored them to liberty.[2]

From the synagogue, they went home to their dwellings and families, which many had not seen for six months. Members of the Jewish community and Muslim merchants paid them visits of congratulation as the whole Jewish quarter broke out in a huge celebration. The names of Montefiore, Crémieux, and the Jewish leaders in Alexandria who had championed the cause were sung out in praise. Muslim visitors expressed their belief in the innocence of the accused men. A satiric puppet show was put on, mocking al-Talli, Father Thomas, and Ratti-Menton. Sherif Pasha tried to dampen the celebrations, but the invigorated crowds shouted, "Up with Austria! Down with France! Hurrah for the Ottomans! Down with the Cross!" Isaac Loria, who had been active on the case from the beginning, threatened to bring a legal action against Ratti-Menton for "full and complete satisfaction . . . for the injury done to the honor of the Jewish nation."[3]

The predictable exception to the celebration was the Christian community of Damascus, which, "forgetting the . . . most sacred precepts of their religion, remained silent and were even astounded." The Christian notables later offered their congratulations to the former prisoners, but Caspar Merlato thought their expressions insincere. Many Christians, and a few Muslims, came to the French consulate to find out what could have motivated the "incomprehensible" development, asking how Muhammad Ali, "without waiting for a French initiative," could have liberated men who had been "condemned . . . for the murder of a French protégé." No one was more shocked than the French consul, who only a few months before had been on the verge of a triumphant prosecution, enjoying his status and using his authority to press his advances on the women of the Jewish community. Ratti-Menton was especially galled when the Jewish community celebrated the good news at a gala garden party hosted by Caspar Merlato and attended not only by the liberated

Jews and other notables of the community but by Picciotto's beautiful young wife, Rebecca, and "several Jewesses."[4]

In Alexandria Dr. Madden had already left by steamer directly to England. Of Montefiore's entourage, Madden had always been the most sympathetic to Crémieux, and the Frenchman had reciprocated, acknowledging that Madden had "a good understanding" of Montefiore. Toward the other members of Montefiore's party, Crémieux was less sympathetic. He called Dr. Loewe a "valet who was with him [Montefiore] as his translator."[5]

The remaining members of the mission ate dinner together on September 12 after they received reports confirming the release of the prisoners in Damascus. Montefiore solemnly announced to Crémieux that nothing more could be gotten from the pasha and that with the foreign consuls leaving Egypt in anticipation of war, there was nothing else they could do until it was known whether Syria would be returned to the sultan. A visit to Damascus, he declared once more, would be "not only a most rash and unwarrantable act, but almost an impossibility."[6] Montefiore planned to leave Alexandria by the same French packet steamer that British consul-general Hodges was taking. En route to England Montefiore planned to make a stately tour to call on the sultan, the pope, and reigning monarchs to whom he would present the triumphant news of the success of the mission.

Crémieux agreed that there was nothing else to be accomplished in Alexandria. For months, since well before they arrived in the Egyptian capital, he had tried to persuade Montefiore that their cause was inextricably linked with the diplomatic issues that had pitted the sultan and the four great powers against Egypt and France. Now he had to listen politely while the phlegmatic Montefiore uttered the same assessment as if it were his own.

Their final joint activity was a letter of gratitude to Muhammad Ali. Unlike the petitions they had presented at the viceroy's divan, which had always brought to the fore their different perceptions of the situation and divergent tactics, this time the Englishman and the Frenchman could agree on the wording. Comparing Muhammad Ali's proclamation ordering the imprisoned Jews freed with the firmans of illustrious sultans, Christian princes, and "even popes," they wrote that "Your Highness has shown the world that you throw back with contempt the infamous calumny that our enemies wished to lay on the Jewish people . . . the shedding of human blood to mix with the unleavened bread—an accusation which would make our ancient and pure religion barbarous and sanguinary."[7] In fact, Muhammad Ali had done nothing of the sort. But it was convenient and artful to use the flattering phrases of a court petition to tie Muhammad Ali to the revocation of the charges of ritual murder he had refused to issue over his own signature. The letter was the last act of the joint mission.

Unlike Montefiore and his entourage, who as British subjects would have been uncomfortable in Alexandria after the British consular staff departed the city under the increasing threats of war, Crémieux, his wife, and Salomon Munk, as French subjects, were welcome to remain in Egypt. That suited Crémieux. Even before his arrival in Egypt he had been contemplating a second mission for the journey.

At one point during the long recesses between calls on the viceroy, Crémieux had visited a local Jewish elementary school. He was appalled at what he saw. The facilities, staff, and curriculum were unimaginably primitive. Children squatted on mats or on the bare soil, rocking themselves as they parroted verses from the Pentateuch, translating the phrases into Arabic without understanding what they were saying. "A little Hebrew, a little Arabic" were the only languages they learned; they were taught nothing of modern European languages like French and Italian and no mathematics, no geography and, for the girls, none of the domestic skills they would need to function in a modern economy.[8]

Crémieux was not the first to focus attention on the schools of the Ottoman Empire. In his fifteen years in Alexandria, Antoine Clot-Bey, the viceroy's physician and Crémieux's new friend and collaborator, had established a medical school and introduced public health reforms. He was part of a wave of French interest in Africa and the Middle East that blended aggressive colonialism and Saint-Simonian optimism. Engineers and entrepreneurs had come to Egypt to build canals and dams, doctors like Clot-Bey came with medical and organizational skills, and French industrialists explored the Egyptian market. Crémieux shared the French belief that their language, culture, literature, and history were the key to modernization and civilization. Montefiore believed that Crémieux had secretly brought 1,000 ducats from Baroness de Rothschild to Egypt for the purpose of establishing a school.

Crémieux spoke to leaders and the chief rabbis of the Jewish communities in Cairo and Alexandria about the idea of establishing new schools with modern, primarily European curricula and found surprisingly little opposition to the idea, especially when Crémieux suggested that half of the funding for the schools could come from contributions from the Jewish communities of Europe. Salomon Munk, with his fluency in Arabic and Turkish and knowledge of the region, was a key aide in the exploration of the idea, translating Crémieux's speeches and explaining that new schools with curricula of modern languages, mathematics, and science would ultimately enable the Jews of the East to enjoy the equality and privileges that the Jews of Europe had already gained. Crémieux suggested that Montefiore might interest himself in a parallel effort by establishing a hospital, but the Englishman answered that he would reserve his funds and efforts for the Holy Land.[9]

For Crémieux, a French patriot even as he criticized and attacked the excesses of the French administration in Damascus and the cover-up of the prosecution by the Quai d'Orsay and the Thiers government, the focus on French in the curricula of the new schools was the most important reform and innovation: by learning French language and history, and gaining access to French culture and technology, the students would no longer be isolated from the benefits of modern civilization. Crémieux believed the linguistic isolation of the Jews of the Ottoman Empire—some communities spoke only Judeo-Spanish (Ladino), and even in Arabic-speaking communities like Damascus, well-educated Jews like Rabbi Antabi often could not write or read Arabic—left the Jews of the East open to the charges of barbarism, isolation, and backwardness that ultimately led to heinous accusations like those that had been made in Damascus. When he had agreement for the establishment of a few new schools, Crémieux recruited a local board of prominent resident Frenchmen in Cairo to advise the school; Antoine Clot-Bey agreed to be a medical supervisor. To Crémieux's delight, the new schools were named after him. When he left Cairo to return to Alexandria, he was already planning how the Crémieux schools in Cairo could lead to the establishment of others in Aleppo, Alexandria, Damascus, and Jerusalem. "My name henceforth will be linked to a truly useful enterprise of immense significance," he wrote in his journal.[10]

With the school project established, Crémieux got ready to sail from Alexandria on his way home. As a final gesture, he paid 10,000 francs each to Clot-Bey and Gaetani for their help in putting the case of the Damascus Jews before Muhammad Ali. Clot-Bey told Crémieux that to have secured more than the release of the Jews would have required considerable baksheesh, at least 500,000 francs and a campaign of at least half a year at the viceroy's divan. "Sir Moses' haste spoiled everything," Clot-Bey said.

On October 7 Adolphe and Amélie Crémieux and Salomon Munk boarded a steamer for the journey home. Their route was circuitous: the Syrian coast, Athens, Corfu, and Trieste by ship then overland to Venice, Vienna, Frankfurt, Mainz, and finally Paris. They were quarantined in Syria and Trieste, where plague fears were still rampant, but everywhere they landed the local Jewish communities feted them with celebratory dinners, speeches, special services in the synagogues, gifts, songs, poetry, testimonials, and proclamations to the glorious achievements of the mission to the East. In most of the communities the synagogues were too small to hold all who came to honor Crémieux, and crowds ended up filling the streets. When their carriage left Trieste, a parade escorted them from the city. In Vienna Crémieux met with Metternich and was banqueted, serenaded, and presented with a cylindrical box of solid gold encircled with diamonds and inscribed "To the worthy champion of his persecuted brethren." (The box was later estimated to be worth 14,000 florins [30,000 francs]). The Jewish community of Vienna, and communities in cities he did not visit, like Prague and Nikolsburg, conferred on him the august title of *Morenu* ("our teacher"), traditionally reserved for the most distinguished of rabbis.[11]

Famed as an orator long before the mission, Crémieux gave speeches in many cities, proclaiming the triumph of the mission, which had been "crowned with success [as the] chains fell away [and] the prisons released the victims of torture," and the future that the new Jewish schools in Egypt would provide as they brought "the cause of civilization and progress to those lands of ignorance and fanaticism." Only a few detractors shied away from Crémieux's celebratory procession. In a few cities where the younger generation treated his arrival as the impetus for public rallies, the older generation cautiously wanted to avoid antagonizing the government or the local Christian citizenry. Some conservative Jewish leaders were also put off by Crémieux's self-promotion and aggressive secularism. "The little man [Crémieux] has a great dose of vanity," Anselm Rothschild wrote from Frankfurt. "Here they want to give him public dinners, but I am decidedly against any public demonstration."[12]

Never one to be outdone, Montefiore mounted his own triumphal procession home after leaving Alexandria. From his earliest negotiations with Muhammad Ali, Montefiore had been frustrated with both the difficulties of dealing with an obstreperous ally of France and with what he saw as the provincialism of the court in Alexandria. He would have preferred to negotiate with the sultan in Constantinople, where his uniform and rank would be received with greater deference and respect and where he would have been negotiating with a formal ally of England instead of Muhammad Ali and his French advisers. At one point during a lull in the negotiations, he even planned an early departure on HMS *Cyclops*. Crémieux claimed credit for talking Montefiore out of leaving.[13]

The Montefiores, with Wire and Dr. Loewe, sailed from Alexandria in mid-September, departing on the same day as the British consul-general. Their ship was bound for Constantinople via Syra, in the Aegean, where they stopped for quarantine. On the condition that they and their servants took baths, changed all of their clothes, had their luggage fumigated with pots of burning sulphur, and followed a physician's directions to strike themselves with a fist under each arm and elsewhere on their bodies, their quarantine was truncated from the exhaustive measures usually imposed during plague epidemics.[14]

In Constantinople Montefiore was received with the pomp and flourishes he craved. Abraham Camondo, the wealthy financier and Jewish shtadlan, allowed Montefiore the use of one of his houses in the Galata area. There Montefiore received members of the local Jewish community and visitors to the city, including Isaac Picciotto, who was on his way to Paris to press charges against Ratti-Menton, and Haim Nissim Abulafia, the father of Rabbi Moses Abulafia. Montefiore's priority was an audience with the sultan. When Montefiore met with the British ambassador to the Porte, Lord Ponsonby, he suggested that he would ask the sultan for what Muhammad Ali had persistently denied him: a firman formally denouncing the accusations of ritual murder against the Damascus Jews. Ponsonby, aware of Palmerston's notion of extending British protection over the Jews of the Ottoman Empire as a counterweight to French protection of the Catholics, was amenable to the idea and arranged for Montefiore to meet with Rashid Pasha, the architect of the Anglo-Turkish alliance "who would perhaps be able to forward his wishes."[15]

Montefiore's timing was fortuitous. Before and during his stay in Constantinople, there were reports of British victories over Ibrahim Pasha's forces in skirmishes in Lebanon. The Ottoman Empire, eager to reassert its authority over Syria, was also eager for international loans. Montefiore assured Rashid Pasha that he had no authority to conduct financial negotiations and that the most he could promise was to look into matters when he returned to England, but with his relationship to the Rothschild family well known, and his elaborate uniforms and extended entourage, he had the trappings of a man who could get things done.[16]

Montefiore's audience with the sultan was arranged for October 28, during Ramadan. Montefiore recorded every detail of the formal procession and ceremony in his diary, describing the cavalcade of "one carriage with four horses and one with two horses," the six heavily armed guards (*kavasses*) and the eight men carrying "large wax torches," the two horsemen with each coach, the sedan accompanying each, and "three men to close the procession." The carriages could not drive up to his door in the hilly Galata area, so he was carried in a sedan chair to the foot of the hill while the rest of his entourage walked. Montefiore, of course, wore his "full uniform" for the audience in the grand hall where the sultan was seated "on a sofa, wearing a violet cloak, fastened at the neck with two clasps of the finest diamonds." The light in the receiving room was too dim for Montefiore to read, so he recited his speech from memory, praising the sultan, calling the Jewish people "the most peaceful and loyal subjects [who] by their industry have augmented the . . . prosperity of the countries in which they live," and asking for a proclamation against the ritual murder charges in Damascus. The preparatory efforts with Rashid Pasha had gone well. The sultan listened to the Turkish translation of the speech and assured Montefiore that the request would be granted.

Ten days later a draft of the sultan's firman was delivered to Montefiore. Written on thick parchment in florid calligraphy, the proclamation declared that a careful examination of Jewish beliefs and religious books had demonstrated that the charges against the Jews were "pure calumny" and proclaimed that "the Jewish nation shall possess the same privileges as are granted to the numerous other nations who submit to our authority. The Jewish nation shall be protected and defended."[17]

The firman actually cited the blood libel in Rhodes rather than the Damascus case, but Montefiore considered it a triumph, calling the firman "the Magna Carta for the Jews in the Turkish dominions." He and Dr. Loewe gave speeches in Constantinople about education and the future of the Jewish communities—as if Montefiore was determined to compete with Crémieux even on this—with Dr. Loewe on one occasion speaking at one of the large synagogues for three hours in Hebrew, Italian, Spanish, and German. When they finally boarded their ship to leave Constantinople on the night of November 7, a crowd of hundreds gathered to salute Montefiore.[18]

Before his arrival in Constantinople, Montefiore had announced that he hoped it would be only a short time before the diplomatic and war crisis resolved itself and "that Damascus will speedily own the Sultan for its lord; if so, we have a special firman from him to proceed thither with ample power and protection." As with his many earlier announcements of his eagerness to go to Damascus, this too seemed mostly a public relations effort. When Montefiore's ship left the Turkish capital, he was bound not for Damascus but for Naples, armed with copies of the sultan's firman translated into Greek, Arabic, and Hebrew that he hoped to present to dignitaries and world leaders as a symbol of the success of the mission. The competition with Crémieux and the portrayals of him and the mission in the press were still foremost in Montefiore's concerns. "I feel satisfied that you will not let the French run away with the honor due to our country and fellow citizens," he wrote to London, "nor allow the *Times* to give the world reports *ex parte* to implicate the Jews, or to show they were pardoned only, or that there was a spontaneous act of the pasha [Muhammad Ali] done without the urgent solicitation or without the necessity of the mission."[19]

In Malta, where he was briefly quarantined, Montefiore learned that a tomb had been erected for Father Thomas in the Capuchin monastery in Damascus with the hateful Italian epitaph claiming that Father Thomas had been "murdered by the Jews 5 February 1840." The Arabic version of the epitaph was even more accusatory:

Façade of the tomb of Father Thomas	Capuchin. He fulfilled his charge
As an apostolic missionary to Syria	Preaching and displaying his solicitude.
Jews slaughtered him	His perfection did not avail him
On the fifth of Isbāṭ	Here are the remains of his bones.

Dated the year 1840[20]

The indictments in stone gave Montefiore's mission a new focus: he decided that he would proceed to Rome to appeal to Pope Gregory XVI to have the epitaphs removed and to issue a formal proclamation against the ritual murder accusations.

The papacy had given no encouragement on the matter. As early as July Montefiore knew that the pope and his government were "extremely" against the Jews and believed in the murder, and en route to Alexandria he wrote in his diary: "The Christians seem to believe if the Jews [are] innocent, then the Christians must be guilty of conspiring against them. God help us." But Dr. Loewe knew the history of blood libel accusations well enough to remind Montefiore that in earlier centuries other popes had issued bulls condemning accusations against the Jews. Armed with the sultan's firman, Montefiore determined to obtain the same declaration from Gregory XVI.[21]

Despite breakdowns of his carriage and other travails—Sir Moses and Lady Montefiore were not easy travelers—Montefiore and his party made it to Rome, where he spread his calling cards widely and took advantage of the social life of the city. He attended the opera in the box of Prince Torlonia, in the presence of the Queen of Spain and the Duchess of Cambridge. But despite his efforts at ingratiating himself, the pope, and even the pope's secretary of state, Cardinal Lambruschini, refused to see Montefiore. The British representative Mr. Aubin met with a Vatican official and reported that "the people about the Pope were persuaded that the Jews had murdered Father Tomasso and even if all the witnesses in the world were brought before the Pope to prove the contrary, neither he nor his people would be convinced." Montefiore could not even get a written petition delivered to the pope;

Cardinal Lambruschini had one of his servants return it with a note saying that he had read the papers "but he had nothing to do with them."[22]

Montefiore's anxieties in Rome were increased by the communications he had received from London. The *Times* had taken the mission to task for not going to Damascus, and there was widespread talk and commentaries that what the mission had achieved was closer to a pardon than an exoneration of the accused Jews, that Muhammad Ali's firman had left the ritual murder charges unresolved and the accused men in a limbo. Even the Board of Deputies, now under a new president, had declared the necessity of Montefiore proceeding to Damascus in spite of his reports to them that senior officers of the Royal Navy had warned him that travel to Syria for the foreseeable future would be "madness."[23]

In the face of the criticism and questions about his mission, Montefiore determined to achieve a victory on the issue of the objectionable tombstone epitaph in Damascus. He obtained an appointment with the Cardinal Protector of the Capuchin order, Agostino Rivarola, and began his meeting by bringing up the firman from the sultan declaring the Jews innocent of the charges of ritual murder. The cardinal agreed that the firman was an important document, "even if it cost Rothschild's fortune." Montefiore, indignant at the accusation, answered that he had not given a "sudi to any person" and that "the high and important office I filled in my community was a sufficient guarantee of my character." The cardinal was not impressed. When Montefiore suggested that Father Thomas might still be alive in one of the monasteries in Lebanon, the cardinal laughed. As to Montefiore's request that the epitaph on Father Thomas's tomb be removed, the cardinal said he would look into the matter but could not order it, since "the convent was under the protection of French authority."[24]

Montefiore had one more chance to polish the perceptions of his mission. In mid-February he, Lady Montefiore, and Dr. Loewe arrived in Paris, where the British ambassador arranged for Montefiore to be received by the king. Montefiore was too fatigued from traveling to eat, but he eagerly dressed in his "full uniform" and went to the palace, where he and Dr. Loewe were escorted into the presence of the king and the royal family.[25]

Louis-Philippe was his usual droll self but well briefed, or quick witted, enough to mock the ponderous Montefiore. When Montefiore proudly handed him a copy of the sultan's firman, Louis-Philippe said he was glad to receive it, then asked Montefiore if he had been in Damascus, leaving it to the feckless Montefiore to explain why he had not traveled there. When Montefiore explained that the sultan considered the accusations against the Jews nothing more than a "calumny," the king answered that he "was happy it is so," adding that he had agreed to receive Montefiore on short notice lest he detain the Englishman in Paris "longer than I wished." Montefiore, serene in his uniform and the surroundings of the king's private reception, seemed oblivious to the irony in the King's comments. Later, when a member of the Chambre began to "rail against Monsieur Thiers," Montefiore stopped him, saying "the result of my mission had been so completely successful I was desirous of having everything of an unpleasant nature forgotten."[26] The last statement was almost certainly true.

Montefiore reached London at the end of February 1841, seven and a half months after the mission departed for Alexandria and three months after he had obtained the firman from the sultan. It had been more than a year since the first reports of the disappearance of Father Thomas, and the Damascus affair had faded from the British papers. Even the criticisms of the mission for failing to go to Damascus and the suggestions that what the mission had secured sounded suspiciously like a pardon of the accused men without a firm local declaration of their innocence had been forgotten, or at least put aside, in the press. Within the Jewish community there was discussion of establishing a seminary in honor of Montefiore's mission, but the Jewish leadership in Britain settled for a special service in the Portuguese synagogue on the day after Purim, March 9, and the presentation of a silver centerpiece, over forty inches tall and weighing 1,319 ounces, topped with a representation of David rescuing a lamb from a lion, and bearing an inscription describing the mission.[27] Lady Montefiore's contributions are acknowledged in the inscription; Crémieux is not mentioned.

Later, at a private levee at St. James Palace, with Lord Palmerston present, Montefiore presented Queen Victoria with a facsimile and translation of the firman from the sultan. The Queen, "being desirous of giving an especial mark of our royal favor" and "in commemoration of these his unceasing exertions on behalf of his injured and persecuted brethren in the East and the Jewish nation at large," granted Montefiore the exceptional distinction of supporters (figures on either side of the shield) on his personal coat of arms.[28]

Epilogue

THE WAR was short. Ibrahim Pasha's armies had easily defeated the much larger Ottoman armies a decade before, but he seemed overwhelmed by the combination of Druse and Maronite revolts on Mount Lebanon, British and Albanian troops landing on the Lebanese coast under General Napier, and shelling from the British fleet. The sight of British men-of-war and frigates offshore seemed to awaken memories that reached back to Lord Nelson and gave courage to the local revolt. British admiral Stopford fired his first volleys on Beirut on September 9, 1840, while Montefiore was still in Alexandria. By October 10 the city had fallen to the British. A month later Acre was captured.

Ibrahim Pasha fell back with his army of sixty thousand to eighty thousand men in a brilliant retreat. A reformer even in defeat, after Sherif Pasha and the Egyptian regime withdrew from Damascus, Ibrahim Pasha assembled the notables of the city and had them elect a temporary civil governor pending the appointment of a new governor by the sultan. With Sherif Pasha gone, those who had cast their fates with the Egyptians fled. Al-Talli claimed he had been driven out by "the hatred of the Jews." Count Ratti-Menton remained at his post as French consul; the Quai d'Orsay would not admit defeat by transferring him. When opportunity presented itself, like New Year's Day or the celebration of the official birthday of the king of the French, Ratti-Menton dressed in his official uniform and led a procession of the Catholics to the Latin Convent of Terra Sancta on Monastery Street. The Arabs said of his gaudy uniform that he was "dressed like a king."[1]

Ratti-Menton was playacting. The release of the incarcerated Jews was only one element of the tremendous diplomatic defeat the French had suffered as Muhammad Ali gave up his territories in Syria and the Arabian peninsula and was forced to beg the sultan to allow him to continue as viceroy of Egypt. Premier Thiers also paid the price for his adherence to the toothless alliance with Egypt. In October 1840 King Louis-Philippe, true to the warnings his ministers had given Muhammad Ali, decided against committing French ships and troops to the defense of a greater Egypt, and Thiers was sacked, to be replaced by his predecessor Marshal Soult. Public opinion, especially on the right, was outraged by the French humiliation, but there were many who welcomed the peace that followed the short war, and a chance for French business interests to advance where the diplomats had retreated. Baron James de Rothschild especially was delighted. Heine wrote that "the prophets of the stock exchange, who know exactly how to decode the facial expressions of the great baron [Rothschild], assure us that the swallows of peace are nesting in his smile. . . . Even the baron's sneezes, they add, speak of peace."[2]

The Quai d'Orsay could only try to save face. In May 1841 des Meloizes finished the final report of his inquiry into the Damascus affair with predictable conclusions. In five hundred manuscript pages of testimony, exhibits, and summary, he blamed the Austrians and the British for elevating a simple murder case into a cause célèbre, noted that the accused Jews had never fully recanted their original testimony, and, in a slight mitigation of the original charges of ritual murder, concluded that the murder of Father Thomas and his servant could only be explained as acts of "fanaticism." Des Meloizes tried to characterize Muhammad Ali's decree as a pardon that implied the guilt of the accused Jews, but by 1841 much of the world had already read about the sultan's firman declaring the Jews innocent.[3]

Shortly after the appearance of des Meloizes's report, Count Ratti-Menton was made a chevalier of the Order of St. Maurice and St. Lazare, recalled to Paris, and then quietly transferred to a consular post in Canton in recognition of "his firm probity in Damascus"—despite the objections of Rothschild and others who questioned his fitness to serve in the diplomatic corps. From Canton Ratti-Menton wrote letters and petitions to justify his actions in Syria. He was soon accused of corruption and involvement in a smuggling operation there and had to be recalled after an aggravated dispute with the French attaché in Macao. In 1855 Ratti-Menton was posted as consul in Havana. There his name was connected with corruption in the tobacco trade, and he was forced to leave that final post after it was discovered that he had been involved in the departure of a slave ship. The scandals that marked his later career did not prevent Ratti-Menton from retiring from the diplomatic corps as an officer of the Légion d'Honneur.[4]

The period from 1843 to 1846, when Ratti-Menton was in Paris waiting for a new diplomatic assignment, preceded the publication of a highly edited version of the procès verbal of the investigation and trials in Damascus. The author of the edition was listed as Achille Laurent, with no affiliation other than the *Société Orientale*, and claimed that he was able to collect these documents during his long residence in the East. It seems probable that Ratti-Menton, perhaps with assistance from Beaudin, produced the edition.[5] Ratti-Menton may also have had a hand in the editing of the dossiers of documents that were destined for the Quai d'Orsay archives. Even today they are filed between dividers bearing the notation: "Affaire de P. Thomas de Damas, assassiné par des israélites indigènes."

After his triumphant return to France, Adolphe Crémieux continued to play an active role in the Central Consistory and in the newly founded Alliance Israélite Universelle, which aggressively pursued a program of raising and directing funds and expertise toward the establishment of schools for the Jewish communities of the Ottoman Empire. The new schools were similar in concept to the schools Crémieux had promoted while he was in Alexandria and Cairo, with curricula featuring French and other European languages, written Arabic and Hebrew, mathematics, science, and domestic skills for young women. The schools bearing Crémieux's name all closed within a few years, but the Alliance schools thrived and had major impacts on the Jewish communities of the East, including the gradual replacement of Ladino by French in many Jewish communities and openings of trade, cultural, and educational opportunities for Jews who had previously been isolated by language as well as their minority status.[6]

In 1845 Amélie Crémieux, who had always been suspicious of the Jewish leaders and was especially intolerant of Montefiore's insistent observance, decided to convert their children to Christianity. Crémieux gradually drifted away from formal involvement with Jewish community organizations in Paris, although he never gave up his commitment to the causes of the Jewish community. In the contentious politics of the Second Empire and the Third Republic, he could not escape the legacy of his role in the Damascus affair. In 1870, when Crémieux served as minister of justice, he was accused by an ally of the notorious anti-Semite Henri Desportes of hiding the archives pertaining to the Damascus affair to suppress the truth about the Jewish ritual murders.[7]

Across the Channel Montefiore basked in the glory of his newly awarded honors, watching from his Park Lane home as the British took advantage of the Anglo-Turkish victory against Muhammad Ali to advance their own agenda in the Middle East. Palmerston was only one of many in Britain who had long dreamt of a British presence in the Holy Land. The most ambitious efforts, like Prussian and British plans to put Jerusalem, Bethlehem, and Nazareth under the control of European powers, had to be curbed in the face of the jealous rivalries of the Orthodox, Catholic, and Protestant interests in Jerusalem and the sultan's own ambitions. But the brief vacuum after the Egyptians left was long enough to allow the London Society to complete their ambitious plan for a major church on Mount Zion as a focus for their efforts to convert the Jews. The new church was Anglican in orientation, with a Hebrew rite and a converted Jew, Michael Solomon Alexander, as the bishop of the new Jerusalem diocese.

Nine years after the Damascus affair, Montefiore finally visited Damascus. The occasion was another blood libel accusation, but this one was simpler, and before Montefiore reached the Middle East, the alleged victim was found alive in Baalbek. Montefiore still journeyed from plague-infested Tiberias to Damascus, where his main interest was to record the inscriptions that were still on the Capuchin tomb of Father Thomas.[8] The assurances about the tomb he had campaigned for in Rome had come to naught, and it was clear that there was no hope of a reopened inquiry into the disappearance of Father Thomas.

Life had changed irrevocably for the Jews of Damascus. Some families had fled to Aleppo, Jerusalem, or Cairo, cities with relatively large Jewish communities and without memories of the terrifying accusations of ritual murder. Of those who stayed, many were scarred with wounds that would not heal—souvenirs of the bastinado, the tourniquet, and months of constant fear. Even those who had not been tortured in the dungeons could not easily shake off the crippling insecurity bred by months of hiding and brutal confrontations with Christian mobs in the streets and suqs. Those who had once considered their homes sanctuaries from the terrors of the city now had to live with a permanent sense of vulnerability, a constant awareness that their homes, communities, and persons could again be violated by the pasha's troops and police. The Street Called Straight had become a no man's land between the Jewish and Christian quarters of the city.

The dynamic of the city had changed. Conquerors had come and gone for centuries, indeed millennia, in Damascus. The resilient social fabric of the city had always been able to absorb another reversal. It should have been especially easy to adapt to the return of the once-familiar Ottoman rule, but the bitter hostilities of the accusations against the Jews had left too many raw edges. The swift changes imposed by the new Ottoman governor, Najib Pasha, nurtured instead of smoothed the competitions and antagonisms.

Some of the changes imposed by the new governor were immediate and highly visible. Raphael Farhi was restored to the position of head sarraf and quickly reestablished himself as controller of the pasha's finances and as a leading banker in the city. At his counting house Christian and Jewish clerks once again sat cross-legged on the floor around him as he stood by a great chest, accepting funds due to the sultan and payments on the loans he made to peasants. He and the new governor became partners in maintaining the exchange between piastres and gold; a public crier stood in the street outside Farhi's counting house announcing the exchange rate.

The new governor also lost no time in reintroducing the pre-Egyptian regulations that forbade Christians wearing a white turban, mounting a horse in the city, or girding themselves with a cord instead of a sash or shawl. Although the sultan's Gülhane Decree had declared that the minorities of the empire were to enjoy the full rights of citizens, the new governor in Damascus announced that Christians with petitions were not to gather outside the serail because the sight of infidels early in the morning affected his digestion. The Christian community blamed the oppressive new rulings on Jewish agitation and lobbying.[9]

In March 1841 Raphael Farhi hosted a dramatic victory celebration to salute the officers of the victorious Anglo-Turkish forces. The inner courtyard of his palatial Damascus home was specially illuminated for the occasion, as the guests drank toasts to Queen Victoria, Montefiore, and the Austrian emperor—Crémieux had been forgotten—and were entertained by a concert of Oriental music. A British officer named Major Charles Henry Churchill gave a rousing speech announcing that "the hour of Israel's deliverance" was near at hand, when the Jewish nation would "once more claim her rank among the power of the world . . . [and that] the descendants of the Maccabees will yet prove themselves worthy of their illustrious ancestors." The audience shouted "*Inshallah!*"[10] Churchill's speech was directed toward Protestant evangelical support of the Jews in the Holy Land, but to the Christian community of Damascus it no doubt sounded like a revelation of the conspiracy between the local Jews and the European nations they had long feared.

The social truce in Damascus had always been delicate, woven on the warp of the roles of each group within the social and economic hierarchies of the city. The Muslim notables had been contemptuous of commerce, regarding the haggling of the suqs with unconcealed disdain as they left merchant activities to the Christians and Jews. As long as the ascendancy of the Muslim majority remained unchallenged and the minorities took care not to offend Muslim sensitivities, and the relative isolation of the city kept the temptations of European commerce and culture at bay, the jealousies, resentments, and misunderstandings between the Muslims and minorities were held in check by the rigid overlay of manners and conventions. The acceptance of Arabic and Turkish as the languages of the streets, Muslim calendars and time keeping, and traditional Arab dress kept the peace.

The Egyptian occupation, with the accompanying ascendancy of the Greek Catholics, had stretched the social fabric. The sound of Christian church bells, the sight of parades of the cross through the streets, and the flaunting of once-forbidden codes of dress and manners brought long-suppressed resentments to the fore. What the minorities saluted as enlightened reforms—the removal of old sumptuary laws, limits on the privilege of riding horses or carrying arms in the city, and restrictions on public religious festivals—undermined what the Muslims had seen as symbols of the unity of the Islamic state, faith, and law. The Christians could argue that Muslims were not forced to drink wine from the newly allowed wine shops in the suqs, but for the Muslims an encouragement of what was forbidden in the Qur'an was blasphemy and a direct affront to Allah.

Increased trade and cultural commerce with Europe brought on by the introduction of steamships and the 1838 Anglo-Ottoman trade agreement stretched the social fabric in other dimensions, introducing a flood of European goods, merchants, and culture to a city that had once known only the great hajj caravans. The new commerce chipped away at the security of the Muslim community as Muslim notables who had long been contemptuous of merchant enterprise saw fortunes made that ultimately dwarfed their once-lucrative land and property holdings. Once fear for their own economic and social security and future goaded the Christians of Damascus toward open attacks on their rivals in the Jewish community, and the rituals of polite greetings and marketplace bargaining were replaced by the horrifying accusations of ritual murder, all the sultan's horses and all the sultan's men could not put the torn fabric together again.

The Damascus Montefiore visited in 1849 was still uneasy. The celebrations of the release of accused men from the Sherif Pasha's dungeons, the garden parties, and the victory celebration at Raphael Farhi's house, along with the 1849 British instruction to consuls in the Ottoman Empire to extend their protection to Jews, kept the antagonisms of 1840 alive. But as Muslims entered the commercial life of the city, competing openly with Christian and Jewish merchants and the lingering political ascendancy of the Christian minority, the principal axis of confrontation shifted from the rivalry of the Christians and Jews to a new and more bitter rivalry between Muslims and Christians. A Jewish traveler wrote that "the Muslims and Jews do not hate each other . . . but to the

Christians the Muslims bear hate." In the eyes of the Muslims, the Jews had been humble and discreet, while the Christians were resented for the privileges they had flaunted during the Egyptian occupation, for their formal alliances with the European powers, and for their blatant cooperation with the foreign consuls. To the extent that European intervention and trade was blamed for the woes of the economy and the disruption of the social and cultural hierarchies in the city, the local Christian communities, who had always been identified with the European powers, became the focus of blame.[11]

If Montefiore noticed the tensions in the city, he did not record his observations. But only a year after his visit, in 1850, riots broke out between the Muslims and Christians in Aleppo. Six years later similar riots followed in Nablus. Both were rehearsals for the terrible riots that swept through Damascus in 1860 as the Muslim majority vented itself on the Christian minority, pouring out a deadly venom bred of the fears and resentments of the commercial dominance of the Greek Catholics and their usurpation of the social roles and prestige of the Muslim notables. The Jews were left untouched in these riots, while Christians were massacred by the thousands, their houses, churches, and businesses plundered and torched. The final death toll was between thirty-five hundred and six thousand. Even the Capuchin monastery that housed the supposed tomb of Father Thomas was destroyed.[12]

If the struggle of the Muslims against the Christians displaced the accusations and legal proceedings against the Jews in Damascus cafe talk, outside the city the story of the Damascus blood libel would not go away. The victims of the Damascus accusations were quickly forgotten, as their wounds and injuries became one more instance of the crippled limbs and deformed extremities that travelers never failed to mention on their return from the East. But the accusations lived on. As the economies of the Ottoman Empire were opened to competition with the world, and Jews were associated with the newly competitive economies, the pattern of Damascus, where the Christians had put aside their internecine battles to form a bloc against the Jews, repeated itself. The Greeks and Armenians aimed blood libel accusations against the Jews of Palestine in 1847, 1848, 1870, and 1871. In Egypt the Muslims joined the Christians in the accusations: a Muslim accusation of blood libel in Cairo in 1844 was followed by a Greek Orthodox accusation in Alexandria in 1846. The accusations spread even beyond the Ottoman Empire. In Hamadan in western Iran eighteen Jews were massacred in 1866 after being accused of ritual murder; two other Jews were burned alive; many others escaped the violence only by converting to Islam. There were incidents in Alexandria in 1870; Smyrna in 1871 and 1873; Damanhur (Egypt) in 1871, 1873, and 1877; and Mansura in 1877.

A blood libel accusation in Aleppo in 1876 was so serious that the sultan sent troops to guard the Jewish quarters in Smyrna and Constantinople. In some of the later accusations, local Muslims extended the formerly Christian symbolism of the myth by accusing the Jews of kidnapping a Muslim child to use its blood for matzo.[13]

Even in societies where enlightened minds had long dismissed the myth of Jewish ritual murder as barbarous humbug, and where Jews were welcomed into the political, social, economic, and cultural life of modern states, the Damascus affair revived ancient debates.

Jewish historians used the episode to celebrate the collective rallying of the Jewish people and to trace the development of Jewish identity that pointed toward triumphs in the struggle for Jewish rights in established states and to Zionism. Chapters in histories of the Jewish people showcased the episode as a triumph of the selfless organization culminating in the mission to the East, where, with the assistance of well-meaning Christians, the looming specter of hatred, prejudice, and ignorance was vanquished in a glorious victory of reason and truth over barbarity and falsehood.[14]

But the struggle against hatred, prejudice, and ignorance was far from over. Even as Jewish historians wrote their optimistic texts, polemicists from across the political spectrum used the Damascus affair as fodder for ferocious anti-Semitic tracts. German theologians offered the Damascus accusations as evidence that Judaism retained human sacrifice as a ritual. Polemicists from both the Far Left and the Far Right used the theologians' arguments to justify opposition to Jewish emancipation and even to the entire Judaeo-Christian religious tradition. The publication of the Damascus trial protocols in French in 1846,[15] followed by an Italian edition in 1850,[16] provided a wealth of documentation for the polemicists, who proved as adept at selective quotation from the protocols as a previous generation had been at selectively quoting the Talmud. "Who would have imagined that certain fanatics use human blood to moisten their holy unleavened bread?" one New York newspaper wrote in reporting the "rediscovery" of the "mysteries of the Talmud." "Notwithstanding . . . all these [endeavors] on the part of Mr. Rothschild and the Jewish nation, to bury this horrid deed in obscurity, the original copy of the trial has been preserved . . . and will shortly come before the public in the shape of a book, illustrated with the portrait of the two unhappy martyrs, and other engravings, representing some of the horrible scenes of this murderous sacrifice on the altar of religious atrocity."[17]

In the 1860s and 1870s the growth of liberalism, socialism, Darwinism, and German and Italian nationalism spurred a wave of conservative reaction that was often quick to cite blood libel accusations as yet another proof of the profound threat of these supposedly "Jewish" movements. Richard Burton, the famous traveler and explorer, served briefly as British consul in Damascus in 1869–71. He had previously written, "Had I a choice of race there is none to which I would more willingly belong than the Jewish." Once in Damascus he spent his time with the Algerian master-Sufi Abd al-Kader al-Jazairi and managed to offend the pasha, who considered Burton an infidel for his unauthorized participation in a hajj; to offend the Muslims by spreading rumors and publicizing Turkish atrocities against the Jewish population; and to offend the Jewish community by refusing to provide mandated protection to several members. After a dispute in which he lost the "composure befitting the Diplomatic Service," Burton was recalled to England, where he justified his behavior as consul in an angry manuscript which claimed that the Damascus affair was perpetrated by Sephardic Jews, who if more intellectual lack the "manliness of bearing, a strongness of spirit and a physical hardiness" of the Askenazic Jews. Burton's manuscript was published as *The Jew, the Gypsy and El Islam*, and despite the objections of the Board of Deputies was popular.[18]

In France Edouard Drumont and Henri Desportes repeatedly cited the Damascus affair in their lurid anti-Semitic tracts of the 1880s, providing polemical ammunition for the later cultural civil war of the Dreyfus affair. Their polemics no doubt contributed to the revival of the blood libel myth in Eastern Europe, where heavily publicized ritual murder accusations were brought to trial in Hungary, the Rhineland, Prussia, Bohemia, and the Ukraine. The last of these trials, the Beilis case of 1913 in Kiev, was the basis for Bernard Malamud's novel *The Fixer*. Even today, on some American university campuses, posters with blatant blood libel accusations are used in demonstrations against American and Israeli policies.[19]

The French Foreign Ministry became a willing ally of the anti-Semitic campaigns when their archivists filed the dossiers on the disappearance of Father Thomas, including the des Meloizes report, in a "classified" section of the Quai d'Orsay archives. Researchers who asked for the material were variously told that the papers did not exist, could not be found, that "France is now directly interested in maintaining public order in the Levant where our Mandatory status creates its own responsibilities," or that "bloody troubles which have been provoked in Palestine in 1929" prevented release of the documents.[20] Despite the French archivists' long-term insistence that the documents relating to the disappearance of Father Thomas were not available, during the wartime occupation German Foreign Office agents had no difficulty locating the material and making photocopies for propaganda use. *Der Stürmer* had regularly devoted space to alleged Jewish ritual murders, and the Nazi propagandists had plans to make a movie about the Damascus affair. The German photocopies, framed with the letterhead of the German Foreign Office, are presently part of the official dossiers on the case in the Quai d'Orsay archives. With the exception of the Nazis, it was not until 1985 that a determined British scholar, Tudor Parfitt, first gained research access to the documents.

Even long after researchers finally got access to the trial protocols and inquiry records, with their cumulative documentation of torture, coerced confessions, manufactured evidence, and perverted judicial procedures, the Damascus affair remains in the news. In 1983 the Syrian minister of defense, General Mustafa Tlass, wrote *Matzo of Zion*, a haphazard collection of alleged revelations about the Damascus affair, to demonstrate what he claims is "the historical reality of Zionist racism." To bolster his credentials, Tlass repeatedly attempted to obtain a doctorate from the Sorbonne, unsuccessfully submitting a thesis to several departments in Paris. His book remains popular in the Arab world and is sold in bookstores and at airports alongside stacks of *The Protocols of the Elders of Zion*. Recently Arab polemicists, including newspaper editorialists and heads of state, have cited the book in renewed blood libel accusations against the Jews. In 2001 an Egyptian film producer announced that a script for a film version of Tlass's book had been written with the title *Harari's List*, as an answer to *Schindler's List*, and that Omar Sharif was being considered for the lead role.[21]

No trace of Father Thomas or his servant Ibrahim Amara was ever found. In 1866 his tombstone, with its epitaphs in Italian and Arabic, was moved from the ruined Capuchin monastery to the Franciscan church at the corner of Monastery and Bab Touma Streets, where it sits today. In the floor of the opposite nave is a stone marking the tomb of eight Franciscan monks who died in the anti-Christian rioting of 1860. One of the friars tells visitors to the church that the troubles in Damascus were always brought on by outsiders.

Acknowledgements
Notes
Index

Acknowledgements

The disappearance of the Capuchin monk in Damascus is a story of unexpected history.

Much of the task of the historian is to winnow sources, asking of a long-dead letter-writer or diarist, "How do you know that?" or "Why should I believe what you have written?" In a process sometimes compared to peeling an onion, the historian strips away layers of collective memories added by successive generations before crafting an orderly narrative from the sources that survive. But the coherence and clarity of the historian's narrative can be misleading. Events are untidy. Those living through a revolution do not always realize they are in the midst of a revolution. Those living in Damascus saw events through distorting prisms of mutual fears, misperceptions, and age-old antagonisms. The geography of information before the telegraph kept news of the horrible events from the outside world for months.

I have tried to tell the story as the contemporaries saw it unfolding, allowing the changing perceptions of participants to be confined and constrained by the isolation of the Middle East and the geography of information. The risk of this approach is that at moments in the narrative the preponderance of apparent evidence may seem to falsely condemn those who would later be exonerated. A more analytic approach, stripping away the myths that have entangled the affair, would risk obscuring the confused perceptions that motivated participants on every side in 1840.

Any historian venturing into the Damascus affair owes a debt to Jonathan Frankel, the author of the superb *The Damascus Affair: "Ritual Murder," Politics, and the Jews in 1840*. Frankel's pathbreaking and voluminous research in archives, newspapers, and published materials has provided invaluable aides to navigation in the sources. The focus and tone of this work are very different from his, but I have profited immeasurably from the routes through the tangles of diplomacy, press coverage, and the wider manifestations of the affair that Frankel pioneered. By rescuing the story of the Damascus affair from a century and a half of myths, Frankel has made this narrative reconstruction possible.

I incurred many other debts in the research and writing of this book. The archivists at the Ministère des Affairs Étrangères and the Archives Nationales in Paris and at the Public Records Office in Kew Garden as well as the librarians at the Rockefeller Library at Brown University, Widener and Lamont Libraries at Harvard University, the Bibliothèque Nationale in Paris, the British Library in London, and the J. Paul Getty Museum in Los Angeles were unfailingly helpful. Members of the Brown University Judaic Studies Faculty Seminar and the Providence Academic Havurah read and offered comments and advice on portions of an early draft. Wayne Franklin, David Kertzer, Jeffrey Lesser, Maud Mandel, and Kenneth Stow read the manuscript at various stages, helping to shape a sometimes unruly narrative, correcting myriad details, and sharpening elements of the story and background. Judith Romney Wegner provided invaluable help with transcriptions and diction, as did Mark Wegner with translations from the Arabic. John Edmunds and Ron Verga provided unexpected information on orthopedic research procedures. My wife, Heather, has put up with years of obsession with this story, used her considerable critical talents to question assumptions, and accompanied me on a challenging journey to Damascus. My son, Justin, offered his fine eye for narrative and his broad readings in historiography.

Finally, I would like to acknowledge the many people in Damascus—Muslim, Christian, and Jew—who for their own protection cannot be credited by name. Although I was unwilling to compromise their safety by revealing the purpose of my queries, my questions to them were many and persistent. That they readily accommodated requests to visit houses, cafes, places of worship, and what must have seemed an odd predilection for certain street corners and alleyways is testimony to their friendliness, politeness, and eagerness to help. I am deeply appreciative of their generosity.

For the errors that remain, especially those which can most accurately be ascribed to my own stubbornness, I claim full credit.

Notes

Abbreviations

AAE   Archives des Affaires Étrangères (unless otherwise noted, Quai d'Orsay, Paris)

AN   Archives Nationales, Paris

APT   Turquie/Affaires Diverses: Assassinat du Père Thomas (microfilm)

FO   Foreign Office Archives, Public Record Office, Kew Gardens, London

The procès verbal of the investigation of the disappearance of Father Thomas and his servant was translated from the Arabic to French, mainly by Beaudin, and collected in what Count Ratti-Menton called a *Journal Arabe*. The microfilm copy in AAE: APT is accompanied by the correspondence between Ratti-Menton and Paris and the documentation of des Meloizes's investigation and includes some testimony and auxiliary documents that were edited out of later versions of the trial record. The manuscript copy of *Journal Arabe* in FO 78/410 is essentially the same as the copy in AAE: APT but is often easier to read. The published version in Achille Laurent, *Relation historique des affaires de Syrie: Procédure complète dirigée en 1840 contre des Juifs de Damas à la suite de la disparition du Père Thomas, Publiées d'après les Documents recueillis en Turquie, en Égypte et en Syrie,* volume 2 (Paris, 1846), omits some embarrassing material from the original and adds other material not present in the original procès verbal.

The definitive study of the Damascus affair is Jonathan Frankel, *The Damascus Affair: "Ritual Murder," Politics, and the Jews in 1840* (New York: Cambridge University Press, 1997). Frankel's prodigious archival

221

and newspaper research and his deft exploration of the wider impact of the affair on diplomacy, the internal politics of European nations, Jewish nationalism, and in the popular press is invaluable.

Chapter 1.   Damascus, February 1840

1. Nathaniel Werry, "On the character and occupation of the Father Tomasso . . . ," (enclosure No. 1), FO 78/410, 198–201; N. Werry to Col. Hodges, June 10, 1840, FO 78/405, 122; Ratti-Menton to Marshall Soult, Feb. 29, 1840, AAE: APT, 1ff; Laurent, *Relation historique des affaires de Syrie* 2:7ff. See also [Andrew Archibald Paton], *The Modern Syrians; or, Native Society in Damascus, Aleppo, and the Mountains of the Druses, from Notes Made in Those Parts during the Years 1841–2–3 by an Oriental Student* (London, 1844), 24.

2. *Journal Arabe,* FO 78/410, 60.

3. John Bowring, *Observations on the Oriental Plague and on Quarantines* (Edinburgh, 1838), 12. Asian cholera first came into the Ottoman Empire from Russia via Iraq in 1821. Donald Quataert, "The Age of Reforms, 1812–1914," in *An Economic and Social History of the Ottoman Empire, 1300–1914,* ed. Halil Inalcik and Donald Quataert (Cambridge, 1994), 788. Many of the manuscript letters of the era in the Foreign Office archives still carry the punch holes or knife marks of the inspections.

4. Rev. J. L. Porter, *Five Years in Damascus,* 2 volumes (London, 1855), 1:139, gives the population from government registers as 74,464 Muslims, 5,995 Greek Orthodox, 6,195 Greek Catholic, fewer than 500 each for other Christian churches and the Druses, 4,630 Jews, and 15,000 strangers/soldiers/slaves. Porter, generally a reliable observer, believed that the number of Muslims was 50 percent higher than the government figures and the number of Jews 25 percent higher, which would have made the total population approximately 150,000. Ursula R. Q. Henriques, "Who Killed Father Thomas?" in *Sir Moses Montefiore: A Symposium,* ed. V. D. Lipman (Oxford, 1982), 50, reports the government figures but suggests that hidden harems would have raised the total numbers.

5. One of the original notices is in FO 78/460, 198.

6. *Journal Arabe,* FO 78/410, 59.

7. Laurent, *Relation historique des affaires de Syrie* 2:7; Ratti-Menton to Soult, Feb. 18, 1840, AAE: APT.

8. Inventory statement, Feb. 10, 1840, AAE: APT, 661ff.

9. Laurent, *Relation historique des affaires de Syrie* 2:7; Ratti-Menton to Soult, Feb. 18, 1840, AAE: APT.

Chapter 2.   The Usual Suspects

1. In Arabic it is called Bab Sharqi Street, after the eastern gate of the city at the end of the street; in Latin it is the Via Recta.

2. Acts 9:3. The story of Paul's conversion is also told in Acts 22 and 26:12–23. Acts 23 describes the alleged plot of the Jews to kill and "dispose of" Paul. The passages were not mentioned in the procès verbal of the Damascus affair.

3. James A. Riley, "Local and Regional Economies of Ottoman Syria during the Eighteenth and Nineteenth Centuries," in *Ownership, Contracts and Markets in China, Southeast Asia and the Middle East: The Potentials of Comparative Study*, ed. MIURA Toru (Tokyo, 2001), 83–84; Bernard Lewis, *What Went Wrong? Western Impact and Middle Eastern Response* (New York, 2002), 50.

4. *La Dépêche de Damas*, No. 23, Apr. 20, 1840 (translated into French), AAE: APT.

5. Antoine Abdel Nour, "Types architecturaux et vocabulaire de l'habitat en Syria," in Dominique Chevallier, ed., *L'Espace social de la ville arabe* (Paris, 1979), 82–83, quoted in André Raymond, *The Great Arab Cities in the 16th–18th Centuries* (New York, 1984), 57.

6. William C. Prime, *Tent Life in the Holy Land* (New York, 1857), 434–35, quoted in Norman A. Stillman, *The Jews of Arab Lands: A History and Source Book* (Philadelphia, 1979); Isabel Burton, *The Inner Life of Syria, Palestine, and the Holy Land* (London, 1879), 102ff., 129, cited in Walter P. Zenner, "Jews in Late Ottoman Syria: External Relations," in *Jewish Societies in the Middle East: Community, Culture and Authority*, ed. Shlomo Deshen and Walter P. Zenner (Washington, D.C., 1982), 193.

7. Laurent, *Relation historique des affaires de Syrie* 2:37.

8. See the Italian translation of Ratti-Menton's journal of the arrests and searches, FO 78/410, 213–22; N. Werry, "On the researches and domiciliary visits made by the local authorities in conjunction with the French Consul . . . ," (enclosure No. 4), FO 78/410, 209–12; Laurent, *Relation historique des affaires de Syrie* 2:10–12; G. W. Pieritz, *Persecution of the Jews at Damascus* (London, 1840), 1; Col. Hodges to Mehmet Ali, May 28, 1840, FO 78/405, 44. Hodges cites as his source a letter the Jewish community sent to Constantinople.

9. Laurent, *Relation historique des affaires de Syrie* 2:10.

10. In the French and Italian versions of the procès verbal, and in contemporaneous correspondence in French, Italian, German, and English, the transcriptions from Arabic are stylized or phonetic. I have substituted modern standard transcriptions or contemporary versions of names: al-Talli instead of el-Telli, Farhi instead of Farkhi or Farḥi, and Abulafia instead of Abu-el-Afieh. I have also used modern English versions of given names: David instead of Daoud, Moses instead of Moussa, and Joseph instead of Yussef. I am indebted to Judith Romney Wegner for help with transliterations.

11. *Journal Arabe*, note 38, FO 78/410, 151; interrogation of al-Talli, Aug. 12, 1840, AAE: APT; N. Werry, "On the character of Mohammed el Tilly, an Egyptian subject . . . ," (enclosure No. 8), FO 78/410, 235–38; Pieritz, *Persecution*, 2.

12. Ratti-Menton to Soult, Feb. 17, 1840, AAE: APT; Laurent, *Relation historique des affaires de Syrie* 2:122.

13. Pieritz, *Persecution*, 3; N. Werry, "On the researches and domiciliary visits . . . ," FO 78/410, 209–12; Ratti-Menton to Soult, Feb. 17, 1840, AAE: APT; Laurent, *Relation historique des affaires de Syrie* 2:10; N. Werry, "On the character of Mohammed el Tilly . . . ," FO 78/410, 237. Ratti-Menton gave no names for the other three arrested men, writing only that they were "de la classe du peuple"; the British consul called them "men of bad character."

Chapter 3.   The Jewish Quarter

1. Appendix 3, des Meloizes submission, July 23, 1840, AAE: APT.

2. [Moses Montefiore], *Diaries of Sir Moses and Lady Montefiore*, 2 volumes, ed. L. Loewe (London, 1890), 1:48.

3. Efraim Karsh and Inari Karsh, *Empires of the Sand: The Struggle for Mastery in the Middle East 1789–1923* (Cambridge, Mass., 1999), 21.

4. On the taxes, see the appendix to Rev. J. L. Porter, *Five Years in Damascus*, 2:322, which reprints the firmat exempting him from the various special taxes; Colonel Churchill, *The Druzes and the Maronites under the Turkish Rule from 1840 to 1860* (London, 1862), 27.

5. Benjamin Braude and Bernard Lewis, *Christians and Jews in the Ottoman Empire: The Functioning of a Plural Society*, 2 volumes (New York, 1982), 1:5.

6. Moshe Ma'oz, *Ottoman Reform in Syria and Palestine 1840–1861* (Oxford, 1968), 4, 21. "Farhi," *Encyclopedia Judaica* (Jerusalem, 1971); Moshe Ma'oz, "Changes in the Position of the Jewish Communities of Palestine and Syria in Mid-Nineteenth Century," in *Studies on Palestine during the Ottoman Period* (Jerusalem, 1975), 143ff; Thomas Philipp, "The Farhi Family and the Changing Position of the Jews in Syria, 1750–1860," *Middle Eastern Studies* 20 (Oct. 1984).

7. Moshe Ma'oz, "Communal Conflicts in Ottoman Syria during the Reform Era: The Role of Political and Economic Factors," in Braude and Lewis, *Christians and Jews in the Ottoman Empire* 2:96, 2:101; Richard Clogg, "The Greek Millet in the Ottoman Empire" in ibid., 1:191; Dick Douwes, *Justice and Oppression: Ottoman Rule in the Province of Damascus and the District of Hama 1785–1841* (Nijmegen, 1994), 130.

8. The Egyptian poet Ḥāfiẓ Ibrāhīm, quoted in A. L. Tibawi, *A Modern History of Syria* (London, 1969), 77.

9. Antabi sent an account of the interview to Moses Montefiore. A. Elhalil, "Te'udah mekorit ḥashuvah 'al 'alilat hadam beDamesk," *Mizraḥ uma'arav* 3 (Tevet-Sivan 5689/1929), 34–49, cited in Frankel, *The Damascus Affair*, 36–37.

10. Interrogation of Antabi, July 11, 1840, AAE: APT; J. B. Levinsohn, *Efés Dammîm: A Series of Conversations at Jerusalem between a Patriarch of the Greek Church and a Chief Rabbi of the Jews, Concerning the Malicious Charge against the Jews of Using Christian Blood*, trans. L. Loewe (London, 1841), vii–ix; Pieritz, *Persecution*, 3.

11. "Marchand de tumbak," AAE: APT; Pieritz, *Persecution*, 3; N. Werry, "On the suicide of Kaffar, an Egyptian merchant . . . ," (enclosure No. 11), July 18, 1840, FO 78/410, 240–42; S. Posener, *Adolphe Crémieux, a Biography*, trans. Eugene Golob (Philadelphia, 1940), 91.

12. Ratti-Menton to Soult, Dec. 21, 1839, AAE: *Correspondence Commercial, Damas*, quoted in Tudor Parfitt, "The Year of the Pride of Israel: Montefiore and the Damascus Blood Libel of 1840," in *The Century of Moses Montefiore*, ed. Sonia Lipman and V. D. Lipman (London, 1985), 138; Ratti-Menton to Thiers, Mar. 24, 1840, AAE: APT.

13. AAE: *Ratti-Menton, le Comte de/Personnel/Série-I*, passim. Baron James Rothschild tried to investigate Ratti-Menton without success. Rothschild

Frères, Paris to K. Rothschild (May 12, 1840), N. M. Rothschild Archives (London), RFamAD/2, Nos. 36 and 53, cited in Frankel, *The Damascus Affair,* 55.

14. Colin Thubron, *Mirror to Damascus* (Boston, 1967), 157.

15. Alphonse de Lamartine, *A Pilgrimage to the Holy Land* (Philadelphia, 1838; reprint, Delmar, N. Y., 1978), 342ff.

16. Beaudin to Paris, Feb. 14, 1834, AAE: *Beaudin/Personnel/Série-I;* Laurent, *Relation historique des affaires de Syrie* 2:226ff. The originals of commercial letters detailing these alleged debts are in AAE: APT. Lamartine complained about the injustice of Beaudin's salary.

17. Interrogation of Antabi, July 11, 1840, AAE: APT.

18. Ratti-Menton and Beaudin later charted the wealth of these men and others they considered especially influential in the community. The figures, apparently wild guesses or broad-brush estimates, are in appendix 3 to the des Meloizes submission, July 23, 1840, AAE: APT. A purse (*bourse*) was equal to 500 piastres (approximately $25).

	Purses	Goods
Murad Farhi	5,000	625,000
David Harari	500	62,500
Isaac Harari	500	62,500
Aaron Harari	500	62,500
Joseph Harari	1,500	187,500
Joseph Leniado	200	25,000
Moses Abulafia	50	6,250
Moses Salonicli	500	62,500
Aslan Farhi	50	6,250
Joseph Farhi	2,000	250,000
Meir Farhi	300	37,500
Jacob Abulafia	100	12,500
Aaron Stambouli	2,000	250,000
Jacob al-Antabi		

19. Laurent, *Relation historique des affaires de Syrie* 2:59–62; N. Werry, "On the reward offered by the Jews for the apprehension of the perpetrators . . . ," (enclosure No. 10), July 18, 1840, FO 78/410, 239; Ma'oz, "Changes in the Position of the Jewish Communities," 149.

20. *Journal Arabe,* FO 78/410, 96; Philipp, "The Farhi Family and the Changing Position," 47.

21. N. Werry, "On the character and reputation of the Chief of Police, Ali Agha . . . ," (enclosure No. 7), July 18, 1840, FO 78/410, 233–34; Ratti-Menton to Soult, Feb. 29, 1840, AAE: APT; N. Werry, "On the researches and domiciliary visits . . . ," FO 78/410, 209.

22. Ratti-Menton to Soult, Apr. 24, 1840, AAE: APT; *Journal Arabe,* FO 78/410, 96.

23. Interrogation of Lisbona, Mar. 27, 1840, AAE: APT; *Journal Arabe*, FO 78/410, 94b.

Chapter 4.   Interrogation

1. Laurent, *Relation historique des affaires de Syrie* 2:11ff. There are conflicting accounts of the barber's testimony in AAE: APT.

2. A later observer, taken to view the wall where the notice was found, reported that it was at a "normal height" for such a notice and within reach of any "normal-sized person." Rev. Joseph Marshall, chaplain of HMS *Castor* (Malta) to Montefiore, Dec. 4, 1840, AAE: APT.

3. *Journal Arabe*, FO 78/410, 147; N. Werry, "On the character and occupation of the Father Tomasso . . . ," FO 78/410, 201.

4. Ratti-Menton to Soult, Feb. 28, 1840, AAE: APT.

5. Interrogation of Solomon al-Hallaq, June 24, 1840, AAE: APT; interrogation of al-Talli, Aug. 12, 1840, AAE: APT.

6. On the use of "hippopotamus-whips," see Eliot Warburton, *The Crescent and the Cross* (London, 1844).

7. Edward B. B. Barker, *Syria and Egypt under the Last Five Sultans of Turkey*, 2 volumes (London, 1876; reprint, New York, 1973), 2:81.

8. The sources vary widely on how many lashes al-Hallaq received. In describing the testimony Ratti-Menton said only that he had been given "some blows with the kurbash." Laurent, *Relation historique des affaires de Syrie* 2:11. In his correspondence to Paris, Ratti-Menton is silent on the bastinado, a subject that would not have been well received in Paris. Ratti-Menton to Soult, Feb. 29, 1840, AAE: APT. Other testimony said al-Hallaq was given 200 lashes, the standard application, refused to talk, and was later given 150 more and the application of a tourniquet around his head. Laurent, *Relation historique des affaires de Syrie* 2:109; N. Werry, "On the punishments and tortures practiced at the Palace and at Sherif pasha's private dwelling . . . ,"(enclosure No. 6), July 18, 1840, FO 78/410, 228. Muhammad al-Talli said in his interrogation that the barber received one thousand lashes (Aug. 12, 1840, AAE: APT). A letter from the Jewish community to Abram Conorte and Aron Coen of the Jewish community in Constantinople claimed the barber had received five hundred lashes. FO 195/162, quoted in Stillman, *The Jews of Arab Lands*. Pieritz, *Persecution*, 6, says the barber was flogged repeatedly and subjected to a machine with screws that were tightened to squeeze his head.

9. N. Werry, "On the punishments and tortures . . . ," FO 78/410, 228–29; Laurent, *Relation historique des affaires de Syrie* 2:14.

10. Ratti-Menton to Soult, Feb. 29, 1840, AAE: APT.

11. Laurent, *Relation historique des affaires de Syrie* 2:20.

12. Ratti-Menton to Soult, Feb. 29, 1840, AAE: APT.

13. On circumventing interest, see James A. Riley, "Local and Regional Economies," 78; on charges of usury, see Vivian D. Lipman, *Sir Moses Montefiore*, 50.

14. John 1:11, 2:14.

15. John 19:6–7, 19:15.

16. H. H. Jessup, *Fifty Three Years in Syria,* 2 volumes (London, 1910), 2:424–25.

17. Nathaniel Werry, the British consul at Damascus, wrote that "I have heard ever since I have been in their country of the Jews being accused of making use of innocent blood, but this is the first occasion of an accusation having been brought solemnly forward on a prosecution related case." Werry to Bidwell, July 20, 1840, FO 78/410, 171.

18. Heinrich Graetz, *Geschichte der Juden von den ältesten Zeiten bis auf die Gegenwart,* 11 volumes (Leipzig, 1870), 11:473; Sherman Lieber, *Mystics and Missionaries: The Jews in Palestine 1799–1840* (Salt Lake City, 1992), 303.

19. N. Werry, "On the general state of the Jew population at Damascus during the accusation and investigation . . . ," (enclosure No. 5), July 18, 1840, FO 78/410, 225–27; Alfandari to Lehren, Mar. 15, 1840, *Archives Israélites de France* (1840): 1:215, quoted in Frankel, *The Damascus Affair,* 67; Yaron Harel, "Jewish-Christian Relations in Aleppo as Background for the Jewish Response to the Events of October 1850," *International Journal of Middle Eastern Studies* 30 (1998): 82.

20. The phrase is from the British consul. N. Werry, "On the researches and domiciliary visits . . . ," FO 78/410, 210.

21. Walter P. Zenner, *A Global Community: The Jews from Alepo, Syria* (Detroit, 2000), 36.

22. Prime, *Tent Life,* 434–35, quoted in Stillman, *The Jews of Arab Lands.*

23. Josef Leniado to Merlato, June 27, 1840; Reverend Schlyntz to Montefiore, Nov. 30, 1840; Esther Leniado to Merlato, Apr. 23, 1840; Rev. Joseph Marshall, chaplain of HMS *Castor* (Malta) to Montefiore, Dec. 4, 1840; interview of Mouna Farhi, Nov. 6, 1840, all in AAE: APT.

24. Laurent, *Relation historique des affaires de Syrie* 2:17. In later testimony Harari claimed he had gone to see Dr. Massari for treatment of the boil on Thursday, the same day the father was expected there for dinner. Ratti-Menton dismissed this claim as a false alibi. AAE: APT.

25. Pieritz, *Persecution,* 7. Pieritz writes that, according to some reports, the men had to stand for three and a half days; this figure does not fit the chronology of the interrogations and seems wildly implausible for merchants as old as some of the arrested men.

26. Laurent, *Relation historique des affaires de Syrie* 2:13–15.

27. Ibid. 2:14–20.

28. Ratti-Menton's notes on the procès verbal, note 11, AAE: APT; Laurent, *Relation historique des affaires de Syrie* 2:22.

29. N. Werry, "On the punishments and tortures . . . ," FO 78/410, 228–32; Ratti-Menton's summary of the case, AAE: APT.

Chapter 5.   The Tumbak Seller & the Watchman

1. N. Werry, "On the suicide of Kaffar, an Egyptian merchant . . . ," FO 78/410, 240–42; Pieritz, *Persecutions,* 2. The story was also reported in the Italian press; see *Gazzetta di Firenze,* May 5, 1840, cited in Frankel, *The Damascus Affair,* 139n.89.

2. It was only in 1870 that the second floor was added to the shops in the Hamidieh suq, the corrugated iron roofs built, and many of the smaller suqs in the city concentrated around the western gate.

3. Col. Hodges to Muhammad Ali, May 28, 1840, FO 78/405, 45–46.

4. Note on the Marchand de Tumbak, AAE: APT.

5. R. Alfandari to Lehren, Mar. 15, 1840, in [Montefiore], *Diaries* 2:212–16.

6. Lt. Shadwell (of HMS *Castor*) to Montefiore, Dec. 5, 1840 (copy), AAE: APT; N. Werry, "On the punishments and tortures . . . ," FO 78/410, 228–32; Pieritz, *Persecution*, 10.

7. Ratti-Menton to Thiers, May 7, 1840; interrogation of Antabi, Aug. 11, 1840, AAE: APT; N. Werry, "On the punishments and tortures . . . ," FO 78/410, 228–32; Pieritz, *Persecutions*, 4. Col. Hodges to Mehmet Ali, May 28, 1840, FO 78/405, 45–46, tells a confused version of the Yavo story, claiming that someone testified that Christians had murdered Father Thomas, that the pasha demanded to know the identify of the Christian who had committed the murder, and that "in order that he should confess, he was beaten to such an extreme that he expired under the blows."

Chapter 6.   The Long Wait

1. Pieritz, *Persecution*, 12.

2. Rev. Joseph Marshall, chaplain of HMS *Castor* (Malta) to Montefiore, Dec. 4, 1840, AAE: APT; Laurent, *Relation historique des affaires de Syrie* 2:235; Pieritz, *Persecution*, 9. The quote from Pieritz may not be correct; Jews were not permitted to own Muslim slaves, and Kittèh would have gotten her master in trouble by calling herself a slave owned by a Jew.

3. N. Werry, "On the punishments and tortures . . . ," FO 78/410, 230; Laurent, *Relation historique des affaires de Syrie* 2:213–14; Pieritz, *Persecution*, 8.

4. Exodus 13:1–2; Numbers 18:16. .

5. Col. Hodges to Mehmet Ali, May 28, 1840, FO 78/405, 42; letter to Abram Conorte and Aron Coen, PRO 195/162, in Stillman, *The Jews of Arab Lands*; N. Werry, "On the punishments and tortures . . . ," FO 78/410, 230; Laurent, *Relation historique des affaires de Syrie* 2:213–14; Alfandari to Lehren, Mar. 15, 1840, in *Archives Israélites de France* (1840): 215, cited in Frankel, *The Damascus Affair*, 38; *Times* (London), Aug. 13, 1840, 3.

6. J. L. Burkhardt, *Travels in Syria and the Holy Land* (London, 1822), 322. One of the Rothschilds had worked with the French consul in Alexandria to provide financial assistance to the Jewish community in Safed after the Druze attack in 1838. R. D. Barnett, "A Diary that Survived," in Lipman and Lipman, *The Century of Moses Montefiore*, 149ff; P. J. W. Steenwijk, "De Damascus-Affaire (1840) en Haar Weerklank in Nederland," *Studia Rosenthaliana* 20 (1986): 70.

7. Ma'oz, "Communal Conflicts," 99–100; Walter P. Zenner, "Jews in Late Ottoman Syria: External Relations," in *Jewish Societies in the Middle East: Community, Culture and Authority*, ed. Shlomo Deshen and Walter P. Zenner (Washington, 1982), 185n.

8. In Arabic the word *alkhan* means both "rotten walnut" and "a stinking uncircumcised person."

9. N. Werry to Bidwell, Aug. 18, 1840, FO 78/410, 286. See also Harel, "Jewish-Christian Relations," 77–96.

10. N. Moore to Palmerston, Jan. 29, 1840, FO 78/412, 142; Carter V. Findley, "The Acid Test of Ottomanism: The Acceptance of Non-Muslims in the Late Ottoman Bureaucracy," in Braude and Lewis, *Christians and Jews in the Ottoman Empire* 1:341.

11. Robert M. Haddad, *Syrian Christians in Muslim Society* (Princeton, 1970), 39.

12. Testimony of al-Talli, Jan. 13, 1841, in Laurent, *Relation historique des affaires de Syrie* 2:260–61.

13. Interrogation of Al-Talli, Aug. 2, 1840, AAE: APT.

14. Interrogation of Aaron Harari, July 4, 1840, AAE: APT.

15. Ibid.; Pieritz, *Persecution*, 6.

16. Ratti-Menton to Soult, Feb. 29, 1840, AAE: APT.

17. Pieritz, *Persecution*, 8, says that the barber confessed to taking the knife from David Harari and slitting the throat himself.

18. James Carroll, *Constantine's Sword: The Church and the Jews* (New York, 2001), 357.

19. This seemingly innocent question was probably included to match up with evidence that was supposedly "discovered" later in the investigation.

20. Laurent, *Relation historique des affaires de Syrie* 2:28–29.

21. Ibid. 2:31–35.

Chapter 7.   Confessions

1. Pieritz, *Persecution*, 9; Lt. Shadwell to Montefiore, Dec. 5, 1840 (copy), AAE: APT; "Journal of the arrests prepared by R[atti-]M[enton]" (copy in Italian in Werry's papers), FO 78/410, 213–22.

2. Ratti-Menton's summary notes, AAE: APT; letter of Rev. Joseph Marshal, chaplain of the HMS *Castor* (Malta) in [Montefiore], *Diaries* 1:230.

3. Lt. Shadwell to Montefiore, Dec. 5, 1840; Rev. Schlyntz (Malta) to Montefiore, Nov. 30, 1840, AAE: APT.

4. The identification of a sewer as the place where alleged Jewish ritual murderers disposed of a body is traditional in the European ritual murder myth; the body of Hugh of Lincoln in 1255 was supposedly discovered in a cesspool. Joshua Trachtenberg, *The Devil and the Jews: The Medieval Conception of the Jew and Its Relation to Modern Anti-Semitism* (Philadelphia, 1983), 131. Several medieval popes condemned this specific accusation; see, for example, the text of Innocent III's condemnation in Solomon Grayzel, *The Church and the Jews in the Thirteenth Century* (New York, 1966), 109. I am indebted to Kenneth Stow of Haifa University for pointing out this reference in his unpublished paper, "The Bollandists and the Authorial Present: Ritual Murder and Its Evolving Perception."

5. The owner of the house was the brother of the woman, a Prussian protégé named Romano who later lodged a protest of Ratti-Menton's behavior. Pieritz, *Persecution*, 11.

6. *Journal Arabe*, FO 78/410, 78; Pieritz, *Persecution*, 11.

7. Ratti-Menton to Soult, Feb. 29, 1840, AAE: APT.

8. Parfitt, "The Year of the Pride of Israel," 144.

9. Leviticus 22:29.

10. The report of Cochelet, the French consul-general in Alexandria, to Soult on Mar. 3, 1840, backing up Ratti-Menton's report and adding that Muhammad Ali "has given the most severe possible orders for the punishment of those guilty" was wishful thinking in early March. Édouard Driault, *L'Égypte et l'Europe: La Crise de 1839–1841*, 5 volumes (Cairo, 1930), 2:169.

11. Count Clermont-Tonnerre, quoted in David Rudavsky, *Emancipation and Adjustment: Contemporary Jewish Religious Movements, Their History and Thought* (New York, 1967), 81; see also Jay R. Berkowitz, *The Shaping of Jewish Identity in Nineteenth-century France* (Detroit, 1989), 47 and passim.

12. Michel Foucault, *Discipline and Punish: The Birth of the Prison* (New York, 1977), 40; Lisa Silverman, *Tortured Subjects: Pain, Truth, and the Body in Early Modern France* (Chicago, 2001), 93–94.

13. N. Werry, "On the punishments and tortures . . . ," FO 78/410, 228–32; Pieritz, *Persecution*, 13; Esther Leniado to Merlato, Apr. 23, 1840, AAE: APT.

14. Palestinian Talmud, *Brakhot* 9:5, 61b.

15. The British consul wrote that with the exception of Moses Salonicli, "none [of the accused men] seem so attached to their Religion as to determine them to die martyrs, indeed their object seemed chiefly to get their lives spared." N. Werry, "On the prosecution, on the crime of murder and on a new trial being granted," (enclosure No. 12), July 18, 1840, FO 78/410, 243–47.

16. Esther Leniado to C. Merlato, Apr. 23, 1840, AAE: APT.

17. On the Prisoner's Dilemma as a philosophical problem and a concept of game theory, see Robert Axelrod, *The Evolution of Cooperation* (New York, 1984), and Richard Dawkins, *The Selfish Gene* (Oxford, 1989).

18. Interrogation of Isaac Harari, July 1, 1840, AAE: APT.

19. Laurent, *Relation historique des affaires de Syrie* 2:76; interrogation of Salonicli, *Journal Arabe*, FO 78/410, 230.

20. Interrogation of Salonicli, July 4, 1840, AAE: APT.

21. Laurent, *Relation historique des affaires de Syrie* 2:78.

22. Ratti-Menton to Thiers, May 7, 1840, AAE: APT.

23. Pieritz to Col. Hodges, May 14, 1840, FO 78/405, 100–102; N. Werry to Col. Hodges, June 10, 1840, [No. 5] FO 78/405, 117; FO memorandum, Nov. 23, 1840 (summary), FO 78/410, 77.

24. There was a notion of bread sanctified for the Jewish priests in Jerusalem in the era of the Temple. The barber, a poor man who was partially supported by the Jewish community, was unlikely to have been educated enough to be referring to an obscure concept that had not been part of Jewish practice for eighteen hundred years.

25. The Christian symbolism of the allegations of ritual murder, which seem to draw so heavily on the Eucharist, are extensions of early versions of the ritual murder accusations which claimed that Jews used the head and intestines of Christian children to make *haroseth*, the mixture of fruits, nuts, and wine eaten at the Passover Seder in memory of the bricks Jews were forced to make in Egypt (Exodus 1:13, 5:6–18). Stow, "The Bollandists and the Authorial Present."

26. *Journal Arabe,* FO 78/410, 76.

27. Laurent, *Relation historique des affaires de Syrie* 2:43; *Journal Arabe,* FO 78/410, 83; Pieritz, *Persecution,* 13–14.

28. N. Werry to Ponsonby, Feb. 28, 1840, FO 195/170, No. 48.

29. Laurent, *Relation historique des affaires de Syrie* 2:146.

30. Ibid. 2:127; "Journal relating to the assassination of the servant, Ibrahim Amara," translated from the Arabic to French by Beaudin, FO 78/410, 155.

31. N. Werry, "On the Egyptian jurisdiction, in the case of the accused Jews . . . ," (enclosure No. 3), July 18, 1840, FO 78/410, 207.

32. "Journal . . . Ibrahim Amara," FO 78/410, 153–66; Ratti-Menton to Soult, Mar. 24, 40, AAE: APT. In a letter to a colleague in Beirut, Mar. 21, 1840, Ratti-Menton attributed the discovery of the details of the murder of the servant to Ayyub Shubli: "In this situation, I had to accept the spontaneous offers of a resident of the country, a Catholic Christian, M. Chubli . . . who has just discovered the murder of Father Thomas's servant." AAE (Nantes): Consulate-Général/Beyrouth, 1840, cartons 25 and 26, quoted in Dominique Chevallie, "Non-Muslim Communities in Arab Cities," in Braude and Lewis, *Christians and Jews in the Ottoman Empire* 2:164n.

Chapter 8.   Evidence

1. "Father Thomas," *Times* (London), May 9, 1840, 6. The report was written by Father Francis. See also *Aceldama ossia processo celebre instruito contro gli Ebrei di Damasco nell'anno 1840* (Cagliari, 1896), 18, quoted in David L. Kertzer, *The Popes against the Jews* (New York, 2001), 88; Rev. Schlyntz (Malta) to Montefiore, Nov. 30, 1840, AAE: APT, wrote that the inscription was finished before the judicial proceedings were completed.

2. N. Werry, "On the general state of the Jew population . . . ," FO 78/410, 225–27

3. J. Wolff, *Missionary Journal and Memoir* (London, 1827), 180–81.

4. N. Werry to Ponsonby, Mar. 30, 1840, No. 49, FO 195/170, 11; N. Werry, "On the reward offered subsequently by the local government for the apprehension of the five missing Jews . . . ," (enclosure No. 9), July 18, 1840, FO 78/410, 238; Pieritz, *Persecution,* 19.

5. N. Werry, "On the condition and character of the accused Jews," (enclosure No. 2), Aug. 18, 1840, FO 78/410, 205–6; Pieritz, *Persecution,* 5; Sherif Pasha to Muhammad Ali, Mar. 24, 1840, *Times* (London), Aug. 17, 1840, 3.

6. Pieritz, *Persecution,* 19.

7. Ibid.

8. N. Werry, "On the condition and character . . . ," FO 78/410, 205; Pieritz, *Persecution,* 19.

9. Laurent, *Relation historique des affaires de Syrie* 2:117.

10. Merlato statement, Mar. 3, 1840, AAE: APT; also in *Journal Arabe,* FO 78/410, 79; Laurent, *Relation historique des affaires de Syrie* 2:37.

11. Pieritz, *Persecution,* 19–20; Lt. Shadwell to Montefiore, Dec. 5, 1840; AAE: APT. I am indebted to John Edmunds and Ronald Verga of Edmunds Maki

Verga & Thorn, Honolulu, Hawaii, for references in the current scientific literature on orthopedic research and testing.

12. Laurent, *Relation historique des affaires de Syrie* 2:37, 2:118; Ratti-Menton,
"*Notes explicatives et pièces à l'appin pour le Journal du P. Thomas,*" AAE: APT;
Merlato statement, Mar. 3, 1840 (certifying the statement of an Austrian doctor),
AAE: APT; statement of Father Francis, Mar. 17, 1840 (in Italian), AAE: APT;
Ratti-Menton to Soult, Mar. 24, 1840, AAE: APT; *Traduction au Journal . . . ensem-
ble aux procès-verbaux . . . assassinat du domestique du P. Thomas, Ibrahim Amara,*
AAE: APT.

13. N. Werry to Palmerston, Mar. 23, 1840, FO 78/410, 42.

Chapter 9. The Rabbis

1. Laurent, *Relation historique des affaires de Syrie* 2:378–93; Kertzer, *The Popes
against the Jews*, 92; Ratti-Menton to Thiers, June 3, 1840, AAE: APT.

2. Laurent, *Relation historique des affaires de Syrie* 2:383–91. Many of these
allegations derive from medieval accusations against Jewish practices; see
Trachtenberg, *The Devil and the Jews*, 148–52 and passim. For the curses the
monk cites Deuteronomy 28:27–28, 35 but not Deuteronomy 28:15, which
explains that the curses are reserved for those who "do not obey the Lord your
God to observe faithfully all His commandments and laws."

3. Trachtenberg, *The Devil and the Jews*, 124–55; R. Po-chia Hsia, *The Myth of
Ritual Murder: Jews and Magic in Reformation Germany* (New Haven, 1988), 208;
R. Po-chia Hsia, *Trent 1475: Stories of a Ritual Murder Trial* (New Haven, 1992),
44–46.

4. For Christian reactions to Jewish public celebrations, see Harel, "Jewish-
Christian Relations," 83. Ratti-Menton and Beaudin discussed conducting a
search at Purim (Mar. 18, 1840). "Journal of the Arrests," prepared by Ratti-
Menton (Italian copy, prepared for N. Werry), FO 78/410, 213–22. On Sephardic
circumcision rituals, see Issachar Ben-Ami, "Customs of Pregnancy and
Childbirth among Sephardic and Oriental Jews," *New Horizons in Sephardic
Studies*, ed. Y. K. Stillman and G. K. Zucker (Albany, 1993), 257. The main synagogue in Damascus still has a circumcision chair, which may date to the era of
the Damascus affair.

5. Pieritz to Hodges, May 14, 1840, FO 78/405, 100–102.

6. Hsia, *Trent 1475*, 31–32, 45; Carroll, *Constantine's Sword*, 272; Trachtenberg, *The Devil and the Jews*, 146. In the traditional ritual murder myth, the
hanging in effigy of Haman at Purim was viewed as a reenactment of the
Crucifixion. See Kenneth Stow, "The Church and the Jews, St. Paul to Pius IX,"
typescript 9–10 (forthcoming in *Atalante del Crestianesimo*, ed. Roberto Busconi
et al., Torino).

7. Ratti-Menton to Soult, Mar. 24, 1840, No. 19, AAE: APT.

8. Ibid.; Laurent, *Relation historique des affaires de Syrie* 2:17, 24, 29, 31, 41, 76;
N. Werry to Ponsonby, Feb. 28, 1840, FO 195/170, No. 48; N. Werry to Ponsonby,
Mar. 30, 1840, FO 195/170, No. 49, 10.

9. See Ecclesiastes 4:12: "A threefold thread is not quickly snapped."

10. Stow, "The Church and the Jews," typescript 41.

11. Laurent, *Relation historique des affaires de Syrie* 2:38, 49, 151.

12. Rev. Schlyntz (Malta) to Montefiore, Nov. 30, 1840, AAE: APT; Laurent, *Relation historique des affaires de Syrie* 2:214–15.

13. Interrogation of Antabi, July 8, 1840, AAE: APT.

14. A. Elhalil, "Te'udah mekorit ḥashuvah 'al 'alilat hadam beDemesk," *Mizraḥ uma'arav* 3 (Tevet–Sivan 5689/1929), Antabi's account, sent to Montefiore, quoted in Frankel, *The Damascus Affair*, 43.

15. Interrogation of Jacob Antabi, July 8, 1840, AAE: APT.

16. Interrogation of Moses Abulafia, June 25, 1840, AAE: APT.

17. Statement of Ora Abulafia, May 5, 1840, AAE: APT; Col. Hodges to Mehmet Ali, May 28, 1840, FO 78/405, 46.

18. Laurent, *Relation historique des affaires de Syrie* 2:45–47; "Declaration of Rabbi Abulafia after his conversion to Mohammedanism," in Éduoard Driault, *L'Égypte et l'Europe: La Crise de 1839–1841* (Cairo, 1930), 2:226–27.

Chapter 10.   The Talmud

1. Haim Nissim Abulafia to Lehren, June 19, 1840, in "Persecution of the Jews in the East," *Sun* (London), July 6, 1840; Frankel, *The Damascus Affair*, 47, cites other sources of this letter. Interrogation of Moses Abulafia, June 1840, AAE: APT. Moses Maimonides, *Letters of Maimonides*, trans. Leon D. Stitskin (New York, 1977), 64.

2. Stanford J. Shaw, *The Jews of the Ottoman Empire and the Turkish Republic* (New York, 1991), 78; Ma'oz, *Ottoman Reform in Syria and Palestine*, 12.

3. Gershom Scholem, *Sabbatai Ṣevi: The Mystical Messiah 1626–1676* (Princeton, 1973), 681.

4. Ibid., 32–37, 40–41, 760, 772, 800–802.

5. Interrogation of Moses Abulafia, June 1840, AAE: APT.

6. Pieritz, *Persecution*, 15; Jasper Chasseaud to John Forsyth, Mar. 24, 1840, in Joseph Leon Blau and S. W. Baron, *The Jews of the United States: A Documentary History*, 3 volumes (New York, 1963), 3:926. The French translations prepared for the trial are in Laurent, *Relation historique des affaires de Syrie* 2:394–98. On Ferrari see Kenneth R. Stow, "Expulsion Italian Style: The Case of Lucio Ferraris," *Jewish History* 3 (spring 1988): 51–63.

7. Interrogation of Moses Abulafia, June 1840, AAE: APT. *Leipziger Allgemeine Zeitung*, May 12, 1840, quoted in Frankel, *The Damascus Affair*, 86.

8. A. Ehrman, *Tractate Berakhot* (Jerusalem, 1965), 72n; Adin Steinsaltz, *The Essential Talmud* (New York, 1976), 75–77; James Carroll, *Constantine's Sword*, 309.

9. *Sanhedrin* 57b.

10. *Sanhedrin* 71b.

11. Genesis 22:3–5; Deuteronomy 21:18–21; Laurent, *Relation historique des affaires de Syrie* 2:53–56, 84; *Journal Arabe*, FO 78/410, 92–98b. The citation to Shimon Bar-Yoḥai, misidentified as "Rabbi Solomon" in the debate, is from the Palestinian Talmud, *Kiddushim* 4:66.

12. Interrogation of Jacob Antabi, July 8, 1840, AAE: APT.

13. The prohibitions are against idolatry, blasphemy, murder, incestuous relations, adultery, theft, eating flesh cut from a living animal, and the establishment of courts to uphold the other six laws. See *Sanhedrin* 56a.

14. *Journal Arabe*, FO 78/410, 92.

15. Elhalil, "Te'udah mekorit," 45, in Frankel, *The Damascus Affair*, 48; David Salomons, *An Account of the Recent Persecution* (London, 1840), 34–35, in ibid., 149.

16. Deuteronomy 12:23. There are many other verses in the Hebrew Bible with the same injunction, such as Deuteronomy 12:16: "you must not partake of the blood; you shall pour it out on the ground like water"; or Leviticus 17:10–11: "And if anyone of the house of Israel or of the strangers who reside among them partakes of any blood, I will set My face against the person who partakes of the blood, and I will cut him off from among his kin. For the life of the flesh is in the blood."

17. Laurent, *Relation historique des affaires de Syrie* 2:57–58.

18. N. Werry to Palmerston, Mar. 23, 1840, FO 78/410, 42; N. Werry to Ponsonby, Mar. 30, 1840, No. 49, FO 195/170, 10.

Chapter 11.   A Brief for the Defense

1. Jewish law permits the delegation of some tasks, such as selling Hometz (leavened bread products) at Passover, but if the alleged murders had taken place the supposed "mitzvah" of committing such a crime could not be delegated. This fairly obscure point of Jewish law is not mentioned in the Moldavian monk's book or in the Talmudic passages and other texts Ratti-Menton and the pasha claimed to have consulted.

2. Monsignor Massimo, Patriarch of Antioch, Alexandria and Jerusalem for the Greek Catholics to the [Congregations for the] Propaganda [of the Faith], April 6, 1840, cited in R. F. O'Connor, "Capuchin Missioners in Palestine and Syria," *American Catholic Quarterly Review* 45 (1920): 552.

3. *Sun* (London), Apr. 18, 1840.

4. Von Laurin to Metternich, June 16, 1840, No. 933, in Nathan Michael Gelber, *Österreich und die Damaskusaffaire im Jahre 1840* (Frankfurt-am-Main, 1927), an offprint from *Jahrbuch der Jüdische-Literarischen Gesellschaft* 18 (1927): 37; Adolphe Crémieux's diary, 120, cited in Frankel, *The Damascus Affair*, 87.

5. On Beaudin see the letters from businesses in Genoa and Beirut in Laurent, *Relation historique des affaires de Syrie* 2:245–47; interrogation of Picciotto, Mar. 9, 1840, AAE: APT.

6. Des Meloizes to Guizot, May 20, 1840, No. 9, AAE: APT.

7. Merlato to von Laurin (Beirut), Feb. 29, 1840, AAE: APT; Laurent, *Relation historique des affaires de Syrie* 2:286–87.

8. Merlato to Sherif Pasha, Feb. 21, 1840, Laurent, *Relation historique des affaires de Syrie* 2:118; Merlato to P. Laurella, Feb. 28, 1840, ibid. 2:289; Merlato statement, Mar. 3, 1840 (certifying the statement of an Austrian doctor), AAE: APT; Merlato to Laurin, Mar. 1, 1840, No. 97, AAE: APT; Ratti-Menton to Thiers, June 7, 1840, No. 25, AAE: APT.

9. Ratti-Menton to Merlato, Mar. 6, 1840, No. 13, AAE: APT; and Ratti-Menton to Merlato, Mar. 7, 1840, No. 14, AAE: APT.

10. Merlato to Ratti-Menton, Mar. 8, 1840, No. 16, AAE: APT.

11. Ratti-Menton to Merlato, Mar. 10, 1840, No. 15, AAE: APT.

12. Merlato to Ratti-Menton, Mar. 11, 1840, No. 17, AAE: APT.

13. Des Meloizes to Guizot, June 20, 1840, No. 9, AAE: APT; Merlato to Laurin, Apr. 17, 1840, No. 110, cited in Frankel, *The Damascus Affair*, 95.

14. Cochelet to Thiers, Apr. 6, 1840, in Driault, *L'Égypte et l'Europe* 2:232.

15. Interrogation of Picciotto, Mar. 9, 1840, AAE: APT; interrogation of Mahsud, Mar. 6, 1840, AAE: APT.

16. Interrogation of Picciotto, Laurent, *Relation historique des affaires de Syrie* 2:159–76.

17. Merlato to Ratti-Menton, Mar. 20, 1840, AAE: APT; Ratti-Menton to Merlato, Mar. 20, 1840, AAE: APT.

18. Karl von Hailbronner, *Morgenland und abendland; bilder von der Donau, Turkei, Griechenland Ägypten, Palastina, Syrien, dem Mittelmeer, Spanien, Portugal, und Sudfrankreich* (Stuttgart, 1841), 364.

19. Interrogation of Picciotto, Mar. 20, 1840, Laurent, *Relation historique des affaires de Syrie* 2:175.

20. Interrogation of Murad al-Fatal (on the assassination of the servant Ibrahim Amara), *Journal Arabe*, FO 78/410, 156; testimony of Rabbi Abulafia, Laurent, *Relation historique des affaires de Syrie* 2:49; interrogation of Mahsud, Mar. 6, 1840, AAE: APT. The first public clocks in the Ottoman Empire, on the grounds of the Dolmabahçe Palace in Istanbul and the citadel of Cairo, were put up in the 1850s. Lewis, *What Went Wrong?* 125.

Chapter 12.   The Geography of Information

1. Niall Ferguson, *The House of Rothschild: Money's Prophets, 1798–1848* (New York, 1998), 299. The semaphores are depicted in Stendahl's novel *Lucien Leuwen*. Book 2 is entitled "The Telegraph," the name then used for the semaphores.

2. N. Werry to Col. Taylor (E. I. Company resident, Baghdad), Dec. 29, 1839, FO 618/4; N. Moore (Beyrout) to John Bidwell (superintendent of the Consular Service, Foreign Office, London), Jan. 27, 1840, FO 78/412, 138; F. H. S. Werry to Ponsonby, Sept. 3, 1840, FO 78/412, 117. On Syrian railroads, see Donald Quataert, "The Age of Reforms, 1812–1914," *An Economic and Social History of the Ottoman Empire, 1300–1914* (New York, 1994), 804–8.

3. The British consul at Beirut at the time of the disappearance of Father Thomas wrote that he did not know a single European who knew Arabic or Turkish. N. Moore to Bidwell, Feb. 20, 1840, FO 78/412, 144.

4. N. Werry to Ponsonby, Mar. 30, 1840, FO 195/170, 9–10.

5. Chasseaud to Forsyth, Mar. 24, 1840, in Blau and Baron, *The Jews of the United States* 3:924–26.

6. N. Werry to Palmerston, Mar. 23, 1840, FO 78/410, 42; N. Werry to Ponsonby, Feb. 28, 1840, FO 195/170, No. 48. As an example of the later correspondence, see N. Werry to Ponsonby, Mar. 30, 1840, FO 195/170, No. 49. The

flood of correspondence from Werry to Palmerston is a special situation because of the charges Palmerston had raised against him; see chapter 16.

7. See François Charles-Roux, *Thiers et Méhémet-Ali* (Paris, 1994).

8. N. Werry to Palmerston, Mar. 23, 1840, FO78/410, 42.

9. The incident was reported in the *Allgemeine Zeitung des Judentums* and cited in "Les Juifs de l'Orient," *Archives Israélites de France* (1841): 217.

10. "Persecution of the Jews at Damascus," *Jewish Intelligence* (July): 171, quoted in Frankel, *The Damascus Affair*, 68.

11. Wilkinson (British consul on Rhodes) to Palmerston, July 4, 1840, FO 78/413, 175; "Translation of a Hebrew Letter," *Times* (London), June 25, 1840, 8. For an excellent treatment of the Rhodes case, see Frankel, *The Damascus Affair*, 69–72, 156–63.

12. For an excellent survey and review of the press reports and reaction to the events in Damascus, see Frankel, *The Damascus Affair*, chaps. 4 and 6.

13. *Sémaphore de Marseille*, Mar. 13, 1840. The article carries a byline from Beirut.

14. *Presse*, Mar. 20, 1840.

15. *Allgemeine Zeitung*, Mar. 13, 1840.

16. "Nouveaux détails sur la disparition du R. P. Thomas," *Sémaphore du Marseille*, Mar. 25, 1840, quoted in Frankel, *The Damascus Affair*, 75; P. Francesco da Ploaghe, Mar. 5, 1840, in *Relazione dell' uccisione del P. Tommaso fatta dagli ebrei* (Archives of the Capuchin Mission, Rome: Busta, Sira, 1840), cited in O'Connor, "Capuchin Missioners in Palestine and Syria," 550–52.

17. *Allgemeine Zeitung*, Mar. 31, 1840, quoted in Frankel, *The Damascus Affair*, 75.

18. *Sémaphore de Marseille*, Apr. 2, 1840, sent from Alexandria on Mar. 22, 1840.

19. Kertzer, *The Popes against the Jews*, 95.

Chapter 13.   Seeking Help

1. See, for example, Maimonides, *Mishneh Torah* 8:11.

2. *Journal des Débats*, Apr. 20–21, 1840. On Lehren see Steenwijk, "De Damascus-Affaire," 80–82.

3. The letter, addressed to Conorte and Cohen in Constantinople, is referred to in [Montefiore], *Diaries* 1:208.

4. Esther Benbassa, "Associational Strategies in Ottoman Jewish Society in the Nineteenth and Twentieth Centuries," in *The Jews of the Ottoman Empire*, ed. Avigdor Levy (Princeton, 1994), 457; Aron Rodrigue, "Abraham de Camondo of Istanbul: The Transformation of Jewish Philanthropy," in *Profiles in Diversity: Jews in a Changing Europe, 1750–1870*, ed. Frances Malino and David Sorkin (Detroit, 1998), 48–50.

5. Elders of the Hebrew Community in Constantinople [I. Camondo, Salamon Qm. Mco. Fua, Samuel de N. Treves] to Messrs de Rothschild in London, Mar. 27, 1840, in [Montefiore], *Diaries* 1:206–7.

6. Bidwell to William Young, Jan. 31, 1839, FO 78/368, quoted in A. L. Tibawi, *British Interests in Palestine 1800–1901* (Oxford, 1961), 3.

7. J. Nicolayson, *Journals, 1826–1842*. Jerusalem City Archives, July 4, 1838, 849, quoted in Lieber, *Mystics and Missionaries*, 308; Tibawi, *British Interests in Palestine*, 40–41.

8. The General Journal of the Mission of the London Society, Mar. 16, 1840 (Jerusalem Municipality: Historical Archive), quoted in Frankel, *The Damascus Affair*, 82. On the London Society, see William Thomas Gidney, *The History of the London Society for Promoting Christianity amongst the Jews, from 1809 to 1908* (London, 1908).

9. General Journal of the Mission of the London Society, Mar. 17–18, 1840.

10. Des Meloizes to Guizot, May 20, 1841, No. 9., AAE: APT.

11. N. Werry to Bidwell, Apr. 24, 1840, FO 78/410, cited in Albert M. Hyamson, "The Damascus Affair—1840," *Transactions of the English Jewish Historical Society* 16 (1952): 58.

12. Haim Nissim Abulafia and Isaac Farhi to James de Rothschild, Mar. 15, 1840, *Archives Israélites de France* (1841): 1:260.

13. N. Werry to Palmerston, May 23, 1840 (enclosure), FO 78/410, 119–20; *Journal Arabe*, note 56, FO 78/410, 151.

14. Isaac Roumani to Haim Roumani, Mar. 3, 1840, and R. Alfandari to Lehren, Mar. 15, 1840, in [Montefiore], *Diaries* 1:210–16.

15. [Heine], *Lutèce* (Paris, 1863), 182–83, quoted in Herbert R. Lottman, *The French Rothschilds* (New York, 1995), 33.

16. *Archives Israélites de France* (1840): 216.

17. "Correspondence books of *Hapekidim vehaamarkalim*" (Amsterdam), Mar. 18, 1840, No. 314, Ben Zvi Institute, Jerusalem, quoted in Frankel, *The Damascus Affair*, 84.

18. "Correspondence books of *Hapekidim vehaamarkalim*," Mar. 25, 1840, No. 329.

19. [Montefiore], *Diaries* 1:206–7. The appeal from the Damascus community is also cited in Col. Hodges's letter of intervention to Mehmet Ali, May 28, 1840, FO 78/405, 44.

Chapter 14.   The Powers That Be

1. The inventories are reprinted in Driault, *L'Égypte et l'Europe*, vol. 2.

2. On the viceroy's printing, see Lewis, *What Went Wrong?* 141. Quotes are from Hodges to Palmerston, June 18, 1840, FO 78/405, 28–34. The visitor was George Pieritz.

3. Cochelet to Thiers, Apr. 2, 1840, in Driault, *L'Égypt et l'Europe* 2:225; Des Meloizes to Thiers, Aug. 17, 1840, cited in Frankel, *The Damascus Affair*, 101.

4. Cochelet to Thiers, Apr. 2, 1840, in Driault, *L'Égypt et l'Europe* 2:225.

5. Adolphe Crémieux, *Journal du voyage accompli en 1840 pour la défense des juifs de Damas accusés du meurtre du père Thomas*, AN: 369-AP-1, 24.

6. Von Laurin to Stürmer, Mar. 31, 1840, in Gelber, *Österreich und die Damaskusaffaire*, 13.

7. Merlato to von Laurin, Apr. 22, 1840, in "Affaire de Damas," *Journal des Débats*, July 30, 1840.

8. Col. Hodges to Palmerston, Jan. 4, 1840, No. 1, FO 78/404, 4; Col. Hodges to Palmerston, Feb. 21, 1840, No. 25, FO 78/404, 95; René Cattaui (Bey), *Le règne de Mohamed Aly d'après les archives russes en Egypte*, 3 volumes (Cairo and Rome, 1931–36), 3:855.

9. N. Werry to Palmerston, May 22, 1840, FO 78/410, 55.

10. N. Werry to Bidwell, May 22, 1840, FO 78/410, 113–14.

11. Hodges to Muhammad Ali, May 28, 1840, FO 78/405, 42–46.

12. Von Laurin to Metternich, May 5, 1840, quoted in Frankel, *The Damascus Affair*, 168; von Laurin to Stürmer, May 6, 1840, in Gelber, *Österreich und die Damaskusaffaire*, 24.

13. Von Laurin to Solomon Rothschild, June 5, 1840, and von Laurin to Karl Rothschild, May 6, 1840, N. M. Rothschild Archives (London), RFam AD/2, quoted in Frankel, *The Damascus Affair*, 168; von Laurin to James Rothschild, Apr. 5, 1840, in Gelber, *Österreich und die Damaskusaffaire*, 17.

14. Joseph Meisl, "Beiträge zur Damaskus-Affäre (1840)," in Ismar Elbogen et al., *Festschrift zu Simon Dubnows siebzigsten Geburtstag* (Berlin, 1930), 235–36.

15. Kertzer, *The Popes against the Jews*, 91.

16. "Persecution of the Jews in the East," *Times* (London), July 30, 1840, 5; Rev. Joseph Marshall, chaplain of HMS *Castor* (Malta) to Montefiore, Dec. 4, 1840, AAE: APT.

17. Richard van Leeuwen, *Notables and Clergy in Mount Lebanon: The Khāazin Sheikhs and the Maronite Church (1736–1840)* (Leiden, 1994); N. Werry to Palmerston, June 23, 1840, FO 78/410, 133; Hodges to Muhammad Ali, May 28, 1840, FO 78/405, 45–46.

18. Gelber, *Österreich und die Damaskusaffaire*, 23–24, in Frankel, *The Damascus Affair*, 151. The *bulgrundi* was issued June 3, 1840; the viceroy's special couriers could make the journey to Damascus in five days.

19. Sherif Pasha to Husayn Pasha, June 30, 1840, in Asad Rustum, *Al-Mahfūzāt al-Mālikiyya al-Miṣriyya* (Beirut, 1986), 4:321, quoted in Frankel, *The Damascus Affair*, 150; Hodges to Palmerston, June 18, 1840, FO 78/405, 33.

20. I Kings 19:15.

21. H. N. Abulafia to Lehren, June 18, 1840, in "Persecution of the Jews of the East," (London) *Sun*, Aug. 6, 1840.

22. Hodges to Palmerston, June 18,1840, No. 54, FO 78/405, 34.

Chapter 15.   The Richest Men in the World

1. Quoted in Herbert R. Lottman, *The French Rothschilds: The Great Banking Dynasty through Two Turbulent Centuries* (New York, 1995), 33.

2. Ferguson, *The House of Rothschild*, 158–59.

3. Frankel, *The Damascus Affair*, 120ff, is very good on the diplomacy of the Rothschilds.

4. Metternich to von Laurin, Apr. 10, 1840, in Gelber, *Österreich und die Damaskusaffaire*, 17–18.

5. Von Laurin to James Rothschild, Mar. 31, 1840, in Gelber, *Österreich und die Damaskusaffaire*, 15. Von Laurin's term was *Judenverfolgung*.

6. Ferguson, *The House of Rothschild*, 29. James Rothschild to Solomon Rothschild, June 7, 1840, in Gelber, *Österreich und die Damaskkusaffaire*, 26.

7. Metternich to von Laurin, May 27, 1840, in Gelber, *Österreich und die Damaskusaffaire*, 27–28.

8. Board of Deputies minute books, quoted in Frankel, *The Damascus Affair*, 124–25.

9. Bidwell wrote to William Young, Jan. 31, 1839: "I am directed by Viscount Palmerston to state to you that it will be a part of your duty as British vice-consul at Jerusalem to afford protection to the Jews generally," FO 78/368, quoted in Tibawi, *British Interests in Palestine*, 3.

10. Ashley's diary, Dec. 16, 1839, Royal Commission on Historical Manuscripts, quoted in Frankel, *The Damascus Affair*, 291.

11. Memorandum from P[almerston] to Col. Hodges, Aug. 28, 1840, FO 78/410, 9.

12. [Palmerston] to N. Werry, May 21, 1840, FO 78/410, 5–6.

13. Frankel, *The Damascus Affair*, 128.

14. Palmerston to Hodges, May 5, 1840, No. 9, FO 78/403, quoted in Hyamson, "The Damascus Affair—1840," 53.

15. *Journal des Débats*, Apr. 8, 1840, quoted in Parfitt, "The Year of the Pride of Israel," 143; Frankel, *The Damascus Affair*, 125–26.

16. Genesis 4:10.

17. On Crémieux see Posener, *Adolphe Crémieux*.

18. Heinrich Heine, *Säkularausgabe: Werke, Briefwechsel, Lebeszeugnissse*, volume 10 [Pariser Berichte 1840–1848] (Berlin, 1979), 21. Heine's usual skepticism may have been tempered by his receipt of a "pension" from French government's secret funds. Ernst Pawel, *The Poet Dying: Heinrich Heine's Last Years in Paris* (New York, 1995), 36ff.

19. Frankel, *The Damascus Affair*, 134.

20. Posener, *Adolphe Crémieux*, 73.

21. Thiers to Ratti-Menton, Apr. 17, 1840, No. 9, AAE: APT.

22. James Rothschild to Solomon Rothschild, May 7 and 12, 1840, in Gelber, *Österreich und die Damaskusaffaire*, 25–27.

23. Ratti-Menton to Sa'id Ali, Apr. 16, 1840, Laurent, *Relation historique des affaires de Syrie* 2:314–17.

24. Ratti-Menton to Thiers, May 7, 1840, No. 25; Ratti-Menton to Thiers, June 29, 1840, No. 26, AAE: APT.

25. *Moniteur Universel*, May 7, 1840.

Chapter 16. Inquiries

1. Von Laurin to Karl Rothschild, Aug. 5, 1840, N. M. Rothschild Archives (London), RFam AD/2, quoted in Frankel, *The Damascus Affair*, 176. Hodges to Palmerston, June 18, 1840, FO 78/405, 31–32.

2. Des Meloizes to Thiers, July 23, 1840, No. 4, AAE: APT; des Meloizes to Guizot, June 14, 1841, No. 8, AAE: APT.

3. Interrogation of Abulafia, June 25, 1840, AAE: APT.

4. Interrogation of Abulafia, June 30, 1840, AAE: APT.

5. Interrogation of Isaac Harari, July 1, 1840, AAE: APT.

6. Interrogation of Aslan Farhi, July 9, 1840, AAE: APT.

7. "Der grosse syrische Judenprozess," *Allgemeine Zeitung* (Augsburg), Sept. 13, 1840, 2042. Frankel, *The Damascus Affair*, 180, suggests that this report was probably written by von Hailbronner, who presented himself as much less skeptical about the Jews in his later book. Joseph Leniado had sent his original complaint about Ratti-Menton's behavior toward his wife to Caspar Merlato as well. Statement of Joseph Leniado, June 27, 1840, AAE: APT.

8. Testimony of Lulu Harari et al., June 21, 1840, AAE: APT.

9. Interview of Esther Leniado and Ora Abulafia, July 3, 1840, AAE: APT.

10. Des Meloizes to Thiers, July 23 and 27, 1840, AAE: APT.

11. N. Werry to J. Bidwell, June 22, 1840, FO 78/410, 130.

12. Des Meloizes to Thiers, July 7, 1840, AAE: APT.

13. Des Meloizes interview with Isaac Loria, July 18, 1840, AAE: APT.

14. "Eastern Affairs," *Times* (London), July 28, 1840, 4. Interview of witnesses, July 22, 1840, AAE: APT.

15. Ratti-Menton to des Meloizes, Sept. 7, 1840, AAE (Nantes): Consulat/Beyrout, file 25, cited in Frankel, *The Damascus Affair*, 183.

Chapter 17.   Politics

1. *Österreichischer Beobachter*, Apr. 12, 1840, in *Persécutions contre les Juifs de Damas, à la suite de la disparition du R. P. Thomas, religieux de l'Ordre des Cauchins, et son domestique, recueil des documents* (Paris, 1840), 24; Frankel, *The Damascus Affair*, 138, points out that much of this material was reprinted without attribution in the *Journal des Débats*, Apr. 20, 1840 (English).

2. Steenwijk, "De Damascus-Affaire," 83.

3. [Heinrich Heine], "Die Juden und die Presse in Paris" (June 11, 1840), *Säkularausgabe* 10:43–45. Of the *Journal des Débats*, Heine wrote: "Good God, how bad things are for the French when one has to bestow words of praise on them for waxing indignant against superstition, torture, and knavery." "Affaire de Damas," *Courier de la Meuse*, June 7, 1840; "France," *Univers*, June 5, 1840; both quoted in Frankel, *The Damascus Affair*, 198–99, which is invaluable on the press coverage in Europe and the Americas (esp. 196–214).

4. (London) *Times*, June 25, 1840, 8.

5. "Persecution of the Jews at Damascus," (London) *Times*, June 29, 1840, 5. The newspaper declined to test the proffered matzos. Ibid., June 25, 1840, 12.

6. *Hansard's Parliamentary Debates* 54 (1840): 1383–84. For a superb discussion of the parliamentary debates on the Damascus affair, see Frankel, *The Damascus Affair*, 194–96.

7. *Hansard's Parliamentary Debates* 54 (1840): 1385.

8. Gregory IX (1227–1241), Innocent IV (1243–1254), Alexander VII (1254–1261), and Clement IV (1265–1268).

9. *Moniteur Universel*, June 3, 1840, 1257–58.

10. Heine, *Säkularausgabe* 10:33; Stow, "The Bollandists and the Authorial Present." On the theological politics in Restoration France, see Sheryl Kroen,

Politics and Theater, the Crisis of Legitimacy in Restoration France (Berkeley, 2000), 76–108.

11. On the baptism episode, see David I. Kertzer, "The Montel Affair: Jewish Policy and French Diplomacy under the July Monarchy," *French Historical Studies* 25, no. 2 (spring 2002): 265–93. As a face-saving gesture to allow the circumvention of canon law, Thiers promised that the child would be raised within the Church. The episode was one of many during the nineteenth century. See Kertzer, *The Popes against the Jews*, 38–59, and *The Kidnapping of Edgardo Mortara* (New York, 1997).

12. Crémieux to Lionel Rothschild, June 2, 1840, and Nathaniel Rothschild to London, June 3, 1840, N. M. Rothschild Archives (London), RAL (XI/104/0), quoted in Frankel, *The Damascus Affair*, 215.

13. In 1836 Moses Montefiore approached his aunt, Nathan Rothschild's wife, about the possibility of a partnership in the Rothschild bank. He was told that New Court would never consider the admission of an outsider, but they might be willing to make young Montefiore a junior partner in view of his marriage to a Rothschild and the exceptional patrician luster of his name—provided he change that name to Rothschild. Montefiore, already a knight, decided to keep his own name. Frederic Morton, *The Rothschilds* (New York, 1963), 57.

14. Frankel, *The Damascus Affair*, 214.

15. Minutes, Board of Deputies, June 15, 1840, quoted in ibid., 217.

Chapter 18. The Mission I

1. (London) *Times*, July 25, 1840; "France," *Univers*, July 22, 1840; N. Werry, "On the punishments and tortures . . . ," FO 78/410, 232.

2. Frasis and Figli Kanuna to Salomon Rothschild, May 27, 1840, in Gelber, *Österreich und die Damaskusaffaire*, 30–31; on the Malta papers, see Frankel, *The Damascus Affair*, 228.

3. Quoted in Kertzer, *The Popes against the Jews*, 98–99.

4. Salomon Rothschild to Metternich, June 12, 1840, in Gelber, *Österreich und die Damaskkusaffaire*, 33; Ferguson, *The House of Rothschild*, 397; Kertzer, *The Popes against the Jews*, 99.

5. "Persecution of the Jews at Damascus," *Morning Herald*, June 25, 1840.

6. [Montefiore], *Diaries* 1:215; "Persecution of the Jews in Damascus: Great Meeting at the Mansion House," *Times* (London), July 4, 1840. Bowring later published his *Report on the Commercial Statistics of Syria* (London, 1840; reprint, New York, 1973); others used his figures and the estimates of wealth provided by Ratti-Menton and the pasha to argue that the accused Jews were wealthy and not deserving of aide or sympathy.

7. Frankel, *The Damascus Affair*, 224.

8. "Persecution of the Jews in the East, containing the Proceedings of a Meeting held at the Synagogue Mekveh Israel, Philadelphia, on Thursday Evening, the 28th of AB, 5600, corresponding with the 27th of August, 1840" (Philadelphia, 1840), 15, in *Beginnings: Early American Judaica*, ed. Abraham J. Karp (Philadelphia, 1975).

9. Leon Allen Jick, *The Americanization of the Synagogue, 1820–1870* (Hanover, N.H., 1976), 65; Lehren to Crémieux, Apr. 11, 1840, No. 356, Correspondence Books of the Hapekidim vehaamarkalim, Amsterdam (Ben Zvi Institute, Jerusalem), quoted in Frankel, *The Damascus Affair*, 239; "Report on the Philadephia Meeting," in Blau and Baron, *The Jews of the United States* 3:935–37.

10. "The Damascus Mission," *Voice of Jacob* 24 (Aug. 24, 1842): 191; Frankel, *The Damascus Affair*, 227–28.

11. Quoted by Yehudah Alkalai, "Minat Yehuda," *Kitvei harav Yehudah Alkalai* 1:221; Lehren to Crémieux, May 25, 1840, No. 420, Correspondence Books of Hapekidim vehaamarkalim, Amsterdam (Ben Zvi Institute, Jerusalem), both in Frankel, *The Damascus Affair*, 256.

12. "Munk," *Encyclopedia Judaica*, 12:525–26.

13. Heine, *Säkularausgabe* 10:36–39.

14. John Bowring, in "Persecution of the Jews in Damascus," (London) *Times*, July 4, 1840, 7.

15. Nathaniel Rothschild, ca. June 25, 1840, quoted in Frankel, *The Damascus Affair*, 222; FO to Montefiore, July 2, 1840, FO 78/421, 7–9; Crémieux, *Journal*, AN: 369-AP-1, 4.

16. Anselm Rothschild (in Paris) to London, July 10, 1840, and Montefiore to London, July 13, 1840, quoted in Frankel, *The Damascus Affair*, 332.

17. "From Our Correspondent," *Globe*, July 27, 1840.

18. "Revue des Feuilles Anglaise," *Univers*, Aug. 4, 1840.

19. Diary, July 24 and Aug. 1, 1840, quoted in Edwin Hodder, *The Life and Work of the Seventh Earl of Shaftesbury*, 3 volumes (London, 1886), 1:310–11.

20. Khaled Fahmy, *All the Pasha's Men: Mehmed Ali, His Army and the Making of Modern Egypt* (Cambridge, 1997), passim.

21. Efraim Karsh and Inari Karsh, *Empires of the Sand: The Struggle for Mastery in the Middle East 1789–1923* (Cambridge, Mass., 1999), 36; Palmerston to Col. Hodges, July 18, 1840, No. 16, FO 78/403, 44–50.

22. Thiers in "Chambre des Députés," *Journal des Débats*, Mar. 25, 1840; Cochelet to Thiers, May 6, 1840, in Driault, *L'Égypt et l'Europe* 2:275–76.

Chapter 19.　The Mission II

1. R. D. Barnett, "A Diary That Survived," 150, 154; [Montefiore], *Diaries* 1:220–21.

2. Crémieux, *Journal*, AN: 369-AP-1, 2–3.

3. Montefiore to Board of Deputies, July 13, 1840, quoted in Frankel, *The Damascus Affair*, 339.

4. Barnett, "A Diary That Survived," 156–57; [Montefiore], *Diaries* 1:221; Crémieux, *Journal*, AN: 369-AP-1, 6.

5. Crémieux, *Journal*, AN: 369-AP-1, 17–19; Barnett, "A Diary That Survived", 165.

6. "Private Correspondence: Alexandria, 7 August," (London) *Times*, Aug. 25, 1840, 4; [Montefiore], *Diaries* 1:224, 226; Hodges to Palmerston, Aug. 5, 1840, FO 78/405, 201.

7. Hodges to Palmerston, July 24, 1840, FO 78/405, 177–78.

8. Montefiore to correspondence committee of the Board of Deputies, 10am, Aug. 7, 1840, quoted in Frankel, *The Damascus Affair,* 341.

9. Walewski to Thiers, Aug. 18, 1840, in Driault, *L'Égypt et l'Europe* 3:135, 137. Hodges to Ponsonby (enclosed report), Aug. 16, 1840, No. 24, FO 78/405, 227.

10. Crémieux, *Journal,* AN: 369-AP-1, 19.

11. Crémieux, *Journal,* AN: 369-AP-1, 27.

12. Minute book of the Board of Deputies, quoted in Frankel, *The Damascus Affair,* 343.

13. [Montefiore], *Diaries* 1:243.

14. Ibid. 1:240–42, 244; Montefiore to correspondence committee of the Board of Deputies, July 25, 1840, quoted in Frankel, *The Damascus Affair,* 347.

15. Crémieux, *Journal,* AN: 369-AP-1, 32.

16. Crémieux, *Journal,* AN: 369-AP-1, 29–30.

17. [Louis Loewe], "The Damascus Affair: The Diary of Dr. Louis Loewe (July–November 1840)," *Yehudith: The Organ of the Judith Lady Montefiore Theological College* 1, no. 3 (Ramsgate, 1940): 27; [Montefiore], *Diaries* 1:244.

18. Crémieux, *Journal,* AN: 369-AP-1, 38–39.

19. [Montefiore], *Diaries* 1:245

20. Montefiore to correspondence committee of the Board of Deputies, Aug. 25, 1840, quoted in Frankel, *The Damascus Affair,* 349; [Loewe], "The Damascus Affair," Aug. 24, 1840, 20.

21. [Montefiore], *Diaries* 1:249.

22. Crémieux, *Journal,* AN: 369-AP-1, 40; [Montefiore], *Diaries* 1:250.

Chapter 20. Muhammad Ali's Behind

1. Robert J. McManus, "An Analysis of Health Claims by Disease," *Proceedings of the Casualty Actuarial and Statistical Society of America,* May 28, 1920, 179, 188; Ferguson, *The House of Rothschild,* 296–99.

2. [Montefiore], *Diaries* 1:244, 246; Cochelet to Thiers, Aug. 30, 1840, in Driault, *L'Égypt et l'Europe* 3:186; Allison to Ponsonby, Aug. 30, 1840, FO 78/396, 154.

3. Hodges to Palmerston [enclosed report, No. 92], Aug. 30, 1840, FO 78/406, 151.

4. Cochelet to Thiers, Aug. 30, 1840, in Driault, *L'Égypt et l'Europe* 3:189.

5. Crémieux, *Journal,* AN: 369-AP-1, 40–41.

6. [Montefiore], *Diaries* 1:250–51. Here, and throughout the entries describing the mission to Alexandria, Loewe's edition of Montefiore's diary makes no mention of Crémieux's role in the turn of events. With the original lost, it is not clear whether this was Montefiore's or Loewe's censorship.

7. Crémieux, *Journal,* AN: 369-AP-1, 41–42.

8. Crémieux, *Journal,* AN: 369-AP-1, 43–44.

9. [Montefiore], *Diaries* 1:251; Montefiore to Louis Cohen, Sept. 27, 1840, in Cecil Roth, *Anglo-Jewish Letters (1158–1917)* (London, 1938), 274.

10. Posener, *Adolphe Crémieux,* 117. Montefiore and Loewe claimed that Loewe discovered the offending term and told Munk to inform Crémieux and

Montefiore but that Munk "apparently forgot to call on Sir Moses." [Montefiore], *Diaries* 1:252.

11. Loewe, "The Damascus Affair," 27; [Montefiore], *Diaries* 1:252.

12. Cremieux, *Journal*, AN: 369-AP-1, 48.

13. Crémieux, *Journal*, AN: 369-AP-1, 59–60.

14. [Montefiore], *Diaries* 1:256; Loewe, "The Damascus Affair," 31.

15. Crémieux, *Journal*, AN: 369-AP-1, 49, 64–65.

16. [Montefiore], *Diaries* 1:257; Crémieux, *Journal*, AN: 369-AP-1, 55; Montefiore to correspondence committee of Board of Deputies, Aug. 25, 1840, in Frankel, *The Damascus Affair*, 358.

Chapter 21. Damascus, September 1840

1. N. Moore to Col. Hodges, Aug. 19, 1840, FO 78/412, 189; Napier to N. Moore, Aug. 14, 1840, FO 78/412, 193; N. Werry to Palmerston, Aug. 18, 1840, FO 78/410, 282.

2. Posener, *Adolphe Crémieux*, 118; [Montefiore], *Diaries* 1:257, 260; Merlato to Crémieux, Sept. 7, 1840, *Times* (London), Oct. 10, 1840, 6; Loria to Valensino, Sept. 7, 1840, quoted in Frankel, *The Damascus Affair*, 360.

3. Ratti-Menton to des Meloize, Sept. 6 and 12, 1840, AAE (Nantes): Consulat/Beyrout, 1840, No. 25, quoted in Frankel, *The Damascus Affair*, 360–61.

4. Ratti-Menton to des Meloize, Sept. 17, 1840, AAE (Nantes): Consulat/Beyrout, 1840, No. 25.

5. Crémieux, *Journal*, AN: 369-AP-1, 55.

6. [Montefiore], *Diaries* 1:257.

7. "Persecution of the Jews in the East," (London) *Times*, Oct. 19, 1840, 6.

8. Crémieux, *Journal*, AN: 369-AP-1, 86 and passim.

9. [Montefiore], *Diaries* 1:257.

10. Crémieux, *Journal*, AN: 369-AP-1, 98; Aron Rodrigue, *French Jews, Turkish Jews: The Alliance Israélite Universelle and the Politics of Jewish Schooling in Turkey, 1860–1925* (Bloomington, 1990).

11. "Nouvelles," *Archives Israélites de France* (1941): 38–40; Crémieux, *Journal*, AN: 369-AP-1, 18–19.

12. "Nouvelles," *Archives Israélites de France* (1941): 40; Anselm Rothschild to London, Nov. 24, 1840, quoted in Frankel, *The Damascus Affair*, 374.

13. Crémieux, *Journal*, AN: 369-AP-1, 40, 45. Montefiore and Crémieux regularly used their diaries to "document" the lax attitudes of each other; many entries in Montefiore's diary record that Crémieux or Madame Crémieux were talking of leaving for Constantinople, Athens, or Cairo. [Montefiore], *Diaries* 1:245, 247, 250.

14. [Montefiore], *Diaries* 1:263–64.

15. Ibid. 1:268.

16. Ibid. 1:269–74.

17. Ibid. 1:279.

18. Montefiore to correspondence committee of the Board of Deputies, Oct. 15, 1840, in Frankel, *The Damascus Affair*, 378; Loewe, "The Damascus Affair," 62.

19. Montefiore to correspondence committee of Board of Deputies, Sept. 17, and Oct. 15, 1840, quoted in Henriques, "Who Killed Father Thomas?" 67, and in Frankel, *The Damascus Affair*, 375, 378.

20. Translated from my photograph of the epitaph by Mark Wegner. The translation in [Montefiore], *Diaries* 1:283, presumably by Dr. Loewe, does not capture the florid language or rhyming verse of the original Arabic:

Ziyy turbat al-Āb Tūmā	al Kabūshī. Wa andab maqāmo
Mursal rasūlī lil-Shām	ya'iz wa yubdī htimāmo.
Qad dhabbahūhu Yahūda	wa lam tujdīh bi-tmāmo
Fi khāmis isbāt	Hadhīh bqāya 'izāmo

Urikha Sanna 1840

21. [Montefiore], *Diaries* 1:283; Barnett, "A Diary That Survived," July 27, 1840, 160.

22. [Montefiore], *Diaries* 1:287, 291.

23. Montefiore to correspondence committee of the Board of Deputies, Dec. 7 and 11, 1840, in Frankel, *The Damascus Affair*, 378.

24. Montefiore to Karl Rothschild, Dec. 7, 1841, in ibid., 381; [Montefiore], *Diaries* 1:291–92.

25. [Montefiore], *Diaries* 1:297.

26. Ibid.

27. See I Samuel 17:34–37.

28. Paul Goodman, *Moses Montefiore* (Philadelphia, 1925), 73–75.

Epilogue

1. Testimony of el-Telli, Jan. 13, 1841, Laurent, *Relation historique des affaires de Syrie* 2:258n; [Paton], *The Modern Syrians*, 36–37.

2. *Augsburger Zeitung*, Mar. 31, 1841, in [Heine], *Lutèce*, 181.

3. Des Meloizes to Guizot, May 20 and 27, 1841, AAE: APT.

4. Guizot to Louis Philippe, Sept. 21, 1842, quoted in Parfitt, "The Year of the Pride of Israel," 140; Henriques, "Who Killed Father Thomas?" 72; AAE: Ratti-Menton/Personnel, Série I, passim.

5. Laurent, *Relation historique des affaires de Syrie* 2:3.

6. Rodrigue, *French Jews, Turkish Jews*, 15 and passim.

7. Ibid., 15, 22; Henri Desportes, *Le mystère du sang chez les Juifs de tous les temps* (Paris, 1889), 188n.

8. Goodman, *Moses Montefiore*, 100.

9. Ma'oz, *Ottoman Reform in Syria and Palestine*, 206; [Paton], *The Modern Syrians*, 33–35, 39–40; Colonel Churchill, *The Druzes and the Maronites under the Turkish Rule from 1840 to 1860* (London, 1862), 34.

10. *Times* (London), Apr. 27, 1841; "Syria," *Morning Chronicle*, Apr. 26, 1841, quoted in Frankel, *The Damascus Affair*, 395.

11. Ma'oz, *Ottoman Reform in Syria and Palestine,* 186, 205.

12. Henriques, "Who Killed Father Thomas?" 71.

13. Parfitt, "The Year of the Pride of Israel," 145; Paul Dumont, "Jewish Communities in Turkey during the Last Decades of the Nineteenth Century in the Light of the Archives of the Alliance Israélite Universelle," in Braude and Lewis, *Christians and Jews in the Ottoman Empire* 1:222–23.

14. Frankel, *The Damascus Affair,* 401–31, provides an exhaustive and perceptive history and analysis of the various treatments of the Damascus affair.

15. Achille Laurent, *Relation historique des affaires de Syrie, depuis 1840 jusqu'en 1842; Statistique générale du Mont-Liban, et Procédure complète dirigée en 1840 contre des Juifs de Damas a la suite de la disparition du Père Thomas, Publiées d'après les Documents recueillis en Turquie, en Égypte et en Syrie* (Paris, 1846), 2 volumes.

16. *Aceldama osia processo celebre instruito contro gli Ebrei di Damasco nell'anno 1840 in seguito al doppio assassinio rituale da loro consumato nella persona del Padre Tommaso dall Sardegna Missionario Cappuccino ed in quell del suo garzoncello Christiano Ebrahim Amarah* (Cagliari-Sassari, 1896) is a later reprint.

17. "Mysteries of the Talmud—Terrible Murder in the East," *New York Herald,* Apr. 6, 1850.

18. In 1897 *The Athenaeum* advertised a work by Burton entitled *Human Sacrifice among the Eastern Jews: or the Murder of Padre Tomasso,* ed. W. H. Wilkins (New York). See http://www.fpp.co.uk/BoD/origins/BurtonMS.html.

19. See, for example, http://www.littlegreenfootballs.com/weblog/?entry=3088 from San Francisco State University, where the charges are directed not only at Israeli policy but are attributed to "Jewish rites."

20. Anonymous note in the archives, Mar. 7, 1931, cited in Parfitt, "The Year of the Pride of Israel," 135.

21. Moustafa Tlass, *Matzo of Zion* (Arabic ed., 1986; English ed., Damascus, 1991); Nabila Chaalan, Syrian delegate, quoted in David Littman, "Syria's Blood Libel Revival at the UN: 1991–2000," http://mypage.bluewin.ch/ameland/Libel.html; "The Damascus Blood Libel (1840) as Told by Syria's Minister of Defense, Mustafa Tlass," *Middle East Research Institute* 99 (June 27, 2002), http://www.memri.org/bin/articles.cgi?Pages=archives&Area=ia &ID=IA9902.

Index

blood libel: accusations after Damascus Affair, 212–13; alleged victims found alive, 209; amelioration of myth by Ratti-Menton and the pasha, 81–82; as barbaric, 110–11; blood rites as rabbinical knowledge, 83–84, 96; commercial motive for sacrifices, 101; contemporary instances of, 214–15; crucifixion and, 32–33, 80; in Damascus, 79; as divine punishment for religious transgressions, 170; economic power of Jews and, 212; in European history, 78–79; exoneration as issue, 192, 193, 199; *firman* rejecting, 202, 204; al-Hallaq's testimony and charges against Damascus Jews, 34–35; Jewish identity strengthened by, 213; *kashrut* laws and, 34; throughout Middle East, 112–13; Muslim adaptations of myth, 213; Nazis and, 214–15; newspaper reports of, 113–14; Ratti-Menton and allegations of, 57–60, 81–82; Sephardic Jews as perpetrators of, 214; Shabbetai Zvi and, 91–92; Sherif Pasha and allegations, 19, 81–82; sources of myth, 32–33, 76–79, 158, 172; as threat to Jewish religion, 168, 169, 182–83; victims as young boys or children, 78, 80, 112–13, 213; Werry on, 75, 79

Board of Deputies, 139, 140–41, 164, 165, 167–68, 204

Bowring, John, 168

bread: blood libel myth and consecration of, 65–66, 77, 88, 213; traditional Jewish meals and, 65–66, 78

bribery: alibis and, 155; dragomans and, 22; as evidence of guilt, 26, 128–29; of interrogators during torture, 30; Loria and Ventura accused of, 155; as motive for charges, 70–71; Picciotto and rumors of, 100; rumors of, 121. *See also baksheesh*

Briggs, Samuel, 131, 182, 184, 185, 190

Britain: Anglo-Ottoman trade agreement, 211; blood libel in England, 78; Board of Deputies, 139–40, 141, 164, 165, 167–68, 204; diplomatic efforts in case, 128, 129 (*see also* Werry, Nathaniel); diplomatic ties with Egypt, 160; internal politics of, 115, 173–74; London Society for Promoting Christianity Amongst the Jews, 119–20; mission, support and

involvement in, 167–68, 168–69; as naval power, 130, 185, 195; official support of mission, 173; Pieritz fact-finding mission, 119–20; political responses to case, 159–60, 173; political stake in Middle East, 49, 71, 141, 173–75, 174, 208–9; protest meetings in London, 129; rights of Jews in, 160

Burton, Richard, 214

butchers *(shohet)*, 81–82

Camondo, Abraham de, 118, 201

Catholicism. *See* Christian communities of Damascus; Vatican

censorship: of European press, 157–58; of opposition to blood libel, 161; of Talmud by Christians, 93–94, 95–96

Central Consistory, 142, 144–45, 163, 176

children: arrested and interrogated, 46, 47; kidnap of Jewish child in Rome, 162; release of, 59; as sacrificial victims in blood libel myth, 78, 80, 112–13, 213; tortured, 73

Christian communities of Damascus: administrative positions held by, 18–19, 50; blood libel charges and, 33; described, 8; factions within, 4; France as supporter of Roman Catholicism, 50; Jewish community and, 47, 48–49, 132, 135; Jewish traditions known by, 79; mobs and crowds, 98, 106–7, 132, 135; as murderers of Fr. Thomas, 133; Muslim community and, 210, 211–12; oppression under Ottoman administration, 210; privileged during Egyptian administration, 50; reactions to release of prisoners, 196–97; as second-class citizens of Ottoman Empire, 17; violence against Jews during Holy Week, 32–34

Christian imagery in blood libel myth: crown of thorns, 80; crucifixion, 32–33, 80; trinity, 77, 81

Churchill, Charles Henry, 210

circumcision, 77–78, 79

citizenship: Crémieux and *more judaico*, 142; of European Jews, 109; of French Jews, 21, 59, 109, 143, 144, 173; Gülhane Decree and Ottoman citizenship, 17, 49–50, 118, 126, 210

Clot-Bey, Dr. Antoine, 188, 189, 198, 199

coaching of witnesses, 37, 72

Index

Index